# GUITAR
## TEACHER EDITION 1

**Editor:** Sandy Feldstein
**Cover Design:** Frank Milone and Ken Rehm
**Photography:** Roberto Santos

ISBN 0-7604-0008-3

Copyright (c) 1994 Beam Me Up Music, c/o CPP/Belwin, Inc.
15800 N.W. 48th Avenue, Miami, Florida 33014
International Copyright Secured  Made in U.S.A.  All Rights Reserved

# Contents

Introduction ............................. 3
The Guitar .............................. 5
Technique ............................... 6
Tuning The Guitar ....................... 7
Equipping Your Guitar Class ............. 8
Guitar Chord Chart ..................... 10
Guitar Fingerboard Chart ............... 11
**Lesson 1**
    Guitar Method ..................... 12
    Guitar Theory ..................... 14
    Guitar Rock Shop .................. 16
**Lesson 2**
    Guitar Method ..................... 18
    Guitar Theory ..................... 20
    Guitar Rock Shop .................. 21
**Lesson 3**
    Guitar Method ..................... 22
    Guitar Theory ..................... 24
    Guitar Rock Shop .................. 25
**Lesson 4**
    Guitar Method ..................... 26
    Guitar Theory ..................... 28
    Guitar Rock Shop .................. 29
**Lesson 5**
    Guitar Method ..................... 30
    Guitar Theory ..................... 32
    Guitar Rock Shop .................. 33
**Lesson 6**
    Guitar Method ..................... 34
    Guitar Theory ..................... 36
    Guitar Rock Shop .................. 37
**Lesson 7**
    Guitar Method ..................... 38
    Guitar Theory ..................... 40
    Guitar Rock Shop .................. 41
**Lesson 8**
    Guitar Method ..................... 42
    Guitar Theory ..................... 44
    Guitar Rock Shop .................. 45
**Lesson 9**
    Guitar Method ..................... 48
    Guitar Theory ..................... 50
    Guitar Rock Shop .................. 51
**Lesson 10**
    Guitar Method ..................... 52
    Guitar Theory ..................... 54
    Guitar Rock Shop .................. 55
**Lesson 11**
    Guitar Method ..................... 56
    Guitar Theory ..................... 57
    Guitar Rock Shop .................. 58

**Lesson 12**
    Guitar Method ..................... 60
    Guitar Theory ..................... 61
    Guitar Rock Shop .................. 62
**Lesson 13**
    Guitar Method ..................... 64
    Guitar Theory ..................... 65
    Guitar Rock Shop .................. 66
**Lesson 14**
    Guitar Method ..................... 68
    Guitar Theory ..................... 69
    Guitar Rock Shop .................. 70
**Lesson 15**
    Guitar Method ..................... 72
    Guitar Theory ..................... 73
    Guitar Rock Shop .................. 74
**Lesson 16**
    Guitar Method ..................... 76
    Guitar Rock Shop .................. 77
**Lesson 17**
    Guitar Method ..................... 80
    Guitar Theory ..................... 82
    Guitar Rock Shop .................. 83
**Lesson 18**
    Guitar Method ..................... 84
    Guitar Theory ..................... 85
    Guitar Rock Shop .................. 86
**Lesson 19**
    Guitar Method ..................... 88
    Guitar Theory ..................... 90
    Guitar Rock Shop .................. 91
**Lesson 20**
    Guitar Method ..................... 92
    Guitar Theory ..................... 94
    Guitar Rock Shop .................. 95
**Lesson 21**
    Guitar Method ..................... 96
    Guitar Theory ..................... 97
    Guitar Rock Shop .................. 98
**Lesson 22**
    Guitar Method .................... 100
    Guitar Theory .................... 101
    Guitar Rock Shop ................. 102
**Lesson 23**
    Guitar Method .................... 104
    Guitar Theory .....................06
    Guitar Rock Shop ................. 107
**Lesson 24**
    Guitar Method .................... 108
    Guitar Theory .................... 109
    Guitar Rock Shop ................. 110

# Introduction

This book is intended to guide you through level one of *Belwin's 21st Century Guitar Course*. On average, level 1 should require from six months to one year to complete. This will vary depending on age group, whether lessons are private, group or classroom, individual practice time, and the supplements used.

All new techniques and concepts are carefully described and demonstrated on the available recordings. If the guitar is not your principle instrument the instructional segments of the recordings will prove invaluable in guiding your students through this course. For the students, using the recordings will enhance both their development and their enjoyment of the guitar.

## Lesson Plans

*Teacher Edition Level 1* provides 24 lesson plans each for *Guitar Method 1*, *Guitar Theory 1* and *Rock Shop 1*. Songs in *Guitar Ensemble 1* and *Guitar Song Trax 1* are correlated to the *Guitar Method* lessons. It is not necessary, or even suggested, that you use all of the supplementary books. They are available so that you can customize the course to suit your needs.

You should choose the pacing the best suits your needs and those of your students. The organization of the book into 24 lessons is based on the typical school year: two semesters, 12 weeks each. Often even in private teaching student attendance conforms to a similar schedule.

## Supplement Suggestions for Private Lessons

**Children (5 - 10):**
- *Guitar Method 1* as the lesson basis.
- *Guitar Theory 1* can be used as an in-lesson workbook, or as homework, to reinforce the method.
- *Guitar Ensemble 1* for group ensemble work.

**Pre- and early teens (11 - 14):**
- *Guitar Method 1* as the lesson basis.
- *Guitar Theory 1* can be used as an in-lesson workbook, or as homework, to reinforce the method.
- *Guitar Ensemble 1* for group ensemble work.
- *Guitar Song Trax 1* for easy, play-along style pop songs. Correlated to *Guitar Method 1* and *Guitar Rock Shop 1*.

**Teens (13 - 18):**
- *Guitar Method 1* as the lesson basis.
- *Guitar Rock Shop 1* should be used with those students interested in learning rock guitar. It may be used in conjunction with the method book for a complete overview of guitar styles or used alone as the basis for rock guitar instruction.
- *Guitar Theory 1* can be used as an in-class workbook to reinforce the method.
- *Guitar Ensemble 1* for group ensemble work.
- *Guitar Song Trax 1* for easy, play-along style pop songs. Correlated to *Guitar Method 1* and *Guitar Rock Shop 1*.

**Adults (18 and over):**
- *Guitar Method 1* as the lesson basis.
- *Guitar Rock Shop 1* should be used with those students interested in learning rock guitar. Use in conjunction with the method book for a complete overview of guitar styles or use alone as the basis for rock guitar instruction.
- *Guitar Theory 1* can be used to reinforce the method.
- *Guitar Song Trax 1* for easy, play-along style pop songs. Correlated to *Guitar Method 1* and *Guitar Rock Shop 1*.

# Supplement Suggestions for Classroom Instruction

**Elementary School:**
- *Guitar Method 1* as the lesson basis.
- *Guitar Theory 1* can be used as an in-class workbook, or as homework, to reinforce the method.
- *Guitar Ensemble 1* for class ensemble work.

**Middle School:**
- *Guitar Method 1* as the lesson basis.
- *Guitar Theory 1* can be used as an in-class workbook, or as homework, to reinforce the method.
- *Guitar Ensemble 1* for class ensemble work.

**High School:**
- *Guitar Method 1* as the lesson basis.
- *Guitar Rock Shop 1* should be used with those students interested in learning rock guitar. Use in conjunction with the method book for a complete overview of guitar styles or use alone as the basis for a rock guitar class.
- *Guitar Theory 1* can be used as an in-class workbook, or as homework, to reinforce the method.
- *Guitar Ensemble 1* for class ensemble work.
- *Guitar Song Trax 1* for easy, play-along style pop songs. Correlated to *Guitar Method 1* and *Guitar Rock Shop 1*.

**Adult Ed:**
- *Guitar Method 1* as the lesson basis.
- *Guitar Rock Shop 1* should be used with those students interested in learning rock guitar. Use in conjunction with the method book for a complete overview of guitar styles or use alone as the basis for a rock guitar class.
- *Guitar Theory 1* can be used to reinforce the method.
- *Guitar Ensemble 1* for class ensemble work.
- *Guitar Song Trax 1* for easy, play-along style pop songs. Correlated to *Guitar Method 1* and *Guitar Rock Shop 1*

Student page 3 from *Guitar Method 1*

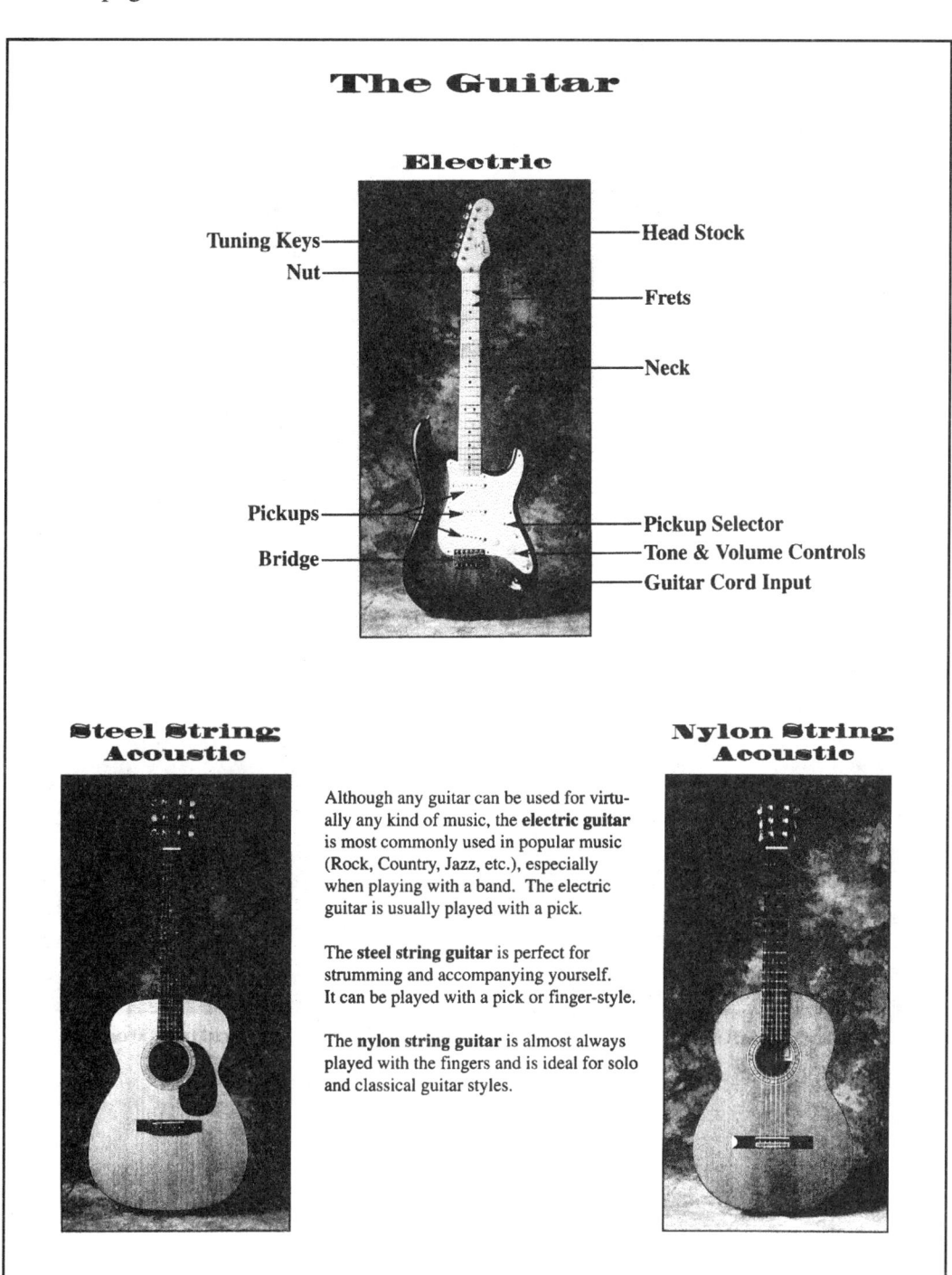

# The Guitar

## Electric

- Tuning Keys
- Nut
- Head Stock
- Frets
- Neck
- Pickups
- Bridge
- Pickup Selector
- Tone & Volume Controls
- Guitar Cord Input

## Steel String Acoustic

## Nylon String Acoustic

Although any guitar can be used for virtually any kind of music, the **electric guitar** is most commonly used in popular music (Rock, Country, Jazz, etc.), especially when playing with a band. The electric guitar is usually played with a pick.

The **steel string guitar** is perfect for strumming and accompanying yourself. It can be played with a pick or finger-style.

The **nylon string guitar** is almost always played with the fingers and is ideal for solo and classical guitar styles.

# Technique

Student page 4 from *Guitar Method 1*

---

## Technique

The pick should be held firmly between the thumb and index finger.

The thumb should be placed behind the neck. The fingers should be placed right behind the frets, not on top of, or in between them.

**Sitting Position**   **Classic Position**   **Standing Position**

---

**Teacher Note:** When seated, the guitar can be held on either the right leg (sitting position shown above) or left leg (classic position). Neither position is right or wrong. Guitarists often shift position from one leg to the other depending on the style and demands of the music. Generally, the classic position places both hands in the best position for awkward stretches and fingerings. The most important thing, whichever position is used, is that the student is comfortable and relaxed.

Student page 5 from *Guitar Method 1*

# Tuning The Guitar

**Electronic Tuners:**

Many brands of small, battery operated tuners, similar to the one shown below, are available. Simply follow the instructions supplied with your tuner.

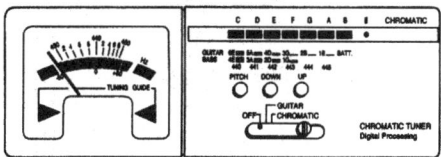

**Tuning the Guitar to a piano:**

One of the easiest ways to tune a guitar is to a piano keyboard. The six strings of the guitar are tuned to the keyboard notes shown in the following diagram:

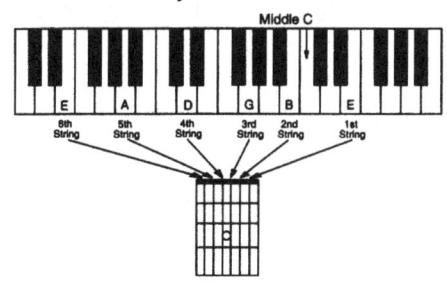

**Tuning the Guitar to Itself (Relative Tuning):**

1. Tune the 6th string to *E* on the piano (or some other fixed pitch instrument). You can also use a pitch pipe or an electronic guitar tuner.

2. Depress the 6th string at the 5th fret. Play it and you will hear the note *A*, which is the same note as the 5th string open. Turn the 5th string tuning key until the pitch of the 5th string matches that of the 6th string.

3. Depress the 5th string at the 5th fret. Play it and you will hear the note *D*, which is the same note as the 4th string open. Turn the 4th string tuning key until the pitch of the 4th string matches that of the 5th string.

4. Depress the 4th string at the 5th fret. Play it and you will hear the note *G*, which is the same note as the 3rd string open. Turn the 3rd string tuning key until the pitch of the 3rd string matches that of the 4th string.

5. Depress the 3rd string at the 4th fret. Play it and you will hear the note *B*, which is the same note as the 2nd string open. Turn the 2nd string tuning key until the pitch of the 2nd string matches that of the 3rd string.

6. Depress the 2nd string at the 5th fret. Play it and you will hear the note *E*, which is the same note as the 1st string open. Turn the 1st string tuning key until the pitch of the 1st string matches that of the 2nd string.

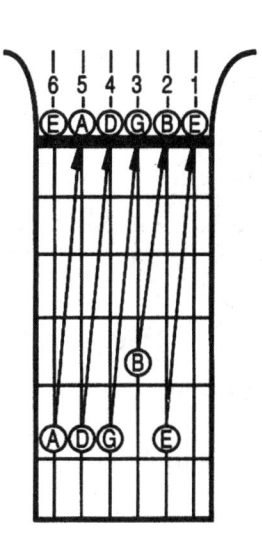

# Equipping Your Guitar Class

For purchasing equipment see your local music dealer or pro-shop. They can usually advise you on everything you'll need. A little comparison shopping will soon show you who provides the best service and prices.

**Guitars:** For elementary or middle school a 3/4 size, nylon-string guitar is suggested. Nylon-string guitars are the easiest to play and even very inexpensive ones can sound pretty good.

For high school, or adult students, a full size guitar would be more appropriate. Again, nylon is suggested as it's less expensive, sounds better and is much more durable than an inexpensive steel-string acoustic or electric guitar. Steel-string acoustics are generally more expensive due to their more complex construction and bracing, which is required to counteract the great force exerted by the steel strings on the neck and body of the guitar.

**Strings:** The guitars will come with strings installed. But guitar strings break often. Also, after a few months of use the strings will become impossible to tune so stock up with about a dozen extra sets. Be aware that with nylon strings the "D" string (4th string) breaks often. On steel string acoustic and electric guitars the high "E" and "B" strings tend to break. You should buy an extra dozen of each of these individual strings.

Three quarter size nylon string guitars use ball-end nylon strings. These are plastic strings with a little ball at the end. Pass the plain end of the string through the little hole in the bridge, the ball-end will catch as you pull it through. Wrap the plain end around the post of the tuning key at least once, then pass through the hole in the post and loop under as shown in the illustration:

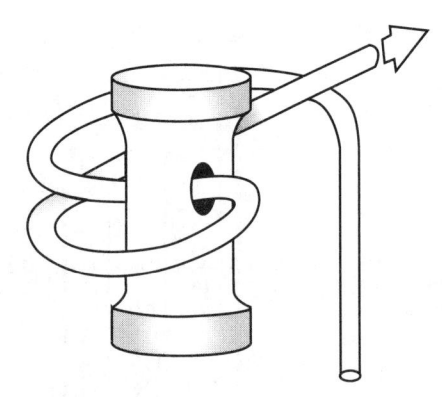

Full size nylon-string guitars can also use the ball-end type of string. Standard nylon strings must be wrapped around the bridge as shown in the illustration:

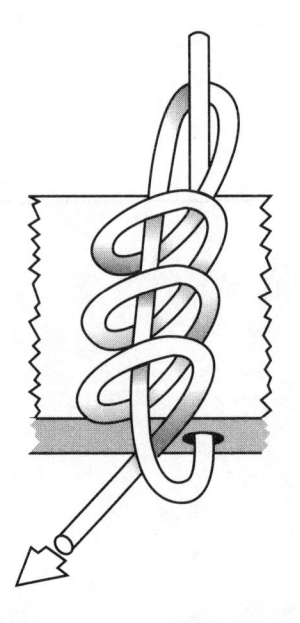

# Equipping Your Guitar Class

Steel strings (both acoustic and electric) use a ball-end type of construction and would be installed the same as the ball-end nylon strings.

**Picks**: Picks come in many shapes and sizes. The type shown below is the most common and useful. I suggest buying a gross for the class.

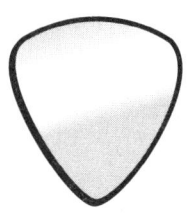

**Tuners:** Electronic guitar tuners, like the one described on page 7 are available fairly cheap. This may be a very worthwhile investment.

**Foot Stools:** It is recommended that you elevate whichever leg the guitar is sitting on. If you are teaching classic position you should use a foot stool to elevate the left leg. When sitting with the guitar on the right leg use it to elevate the right leg. If you don't have any foot stools a guitar case or a stack of books can do the trick.

**Storage:** The guitars should be stored off the floor. Guitar hangers as shown in diagram 4 work for any guitar; they allow you to hang the guitar on the wall when not in use. These hangers are available through your local dealer or you may be able to talk your wood-shop instructor into building a set of hangers (one for each guitar) and mounting them on the wall (diagram 5).

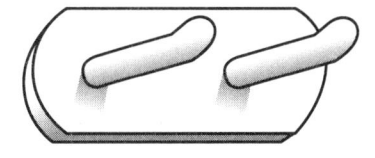

# Guitar Chord Chart

Student page 48 from *Guitar Method 1*

## Guitar Chord Chart

The following chart shows all of the most commonly used guitar chords.
o indicates an open string. x indicates the string is not to be played.

| A | Am | A7 |
|---|----|----|
| B7 | C | C7 |
| D | Dm | D7 |
| E | Em | E7 |
| F | G | G7 |
| E5 | A5 | D5 |

# Guitar Fingerboard Chart

Student page 32 from *Guitar Theory 1*

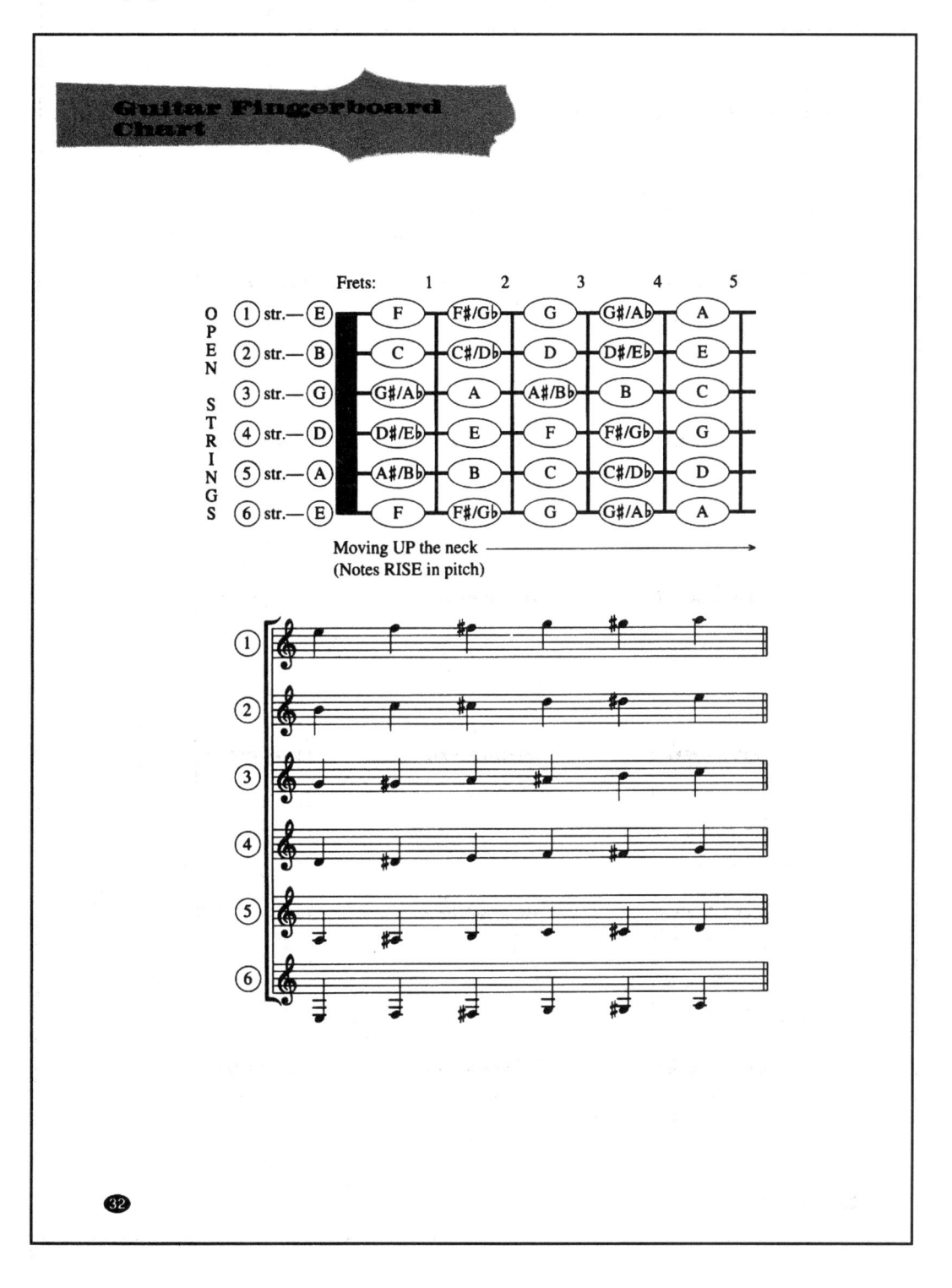

# Guitar Method 1

## Lesson 1: Music and Rhythm Notation

### New Concept
Music Staff
G Clef
Placement of notes on the lines and spaces
Measures
Bar Lines
Tablature

---

**Music Notation**

There are seven natural notes. They are named for the first seven letters of the alphabet: A B C D E F G. After G, we begin again with A.

Music is written on a **staff**. The staff consists of five lines with four spaces between the lines:

At the beginning of the staff is a treble or G clef. (The treble clef is known as the G clef because it encircles the 2nd line G.) The clef determines the location of notes on the staff. All guitar music is written on a treble clef.

The notes are written on the staff in alphabetical order. The first line is E:

Notes can extend above, and below, the treble clef. When they do, **ledger lines** are added. Following is the approximate range of the guitar from the lowest note, open sixth string "E," to "B" on the first string, 17th fret.

The staff is divided into *measures* by *bar lines*. A heavy double bar line marks the end of the music:

**Tablature** is a type of music notation that is specific to the guitar; its use dates back to the 1600's. Tablature illustrates the location of notes on the neck of the guitar. Tablature is usually used in conjunction with a music staff. The notes and rhythms are indicated in the music staff; the tablature shows where those notes are played on the guitar.

The location of any note is indicated by the placement of fret numbers on the strings.

1st string
2nd string
3rd string
4th string
5th string
6th string

In this book, tablature will be used with all new notes and fingerings. "Tab" will also be used on all pop songs and as an aid to learning the more challenging arrangements; thereby making the learning process easier and more fun.

❻

---

### Objective
- This lesson is a primer. It will provide a basic understanding of notation and tablature and how they relate to the guitar.

### Teacher Suggestions
- Present the music staff and treble (G) clef.
- Explain and demonstrate the alphabetical sequence of notes on the staff.
- Draw, as shown on the above student page, the entire range of the guitar from low E to high B (the upper range varies widely).
- Play the low E and high B. Demonstrate that as the notes rise in pitch they are notated progressively higher on the staff.
- Draw the six line tablature staff. Show how it is actually a diagram of the six strings of the guitar. The location of any note can be indicated by the placement of fret numbers on the strings.

**Teacher Note:** Tablature is a type of music notation that is specific to the guitar, its use dates back to the Renaissance period. Because of its ease and immediate accessibility it is currently very popular in the notation of all forms of guitar music. Tablature does not indicate rhythm and is usually used in conjunction with standard notation. Tab works best when the student either already knows how a song should sound or is using it in conjunction with a recorded version of the song. In the *Guitar Method* books, tab is used on all pop and rock songs and as an aid in learning new material and some of the more challenging arrangements.

# Lesson 1: Music and Rhythm Notation

**Guitar Method 1**

### Rhythm Notation And Time Signatures

At the beginning of every song is a time signature. 4/4 is the most common time signature:

$\frac{4}{4}$ FOUR COUNTS TO A MEASURE
A QUARTER NOTE RECEIVES ONE COUNT

The top number tells you how many counts per measure.
The bottom number tells you which kind of note receives one count.

The time value of a note is determined by three things:

1) note head:
2) stem:
3) flag:

○ This is a whole note. The note head is open and has no stem. In 4/4 time, a whole note receives 4 counts.

♩ This is a half note. It has an open note head and a stem. A half note receives 2 counts.

♩ This is a quarter note. It has a solid note head and a stem. A quarter note receives 1 count.

♪ This is an eighth note. It has a solid note head and a stem with a flag attached. An eighth note receives 1/2 count.

| Whole Note: | ○ | | | |
|---|---|---|---|---|
| Count: | 1 | 2 | 3 | 4 |
| Half Note: | ♩ | | ♩ | |
| Count: | 1 | 2 | 3 | 4 |
| Quarter Note: | ♩ | ♩ | ♩ | ♩ |
| Count: | 1 | 2 | 3 | 4 |
| Eighth Note: | ♪♪ | ♪♪ | ♪♪ | ♪♪ |
| Count: | 1 & | 2 & | 3 & | 4 & |

Count out loud and clap the rhythm to this excerpt from *Jingle Bells*.

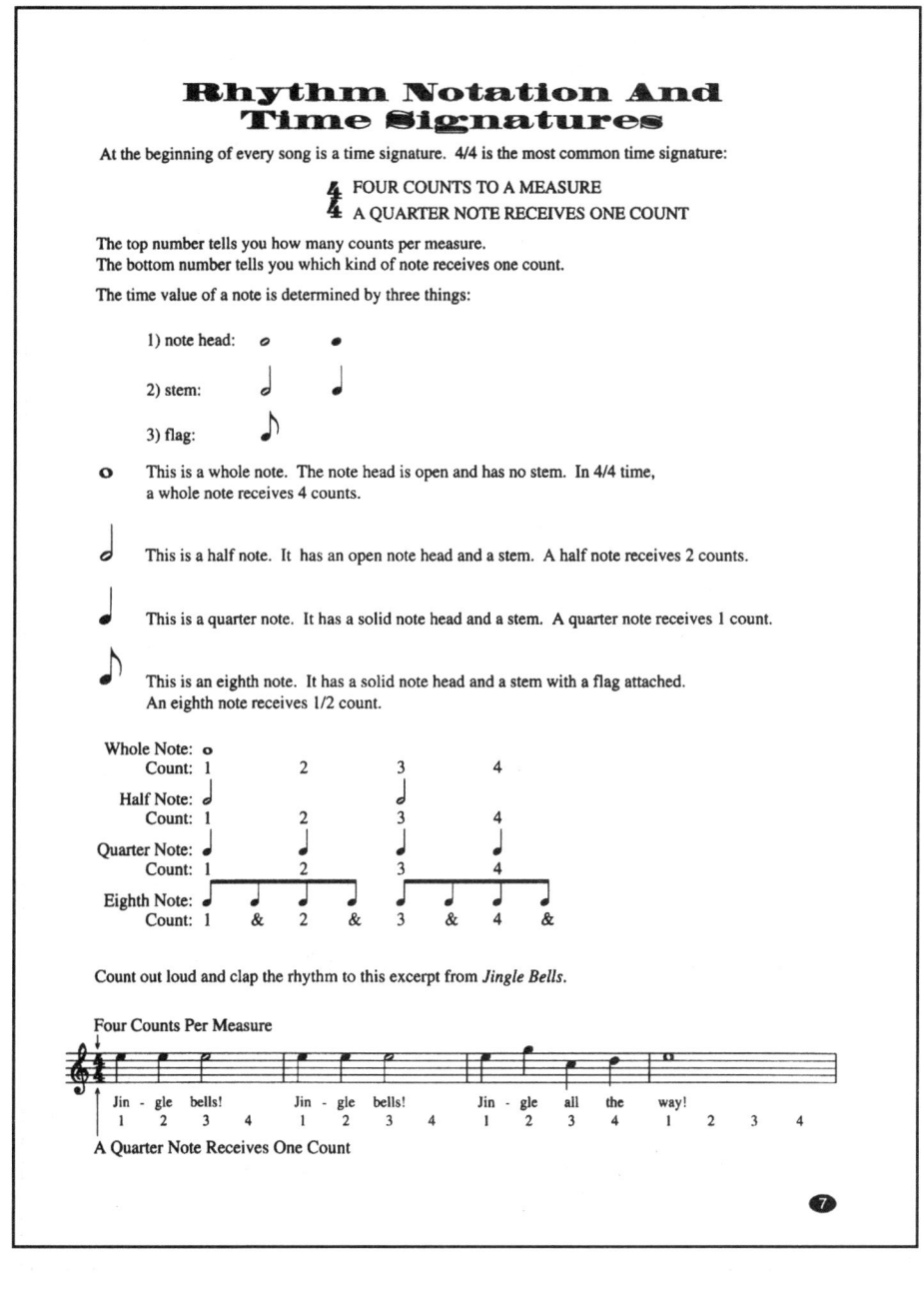

Four Counts Per Measure

Jin - gle bells! Jin - gle bells! Jin - gle all the way!
1  2  3  4   1  2  3  4   1  2  3  4   1  2  3  4

A Quarter Note Receives One Count

⑦

## New Concept

4/4
Note Head
Stem
Flag
Whole note
Half note
Quarter note
Eighth note

## Teacher Suggestions
- Explain the time signature.
- Have students draw note heads (open and closed), stems, and flags (see theory book for more written exercises).
- Explain whole, half, quarter and eighth notes. Demonstrate each by counting and clapping and playing at the piano or guitar.
- Have students count and clap the rhythm to *Jingle Bells*.

**Teacher Note:** Lesson 1 is the same whether using the *Guitar Method* or *Rock Shop* books. *Guitar Method* pages 4 and 5 are the same as *Rock Shop* pages 6 and 7.

# Guitar Theory 1

## Theory Lesson 1: Music & Rhythm Notation

**Reinforces**

Music Staff
G Clef
Placement of notes on the lines and spaces
Measures
Bar Lines

---

### Music Notation

Music is written on a five line staff. Between each line there is a space.

Number the lines and spaces:

line # ___ →
line # ___ →
line # ___ →
line # ___ →
line # _1_ →

space # ___
space # ___
space # ___
space # _1_

At the beginning of each staff there is a clef. The treble clef encircles the second line which is the note G. Therefore, it is sometimes called the G clef:

← G

Notes are named after the first seven letters of the alphabet (A through G):

E  F  G  A  B  C  D  E  F  G

Draw the notes of the musical alphabet:

A  B  C  D  E  F  G

Music is divided into equal parts called **measures.**
**Bar lines** indicate the beginning and end of measures.

The distance between two bar lines is called a measure.
**Double bar lines,** one thin and one thick, show the end of a piece.

Bar Lines          Double Bar Line
Measure  Measure  Measure

1. Divide the staff into seven measures.
2. Name the notes.
3. End the staff with a double bar line.

A ___  ___  ___  ___  ___  ___

Use after page 6 of *Belwin's 21st Century Guitar Method 1*.

❷

---

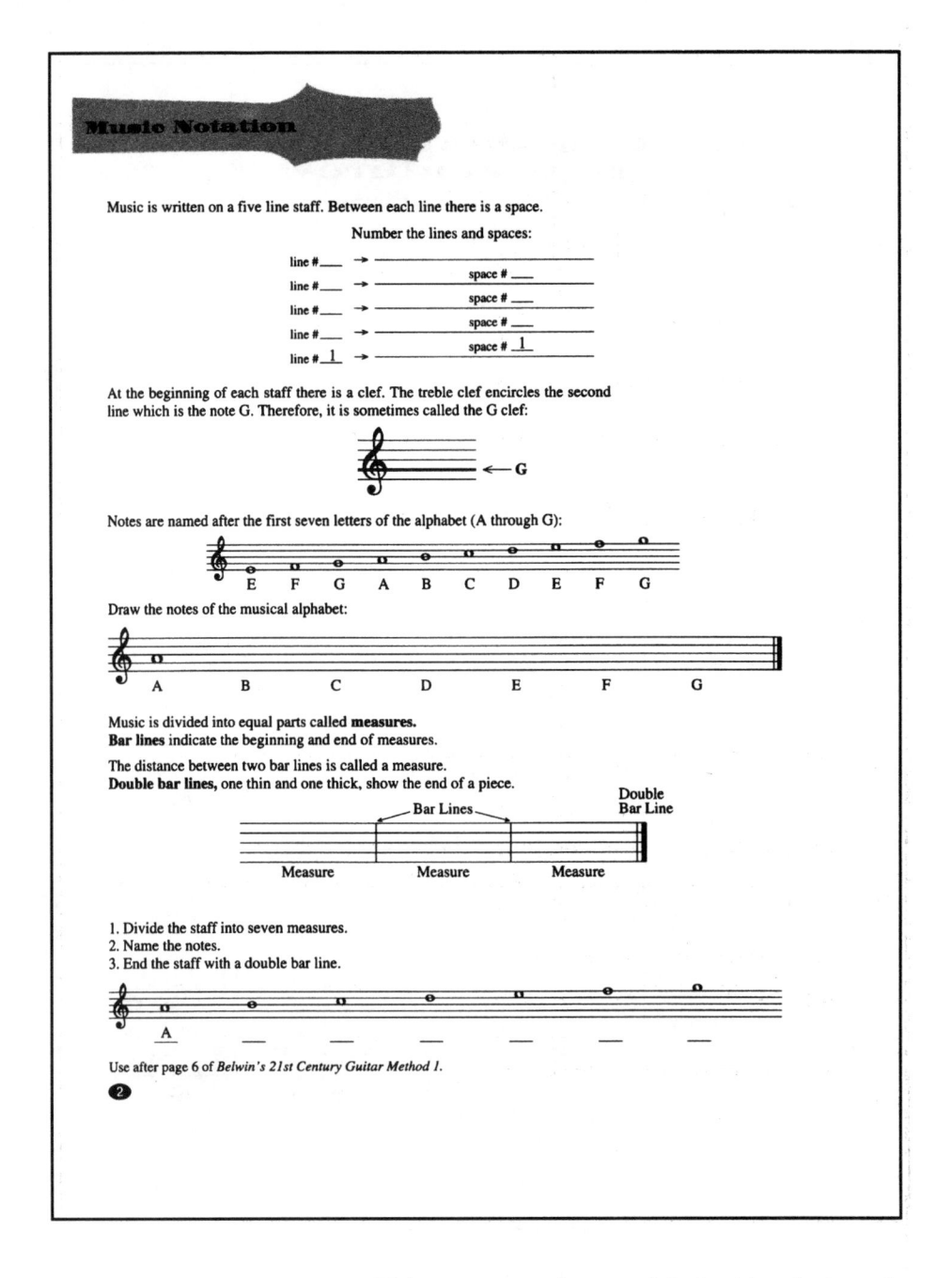

This page correlates to Method book page 6.

*Guitar Theory 1* supports all the new concepts taught in *Guitar Method 1*. The book is written workbook-style with examples and exercises that reinforce reading and writing music; relate music notation to tablature and guitar frames, and build an understanding of the guitar fingerboard.

### Teacher Suggestions
- Explain each fill-in example.
- Do part of each example with students.
- Have students complete the examples on their own or as homework assignments.

# Theory Lesson 1: Music & Rhythm Notation

**Guitar Theory 1**

## Reinforces
4/4
Note Head
Stem
Flag
Whole note
Half note
Quarter note
Eighth note

This page correlates to Method book page 7.

## Teacher Suggestions
- Explain each fill-in example.
- Have students clap each rhythm example.
- Do part of each example with students.
- Have students complete the examples on their own or as homework assignments.

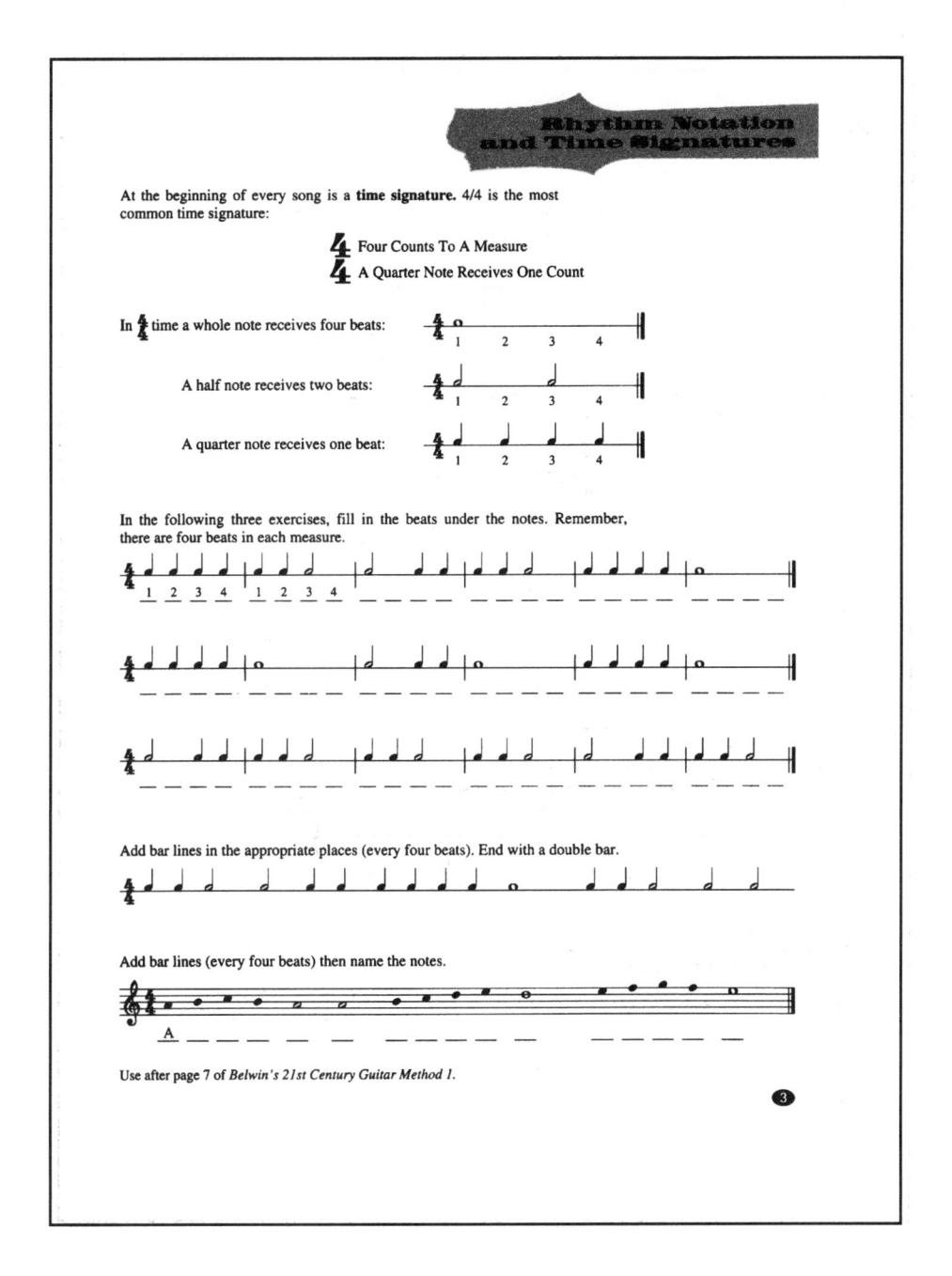

**Guitar Rock Shop 1**

# Lesson 1: Music and Rhythm Notation

## New Concept
Music Staff
G Clef
Placement of notes on the lines and spaces
Measures
Bar Lines
Tablature

---

### Music Notation

There are seven natural notes. They are named for the first seven letters of the alphabet: A B C D E F G. After G, we begin again with A.

Music is written on a **staff**. The staff consists of five lines with four spaces between the lines:

- 5th Line / 4th Space
- 4th Line / 3rd Space
- 3rd Line / 2nd Space
- 2nd Line / 1st Space
- 1st Line

At the beginning of the staff is a treble or G clef. (The treble clef is known as the G clef because it encircles the 2nd line G.) The clef determines the location of notes on the staff. All guitar music is written on a treble clef.

The notes are written on the staff in alphabetical order. The first line is E:

Notes can extend above, and below, the treble clef. When they do, **ledger lines** are added. Following is the approximate range of the guitar from the lowest note, open sixth string "E," to "B" on the first string, 17th fret.

The staff is divided into *measures* by *bar lines*. A heavy double bar line marks the end of the music:

**Tablature** is a type of music notation that is specific to the guitar; its use dates back to the 1600's. Tablature illustrates the location of notes on the neck of the guitar. Tablature is usually used in conjunction with a music staff. The notes and rhythms are indicated in the music staff; the tablature shows where those notes are played on the guitar.

The location of any note is indicated by the placement of fret numbers on the strings.

1st string
2nd string
3rd string
4th string
5th string
6th string

In this book, tablature will be used with all new notes and fingerings. "Tab" will also be used on all pop songs and as an aid to learning the more challenging arrangements; thereby making the learning process easier and more fun.

---

**Teacher Note:** Lesson 1 is the same whether using the *Guitar Method* or *Rock Shop* books. *Guitar Method* pages 6 and 7 are the same as *Rock Shop* pages 4 and 5.

## Objective
- This lesson is a primer. It will provide a basic understanding of notation and tablature and how they relate to the guitar.

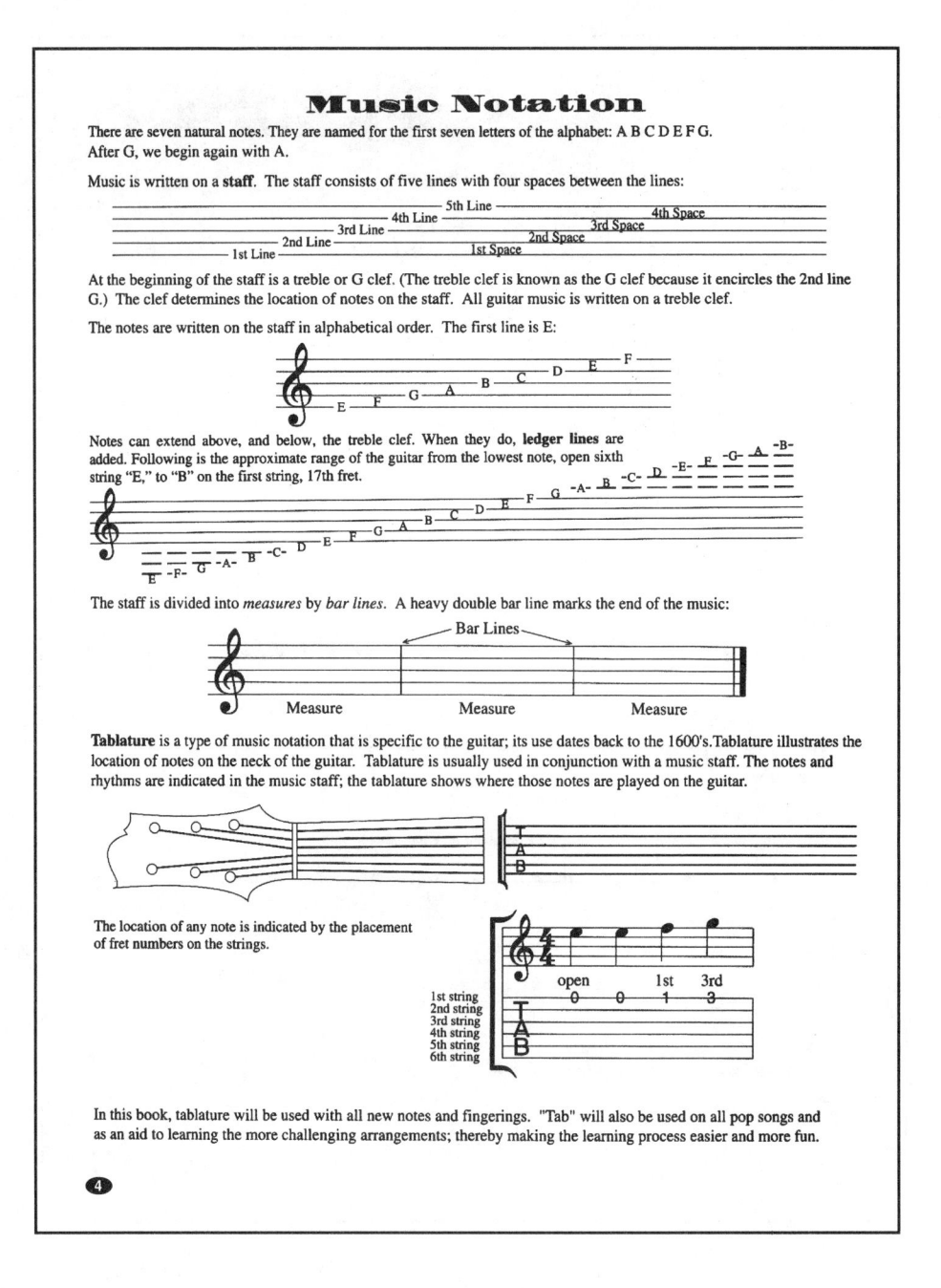

## Teacher Suggestions
- Present the music staff and treble (G) clef.
- Explain and demonstrate the alphabetical sequence of notes on the staff.
- Draw, as shown in the above student page, the entire range of the guitar from low E to high B (the upper range varies widely).
- Play the low E and high B. Demonstrate that as the notes rise in pitch they are notated progressively higher on the staff.
- Draw the six line tablature staff. Show how it is actually a diagram of the six strings of the guitar. The location of any note can be indicated by the placement of fret numbers on the strings.

**Teacher Note:** Tablature is a type of music notation that is specific to the guitar, its use dates back to the Renaissance period. Because of its ease and immediate accessibility it is currently very popular in the notation of all forms of guitar music. Tablature does not indicate rhythm and is usually used in conjunction with standard notation. Tab works best when the student either already knows how a song should sound or is using it in conjunction with a recorded version of the song. In the *Guitar Rock Shop* books, tab is used throughout.

# Lesson 1: Music and Rhythm Notation

**Guitar Rock Shop 1**

## Rhythm Notation And Time Signatures

At the beginning of every song is a time signature. 4/4 is the most common time signature:

**4** FOUR COUNTS TO A MEASURE
**4** A QUARTER NOTE RECEIVES ONE COUNT

The top number tells you how many counts per measure.
The bottom number tells you which kind of note receives one count.

The time value of a note is determined by three things:

1) note head:
2) stem:
3) flag:

This is a whole note. The note head is open and has no stem. In 4/4 time, a whole note receives 4 counts.

This is a half note. It has an open note head and a stem. A half note receives 2 counts.

This is a quarter note. It has a solid note head and a stem. A quarter note receives 1 count.

This is an eighth note. It has a solid note head and a stem with a flag attached. An eighth note receives 1/2 count.

Whole Note:
Count: 1  2  3  4
Half Note:
Count: 1  2  3  4
Quarter Note:
Count: 1  2  3  4
Eighth Note:
Count: 1 & 2 & 3 & 4 &

Count out loud and clap the rhythm to this excerpt from *Jingle Bells*.

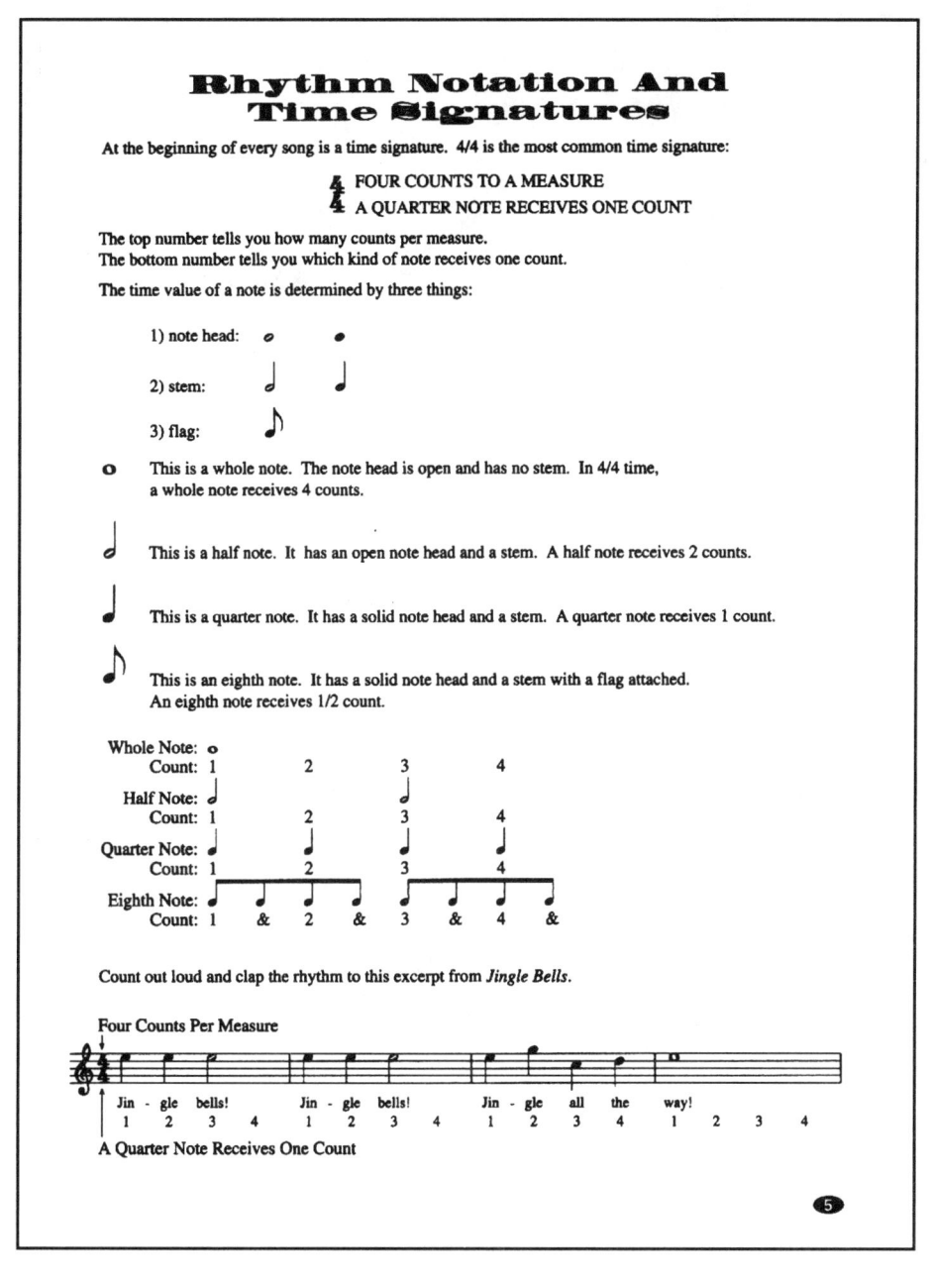

Four Counts Per Measure

Jin - gle bells! Jin - gle bells! Jin - gle all the way!
1  2  3  4    1  2  3  4    1  2  3  4   1  2  3  4

A Quarter Note Receives One Count

## New Concept

4/4
Note Head
Stem
Flag
Whole note
Half note
Quarter note
Eighth note

## Teacher Suggestions

- Explain the time signature.
- Have students draw note heads (open and closed), stems, and flags (see theory book for more written exercises).
- Explain whole, half, quarter and eighth notes. Demonstrate each by counting and clapping and playing at the piano or guitar.
- Have students count and clap the rhythm to *Jingle Bells*.

17

# Guitar Method 1

## Lesson 2: The Notes on the First String

**New Concepts**

First string E, F and G

Using the pick

The downstroke (⊓)

Right- and left-hand position

Relating notation and tab to playing the guitar

**Objective**
- Learn the first string E, F and G
- Be able to play the songs on *Method* page 9 in tempo with the recording or with the optional teacher accompaniments

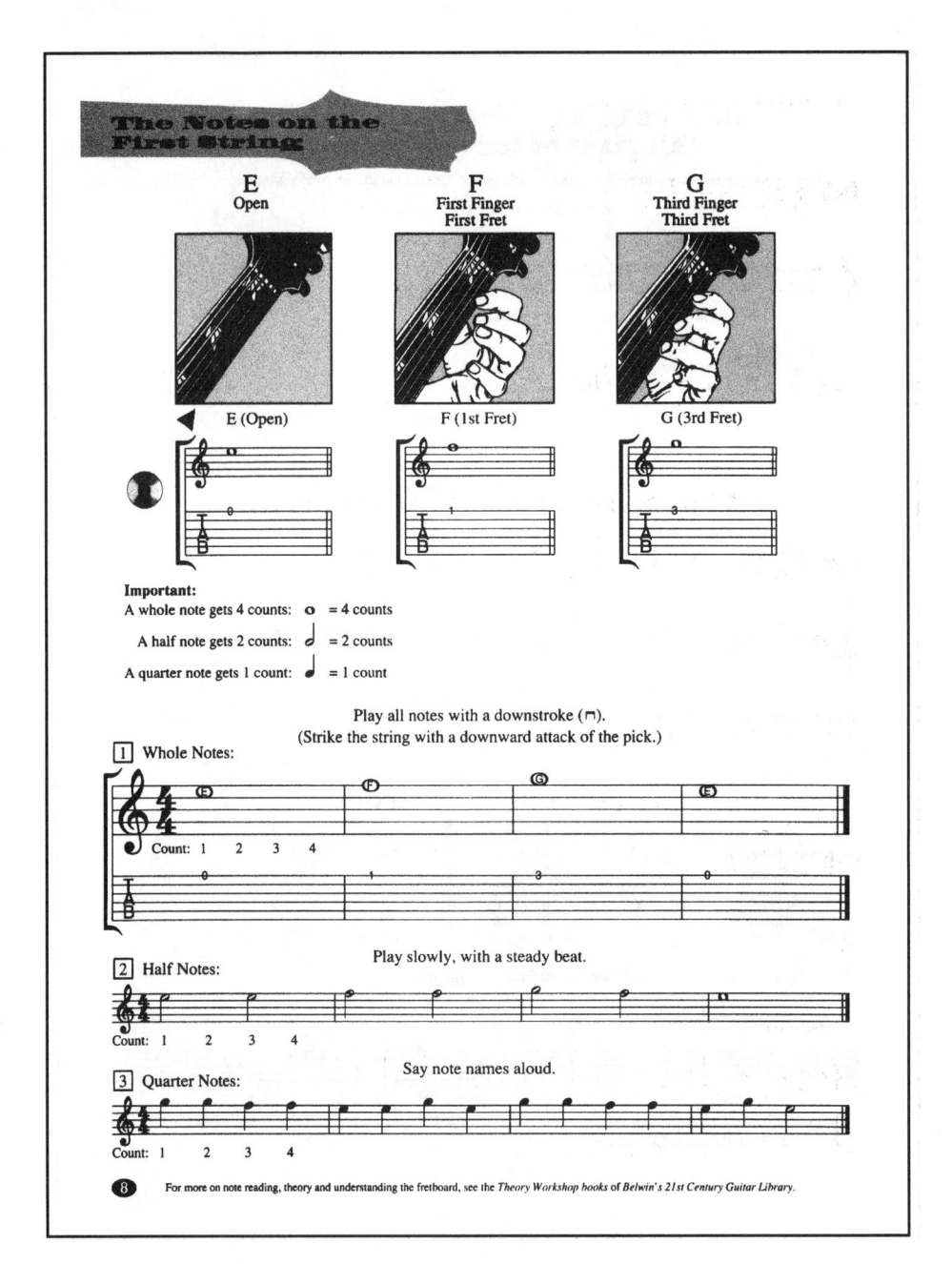

**Teacher Suggestions**
- Have students play E, F and G. Show how the notes they are playing relate to the drawings, notation and tab.
- Demonstrate proper sitting position (see method page 4).
- Have students listen to program 3 on recording.

**Technique:** (See photos, method page 4) The right hand should be held in a loose fist. Hold the pick between the first and second fingers (thumb and index). The fifth finger, or even the third, fourth and fifth fingers can rest gently on the top of the guitar. (Curl the fingers slightly so the finger nail, not the flesh of the finger tip, touches the top.) The left hand thumb should be placed in the center of the neck, behind the second finger, with the elbow moved out in front of the body.

**Teacher Note:** All new techniques and concepts are carefully described and demonstrated on the available recording. If the guitar is not your principle instrument the instructional segments of the recording will prove invaluable in guiding your students through this course.

# Lesson 2: The Notes on the First String

**Guitar Method 1**

## Reinforces
First string E, F and G
Whole notes
Half notes
Quarter notes

## Listening Suggestions
• If possible, play recordings in the styles of the pieces being learned.
• Folk: Any popular guitar/vocal artist like early James Taylor or Joni Mitchell.
• Flamenco: Paco Pena, Paco de Lucia
• Blues: B.B. King, Buddy Guy, Stevie Ray Vaughan

## Teacher Suggestions
- All the music is performed on the accompaniment recordings with full accompaniment tracks—the student part being isolated in the right channel and the accompaniment tracks in the left. The students will learn much faster and enjoy learning the guitar much more if they are able to hear, and play-along with, each song.
- It is suggested that each student have their own copy of the recording. If this is not feasible, have at least one copy for class use.
- Use the following listening sequence for learning all songs.
    Play the recordings of each song four times:
    1) the complete recording
    2) the student part (move your balance control all the way to the right)
    3) the accompaniment part (balance control all the way to the left)
    4) the complete recording
- **Group Class:** When ready, have students perform the songs in unison, playing with the accompaniment tracks. If you have some advanced students in class, have them strum the chords while the rest of the class plays melody.

19

**Guitar Theory 1**

**Theory Lesson 2: The Notes on the First String**

## Reinforces

First string E, F and G
Whole notes
Half notes
Quarter note

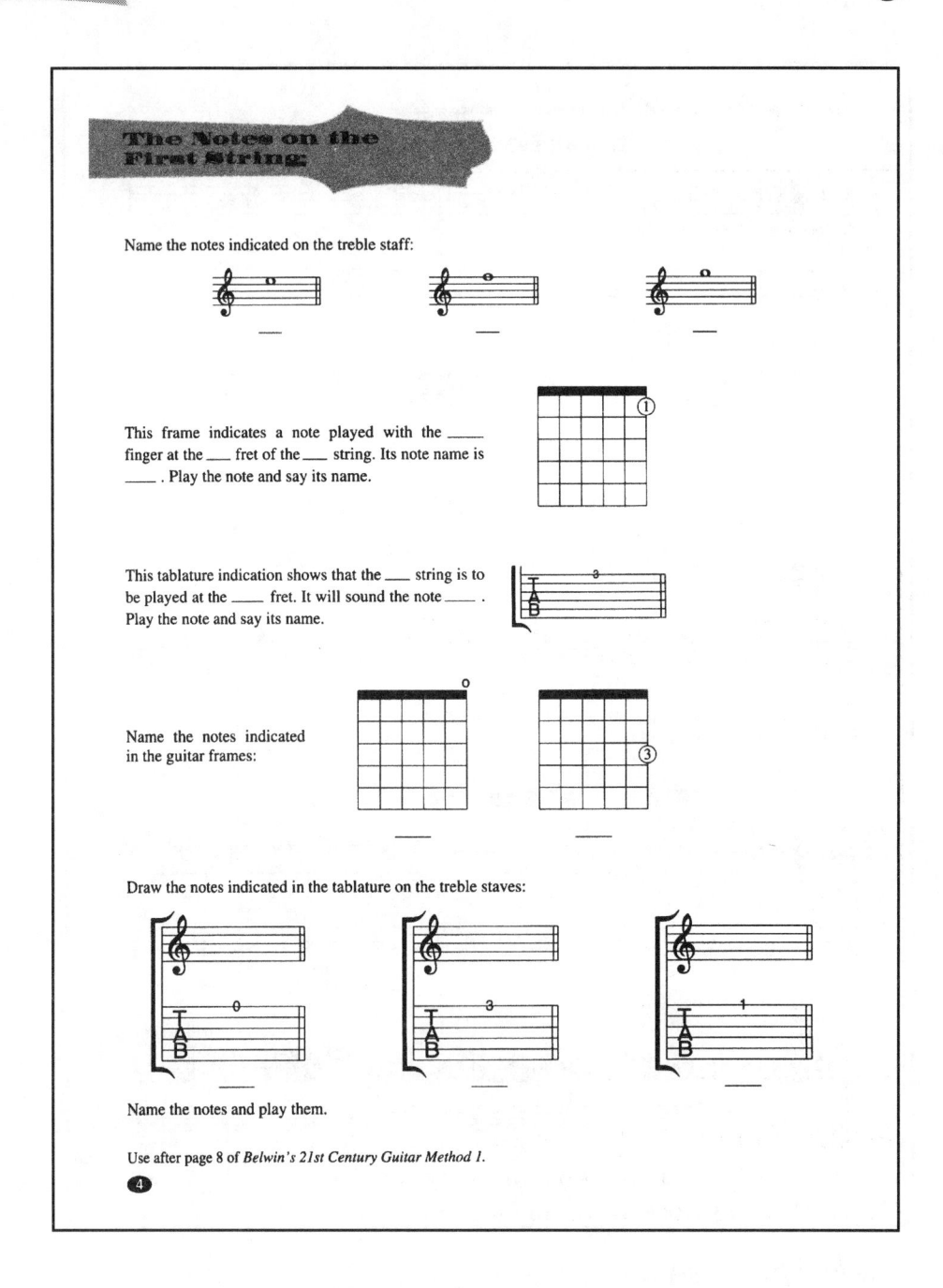

---

**The Notes on the First String:**

Name the notes indicated on the treble staff:

This frame indicates a note played with the ____ finger at the ____ fret of the ____ string. Its note name is ____ . Play the note and say its name.

This tablature indication shows that the ____ string is to be played at the ____ fret. It will sound the note ____ . Play the note and say its name.

Name the notes indicated in the guitar frames:

Draw the notes indicated in the tablature on the treble staves:

Name the notes and play them.

Use after page 8 of *Belwin's 21st Century Guitar Method 1*.

❹

---

This page correlates to *Guitar Method 1* page 8.

## Objective
- The notation, guitar frame and tablature fill-in examples are intended to develop the students ability to understand and visualize note locations on the neck of the guitar.

## Teacher Suggestions
- Explain each fill-in example.
- Do part of each example with students.
- Have students complete the examples on their own or as homework assignments.

# Rock Lesson 2: The E5 Power Chord

**Guitar Rock Shop 1**

## New Concepts
Power Chords, E5, Chord Construction

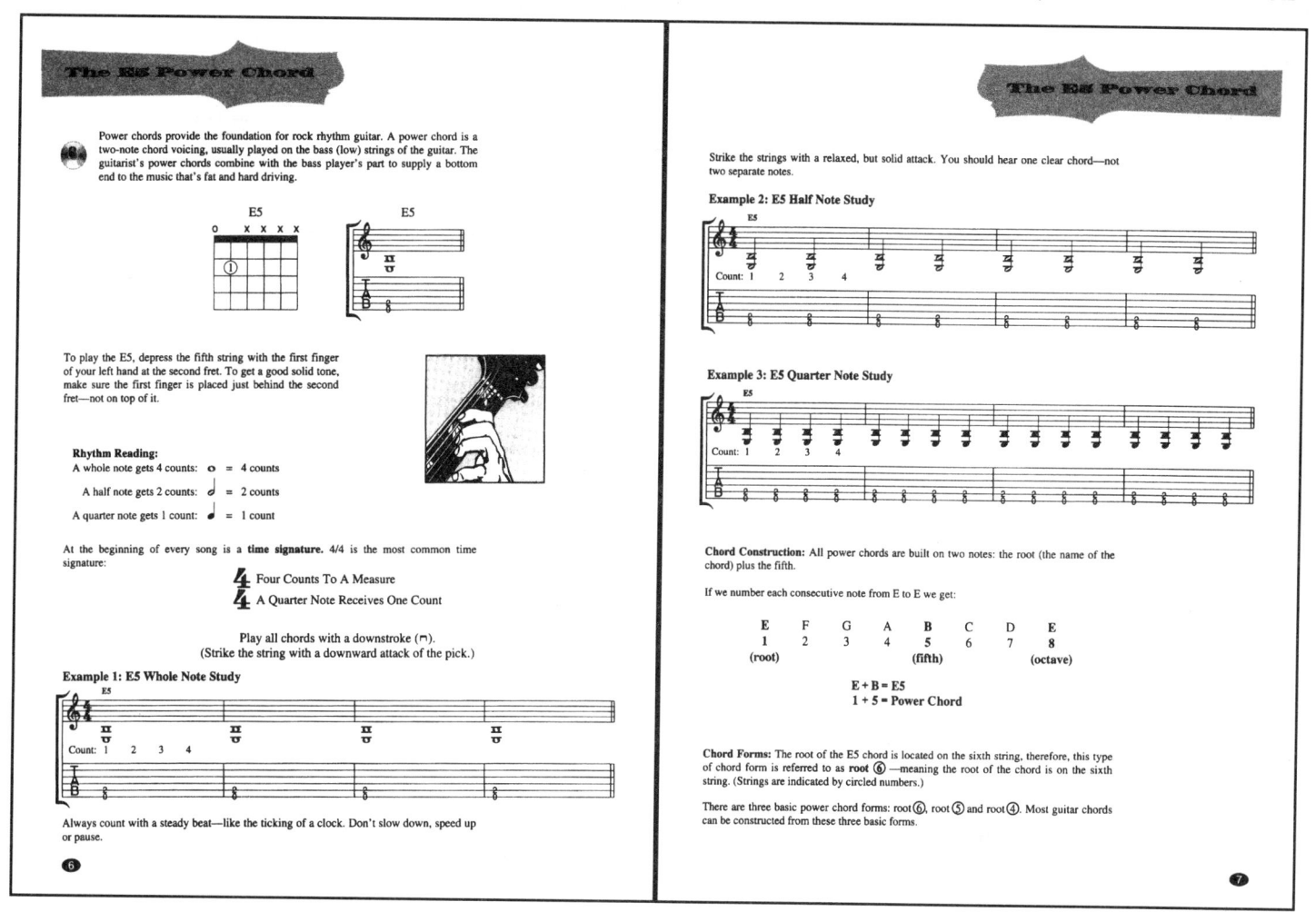

---

### The E5 Power Chord

Power chords provide the foundation for rock rhythm guitar. A power chord is a two-note chord voicing, usually played on the bass (low) strings of the guitar. The guitarist's power chords combine with the bass player's part to supply a bottom end to the music that's fat and hard driving.

To play the E5, depress the fifth string with the first finger of your left hand at the second fret. To get a good solid tone, make sure the first finger is placed just behind the second fret—not on top of it.

**Rhythm Reading:**
A whole note gets 4 counts: o = 4 counts
A half note gets 2 counts: ♩ = 2 counts
A quarter note gets 1 count: ♩ = 1 count

At the beginning of every song is a **time signature**. 4/4 is the most common time signature:

4 — Four Counts To A Measure
4 — A Quarter Note Receives One Count

Play all chords with a downstroke (⊓).
(Strike the string with a downward attack of the pick.)

**Example 1: E5 Whole Note Study**

Always count with a steady beat—like the ticking of a clock. Don't slow down, speed up or pause.

### The E5 Power Chord

Strike the strings with a relaxed, but solid attack. You should hear one clear chord—not two separate notes.

**Example 2: E5 Half Note Study**

**Example 3: E5 Quarter Note Study**

**Chord Construction:** All power chords are built on two notes: the root (the name of the chord) plus the fifth.

If we number each consecutive note from E to E we get:

| E | F | G | A | B | C | D | E |
|---|---|---|---|---|---|---|---|
| 1 | 2 | 3 | 4 | 5 | 6 | 7 | 8 |
| (root) | | | | (fifth) | | | (octave) |

E + B = E5
1 + 5 = Power Chord

**Chord Forms:** The root of the E5 chord is located on the sixth string, therefore, this type of chord form is referred to as **root** ⑥—meaning the root of the chord is on the sixth string. (Strings are indicated by circled numbers.)

There are three basic power chord forms: root ⑥, root ⑤ and root ④. Most guitar chords can be constructed from these three basic forms.

---

**Teacher Note:** The *Rock Shop* series is designed as a complete, stand-alone method for rock guitar. It covers the same rhythms and positions as the *Guitar Method* and is correlated to the sequence of material taught in the *Guitar Method's* Rock Workshop sections.

## Objective
- Learn the E5
- Understand its construction (root/5th)
- Be able to locate the root (E on the sixth string)

## Teacher Suggestions
- Listen to program 3 on the recording, it describes the E5 power chord and demonstrates each of the music examples.
- Help students to locate (hear) and sing the root (E) of the E5 power chord (they should sing it in whichever octave is most comfortable). Have students sing the root, in rhythm, with Examples 1 - 3. They should sing with the play-along tracks and then they can sing and play. This is terrific ear training!

**Technique:** (See photos, *Rock Shop* page 2) The right hand should be held in a loose fist. Hold the pick between the first and second fingers (thumb and index). The fifth finger, or even the third, fourth and fifth fingers can rest gently on the top of the guitar (curl the fingers slightly so the finger nail, not the flesh of the finger tip, touches the top. The left hand thumb should be placed in the center of the neck behind the second finger with the elbow moved out in front of the body.

# Guitar Method 1

## Lesson 3: The Notes on the Second String

**New Concepts**
Second string B, C and D

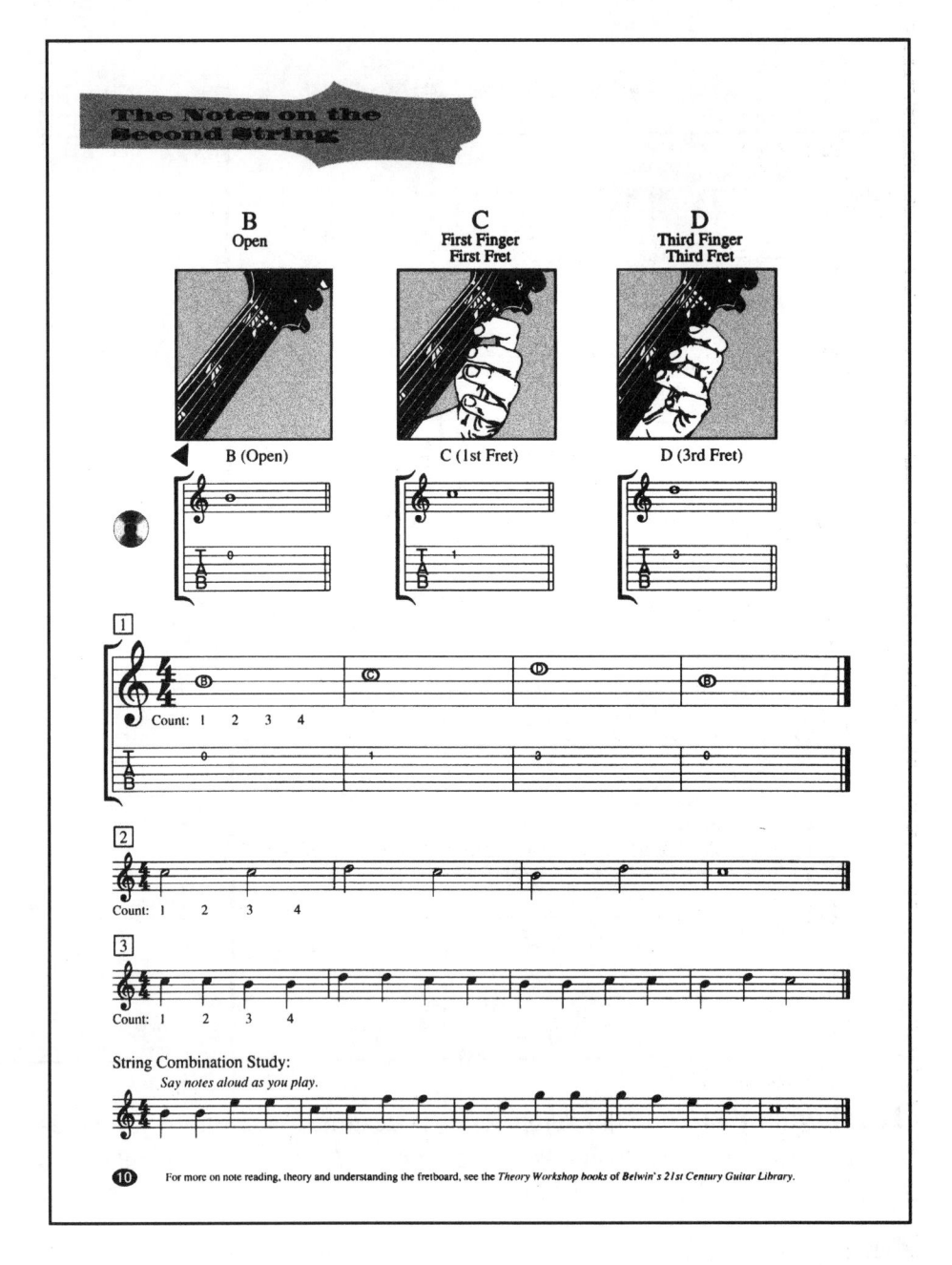

**Objective**
- Learn the second string B, C and D
- Be able to play the songs on Method page 11 in tempo with the recording or with the optional teacher accompaniments
- Review first string E, F and G and rhythms: w, h & q

**Teacher Suggestions**
- Have students play B, C and D. Show how the notes they are playing relate to the drawings, notation and **tab**.
- Have students play B, C, D, E, F and G noting that the notes ascend in pitch as they ascend through the alphabet.
- Technique: Review proper sitting position and left and right hand technique (left-hand thumb behind the neck, pick held loosely between the index and middle fingers).
- Have students listen to program 7 on recording.
- Optional Ensemble Book: Students are now prepared to play *Love Somebody* and *The Trolley Song* on pages 4 and 6 of *Guitar Ensemble 1*.

# Lesson 3: The Notes on the Second String

**Guitar Method 1**

## Reinforces
Second string B, C and D
First string E, F and G

[Sheet music: **Jingle Bells** (Brightly, J. Pierpont) — "Jingle bells! Jingle bells! Jingle all the way! Oh, what fun it is to ride a one-horse o-pen sleigh. Jingle bells! Jingle bells! Jingle all the way! Oh, what fun it is to ride a one-horse o-pen sleigh."]

[Sheet music: **Aura Lee** (Slowly, Traditional American Folk Song) — "As the black-bird in the spring, 'neath the wil-low tree, sat and piped I heard him sing, sing of Au-ra Lee." with Suggested Teacher Accompaniment.]

[Sheet music: **The Boogie Shuffle** (Medium tempo, A.S.) with Suggested Teacher Accompaniment (Medium tempo - shuffle feel).]

11

## Teacher Suggestions
- *Aura Lee* is a popular American folk song from the Civil War era. Elvis Presley recorded it as *Love Me Tender* for the movie of the same name. If possible bring in a recording of that version for the class to hear.
- Use the suggested listening sequence described on page 19.
- Have students sing the melodies to *Jingle Bells* and *Aura Lee* along with the accompaniment tracks. Singing is a valuable ear training device. Also, singing is the most immediate and personal way for anyone to become involved in music. Some students will even discover a talent for it.
- **Group Class:** When ready, have students perform the songs in unison, playing with the accompaniment tracks. If you have some advanced students in class, have them strum the chords while the rest of the class plays melody.

# Guitar Theory 1

## Theory Lesson 3: The Notes on the Second String

**Reinforces**
Second string B, C and D

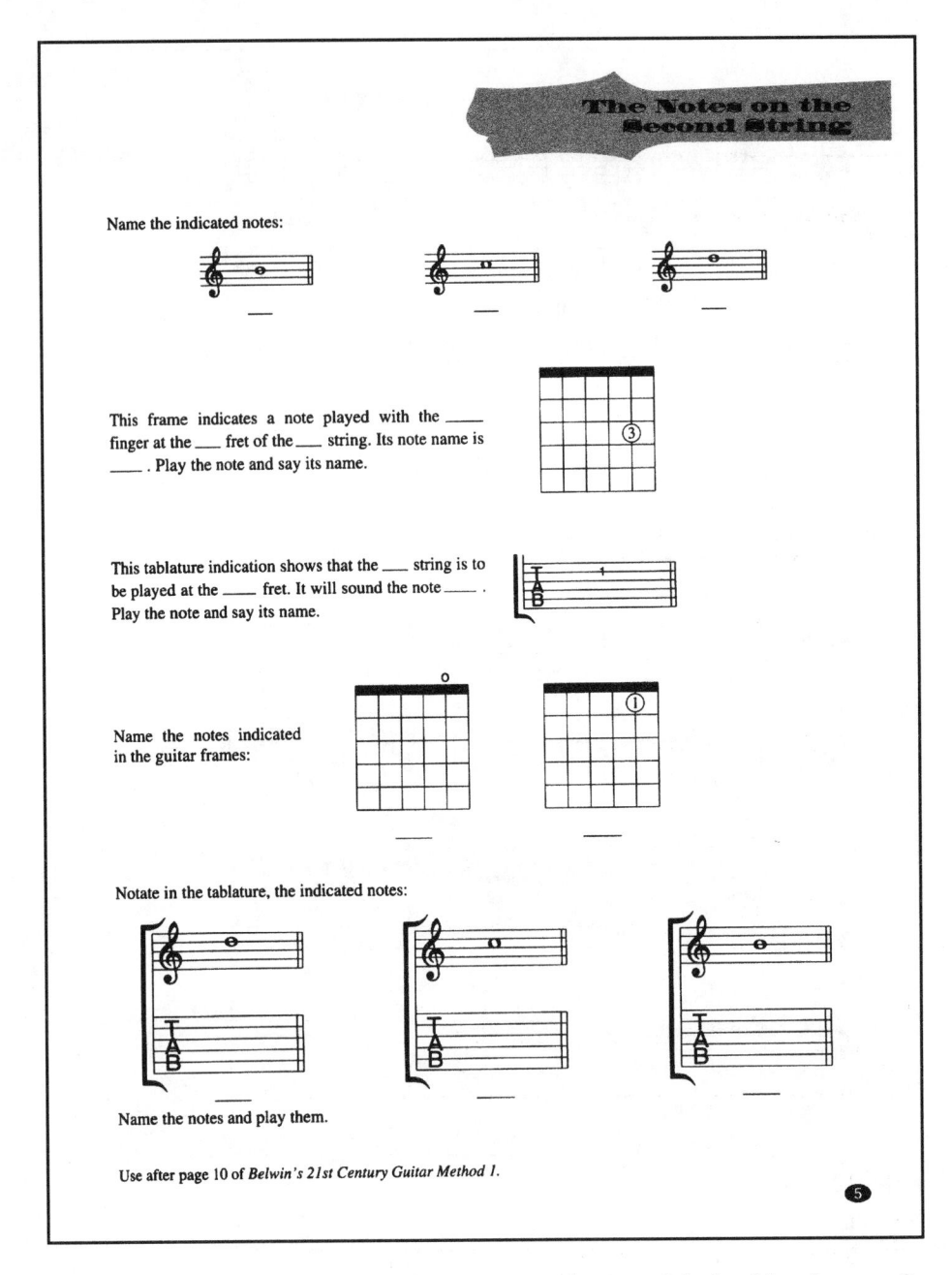

---

### The Notes on the Second String

Name the indicated notes:

This frame indicates a note played with the ____ finger at the ____ fret of the ____ string. Its note name is ____ . Play the note and say its name.

This tablature indication shows that the ____ string is to be played at the ____ fret. It will sound the note ____ . Play the note and say its name.

Name the notes indicated in the guitar frames:

Notate in the tablature, the indicated notes:

Name the notes and play them.

Use after page 10 of *Belwin's 21st Century Guitar Method 1*.

---

This page correlates to Method book page 8.

## Objective
- Develop the students ability to understand and visualize note locations on the neck of the guitar.

## Teacher Suggestions
- Explain each fill-in example.
- Do part of each example with students.
- Have students complete the examples on their own or as homework assignments.

**Teacher Note:** If students are having trouble relating the tab and guitar frame diagrams to the neck of the guitar, lay a guitar flat, horizontally on a desk top in front of the student. Tablature is a horizontal diagram of the neck. Now hold the guitar vertically. Guitar frames are a vertical diagram of the neck.

# Rock Lesson 3: The A5 Power Chord

## Guitar Rock Shop 1

### New Concepts
A5, Combining E5 and A5

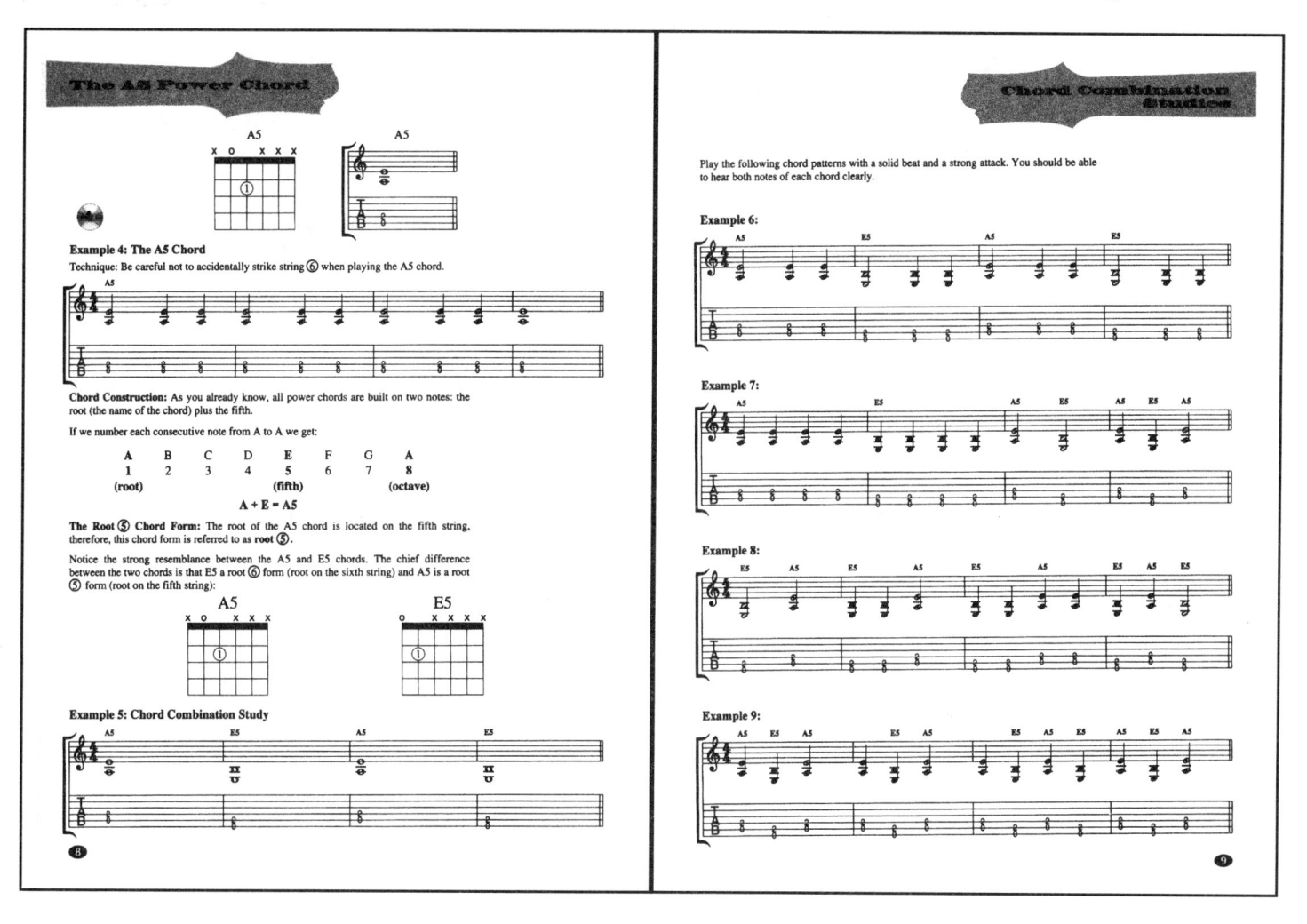

## Objective
- Learn the A5
- Understand its chord construction (root/5th)
- Be able to locate the root (A on the fifth string)

## Teacher Suggestions
- Listen to program 4 on the recording, it describes the A5 power chord and contains each of the music examples.
- Explain the construction of the A5 chord (root/fifth) and compare it to the construction of the E5 chord. (Note: At this time the students have not yet learned sharps, flats, key signatures or scale construction. They should derive the E5 and A5 chords from simple eight-note scales beginning on E and A rather than the complete E and A major scales.)
- Point out the resemblance between the "shape" of the E5 and the "shape" of the A5. The two chords look exactly alike. The only difference being the strings on which their roots are located.
- Have students sing the root (A) of the A5 power chord. Sing the root, in rhythm, with example 4. Help students to locate and sing the root movement (A - E) in examples 5 - 9. Once they can hear and sing the roots in example 5 they will quickly do the same in examples 6 - 9.

# Guitar Method 1

## Lesson 4: Ties and Pick-up Notes

**New Concepts**
Ties

**Reinforces**
First string E, F and G
Second string B, C and D
Whole notes
Half notes

---

### Tied Notes

A curved line connecting two notes of the same pitch is called a *tie*. Play the first note and hold it for the time value of both notes combined. Do not play the second note.

**All Tied Up**

**Mary Ann**
Caribbean

All day all night, Mar-y Ann, ___ down by the sea-shore sift-ing sand. ___ All the lit-tle chil-dren love Mar-y Ann, ___ down by the sea-shore sift-ing sand. ___

**Power Rock**
A.S.

*Suggested Teacher Accompaniment:*
*(Straight-eighth rock)*

---

**Objective**
- Be able to play, and count, ties and pick-up notes
- Review all notes and rhythms learned so far

**Teacher Suggestions**
- Have students count aloud while clapping the rhythm to each song.
- Have the students clap the rhythm of each song while listening to the recording (programs 11 - 13).
- Use the complete listening sequence described on page 19.
- Have students sing the melody to *Mary Ann* along with the accompaniment tracks.
- **Technique:** Review proper left- and right-hand positions.

# Lesson 4: Ties and Pick-up Notes

**Guitar Method 1**

## New Concepts
Pick-up Notes

## Reinforces
Ties

---

Not all songs begin on beat 1. Many songs begin with an incomplete measure. *Notes played before the first complete measure are called **pick-up notes**. The missing beats are usually found in the last measure of the song.*

*Pick-Up Piece* and *When The Saints Go Marching In* both begin on the second beat of an incomplete measure. Count the missing beat (1) out loud and then begin playing on 2.

### Pick-up Piece

(pick-up notes) ... (missing beat)
Count: (1) 2 3 4 ... 1

### When the Saints Go Marching In

Fast — Traditional Jazz

Oh when the saints _____ go march-ing in, _____ oh when the
Count: (1) 2 3 4

Saints go march-ing in. _____ Yes we'll

all get up and join 'em, _____ when the

Saints go march-ing in. _____

---

## Teacher Suggestions
- Describe the pick-up notes as an incomplete measure leading in to the first complete measure of the song.
- Students should count the pick-up along with the recording.
- Use the complete listening sequence described on page 19.
- Have students sing *Oh, When the Saints Go Marching In* with the accompaniment tracks.
- **Group Class:** When ready, have students perform the songs on pages 12 and 13 in unison, playing with the accompaniment tracks. If you have some advanced students in class, have them strum the chords while the rest of the class plays melody.

# Guitar Theory 1

## Theory Lesson 4: Ties and Pick-up Notes

**Reinforces**
Ties
Pick-up Notes

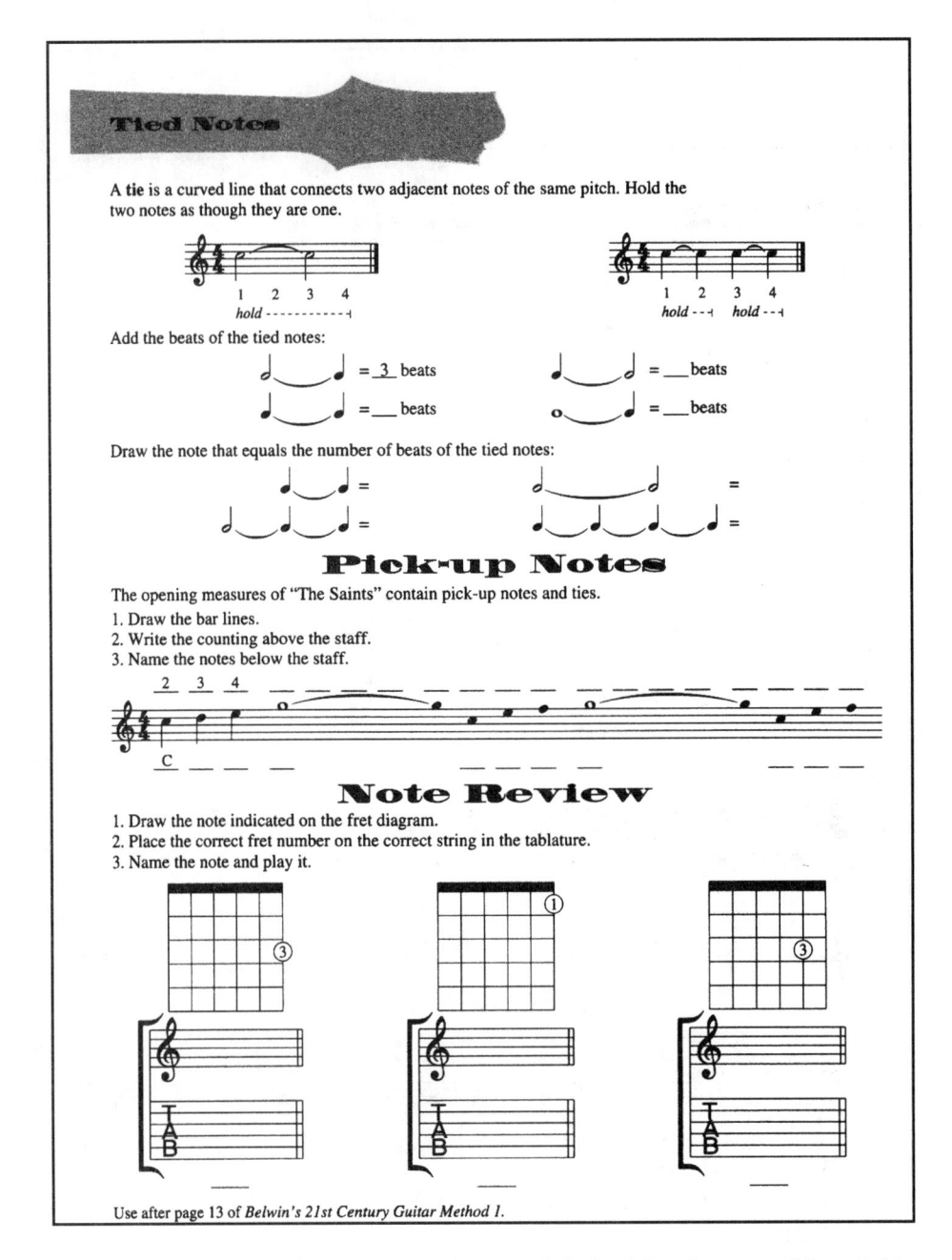

### Tied Notes

A **tie** is a curved line that connects two adjacent notes of the same pitch. Hold the two notes as though they are one.

Add the beats of the tied notes:

Draw the note that equals the number of beats of the tied notes:

### Pick-up Notes

The opening measures of "The Saints" contain pick-up notes and ties.
1. Draw the bar lines.
2. Write the counting above the staff.
3. Name the notes below the staff.

### Note Review

1. Draw the note indicated on the fret diagram.
2. Place the correct fret number on the correct string in the tablature.
3. Name the note and play it.

Use after page 13 of *Belwin's 21st Century Guitar Method 1*.

This page correlates to Method book pages 12 and 13.

## Objective
- Reinforce the counting of ties and pick-up notes

## Teacher Suggestions
- Explain each fill-in example.
- Do part of each example with students.
- Have students complete the examples on their own or as homework assignments.

**Rock Lesson 4: The D5 Power Chord**

# Guitar Rock Shop 1

## New Concepts
D5, Combining E5, A5 and D5

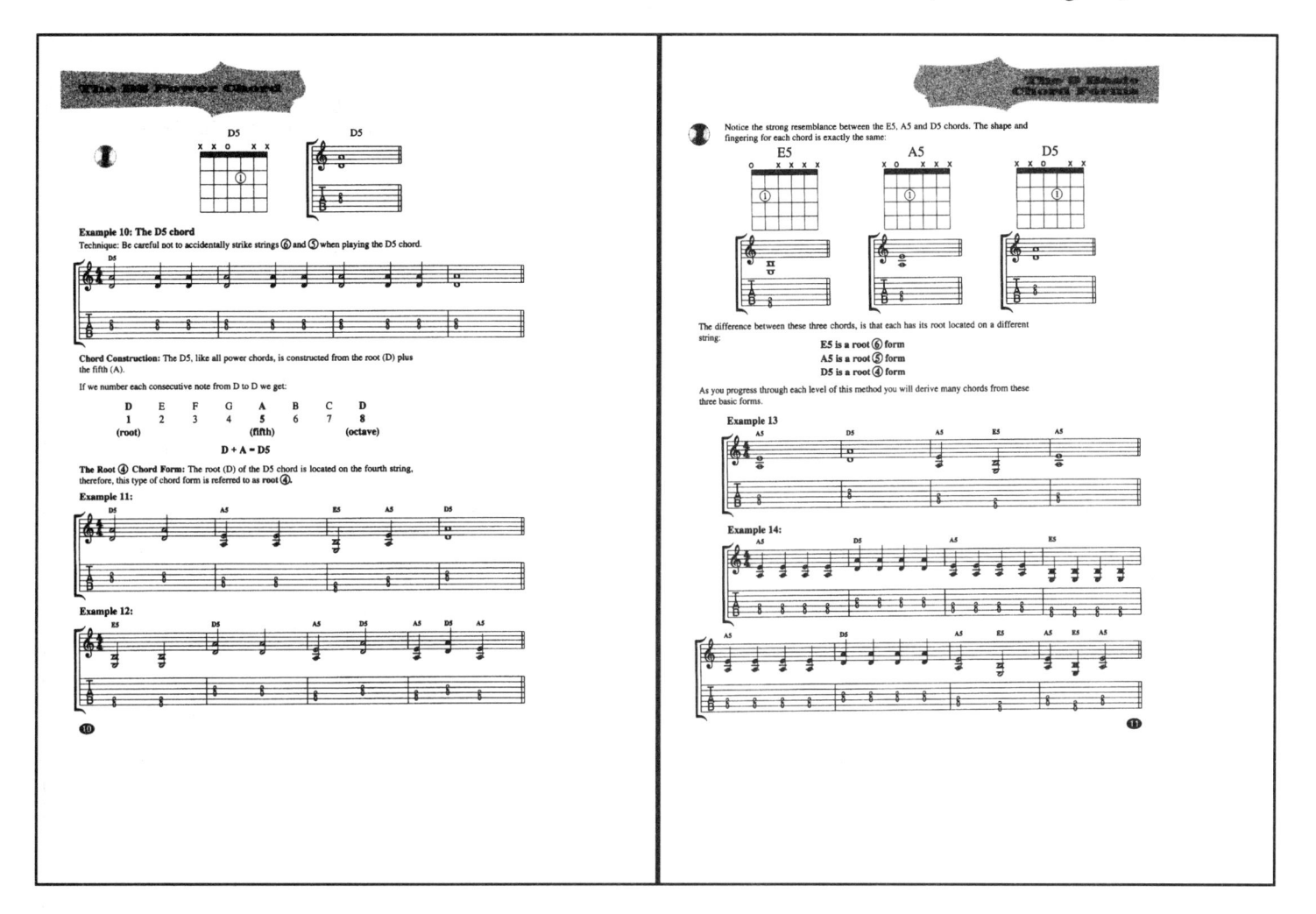

### The D5 Power Chord

**Example 10: The D5 chord**
Technique: Be careful not to accidentally strike strings ⑥ and ⑤ when playing the D5 chord.

**Chord Construction:** The D5, like all power chords, is constructed from the root (D) plus the fifth (A).
If we number each consecutive note from D to D we get:

| D | E | F | G | A | B | C | D |
|---|---|---|---|---|---|---|---|
| 1 | 2 | 3 | 4 | 5 | 6 | 7 | 8 |
| (root) | | | | (fifth) | | | (octave) |

D + A = D5

**The Root ④ Chord Form:** The root (D) of the D5 chord is located on the fourth string, therefore, this type of chord form is referred to as root ④.

**Example 11:**

**Example 12:**

### The 3 Basic Chord Forms

Notice the strong resemblance between the E5, A5 and D5 chords. The shape and fingering for each chord is exactly the same:

The difference between these three chords, is that each has its root located on a different string:

E5 is a root ⑥ form
A5 is a root ⑤ form
D5 is a root ④ form

As you progress through each level of this method you will derive many chords from these three basic forms.

**Example 13:**

**Example 14:**

## Teacher Suggestions
- Listen to program 5 on the recording, it describes the D5 power chord and contains each of the music examples.
- Analyze the construction of the D5 chord (root/fifth) and compare it to the construction of the E5 and A5 chords.
- Point out the resemblance between the "shape" of the D5 and the "shape" of the A5 and E5 power chords. All three chords look exactly alike. The only difference being the strings on which their roots are located.
- Have students sing the root (D) of the D5 power chord. Sing the root, in rhythm, with example 10. Help students to locate and sing the root movement in examples 11 - 14.

**Teacher Note:** E5, A5 and D5 are, respectively, Root ⑥, Root ⑤ and Root ④ chord forms. (Circled numbers are string indications: Root ⑥ indicates the root of the chord is located on the sixth string.) This is an important concept to reinforce. Virtually all chords and scales will be derived from these three basic chord forms. Also important is the concept of similar "shapes." When combined, these two concepts will enable the student to easily visualize chords and scales as moveable patterns (shapes) that can be played anywhere on the neck of the guitar (the key of the chord or scale being determined by its root location).

# Guitar Method 1

## Lesson 5: The Notes on the Third String

**New Concepts**
Third string G and A

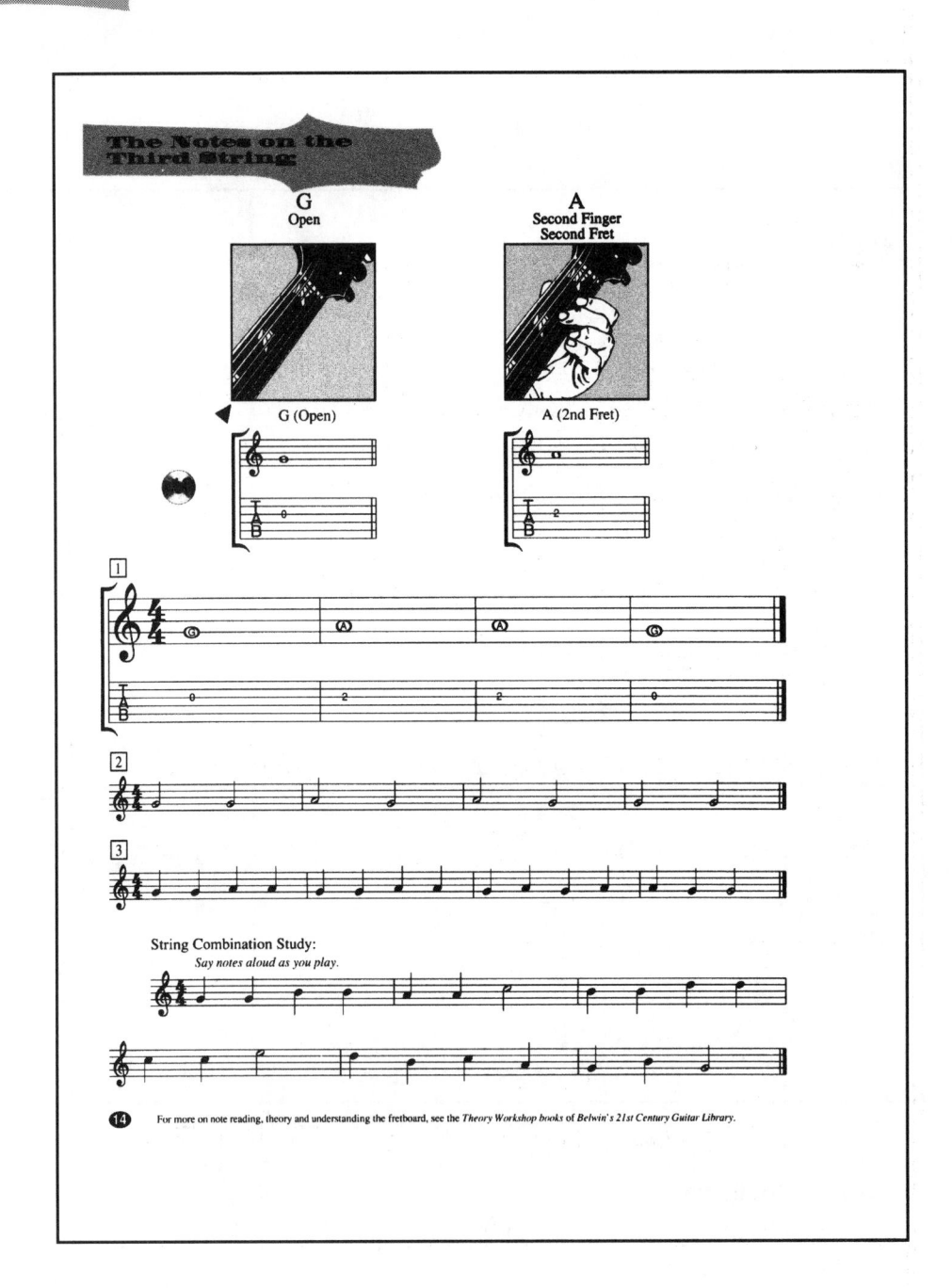

**Objective**
- Learn the third string G and A
- Learn the dotted half note rhythm
- Review all notes and rhythms

**Teacher Suggestions**
- Have students play the third string G and A. Show how the notes they are playing relate to the drawing, notation and tab.
- Have students play G, A, B, C, D, E, F and G, again noting that the notes ascend in pitch as they ascend through the alphabet. **Teacher Note:** Students often memorize the location of each note without understanding the mechanics of the instrument. This is why I feel it is important to constantly reinforce that the guitar neck is logical and that the note locations are sequential.
- Have students listen to program 16 on the recording.

**Optional Song Book:** Students are now prepared to play *As Tears Go By* on page 4 of *Song Trax 1*.

# Lesson 5: The Notes on the Third String

**Guitar Method 1**

## New Concepts
The dotted half note
Reinforces
Third string G and A

## Listening Suggestions
- *Oh, Susanna*, from James Taylor's album *Sweet Baby James*.

## Teacher Suggestions
- *Oh, Susanna* is a another popular American folk song. The "feel" of this arrangement is slower than usually heard and is inspired by the James Taylor version.
- Use the complete listening sequence described on page 19.
- Have students sing *Oh, Susanna* with either the accompaniment tracks or with teacher accompaniment
- **Group Class:** When ready, have students perform *Oh, Susanna* in unison, playing with the accompaniment tracks.
- If you have some advanced students in class, have them strum the chords while the rest of the class plays melody.

**Optional Ensemble Book:** Students are now prepared to play *When The Saints Go Marching In* on page 8 of *Guitar Ensemble 1*.

# Guitar Theory 1

## Theory Lesson 5: The Notes on the Third String

**Reinforces**
Third string G and A

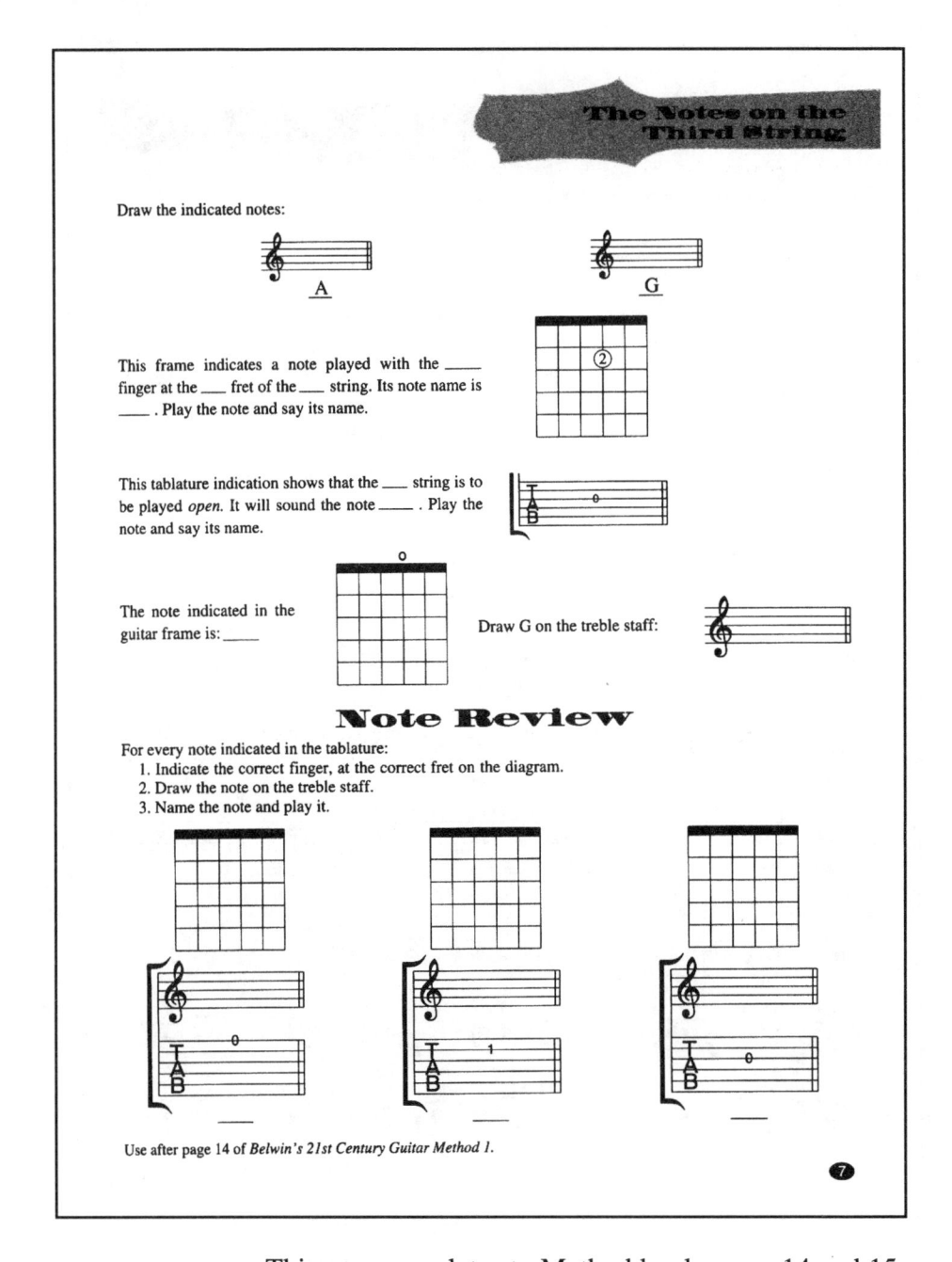

---

### The Notes on the Third String

Draw the indicated notes:

A          G

This frame indicates a note played with the ____ finger at the ____ fret of the ____ string. Its note name is ____. Play the note and say its name.

This tablature indication shows that the ____ string is to be played *open*. It will sound the note ____. Play the note and say its name.

The note indicated in the guitar frame is: ____

Draw G on the treble staff:

### Note Review

For every note indicated in the tablature:
1. Indicate the correct finger, at the correct fret on the diagram.
2. Draw the note on the treble staff.
3. Name the note and play it.

Use after page 14 of *Belwin's 21st Century Guitar Method 1*.

---

This page correlates to Method book pages 14 and 15.

## Objective
- Develop the students ability to understand and visualize note locations on the neck of the guitar

## Teacher Suggestions
- Explain each fill-in example.
- Do part of each example with students.
- Have students complete the examples on their own or as homework assignments.

# Rock Lesson 5: The Blues Progression

## Guitar Rock Shop 1

## New Concepts
The 12-bar Blues Progression, I, IV and V

## Reinforces
A5, D5 and E5

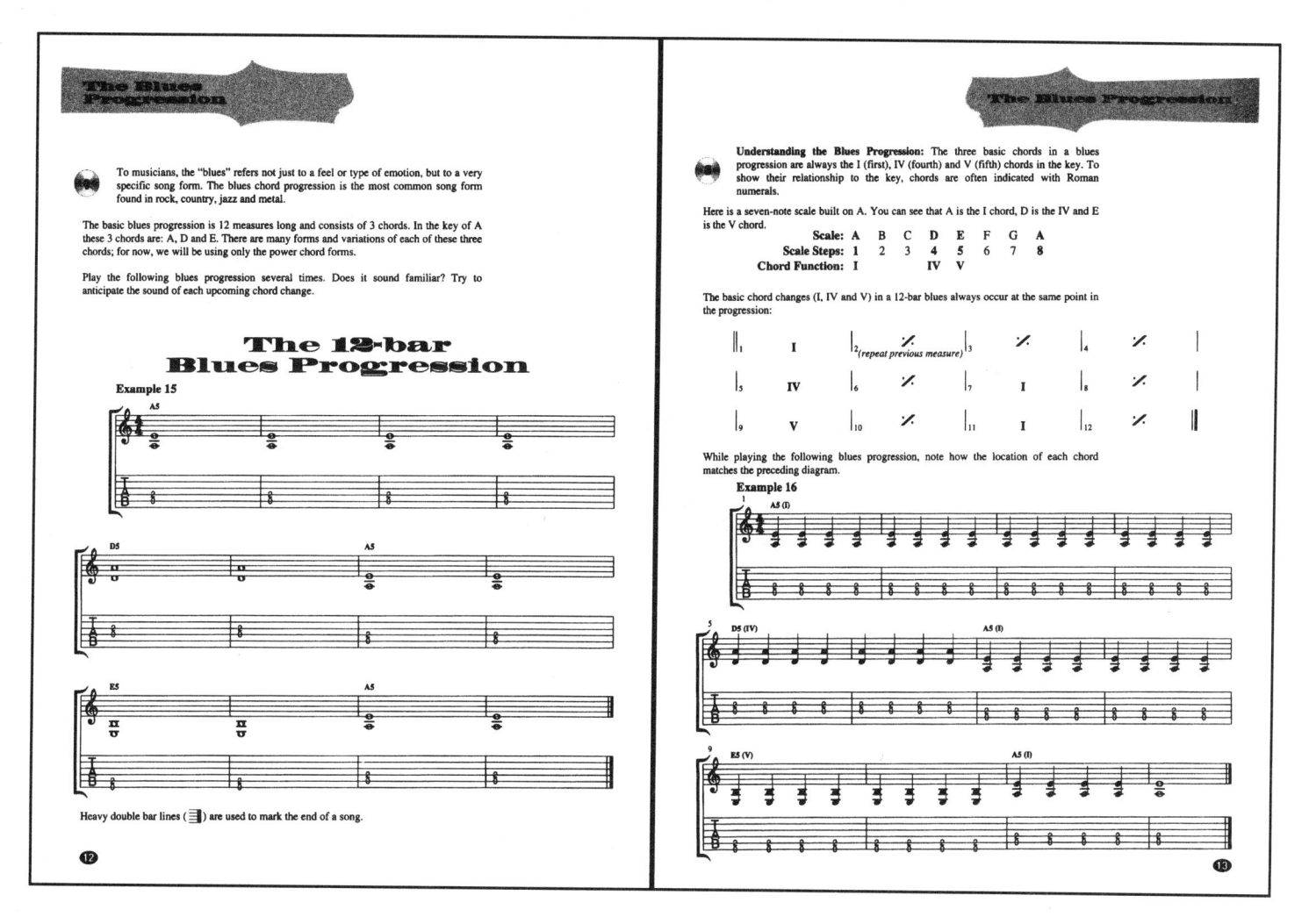

## Teacher Suggestions
- Play program 7.
- Write out an eight-note scale beginning on A (no sharps or flats are necessary at this point). Number each note and show how A, D and E are the 1st, 4th and 5th notes of the scale. Explain that the chords built from those notes are the I, IV and V chords.
- Write out a complete 12-bar blues progression (as shown on above). Use Roman numerals, rather than letter names, to indicate the chords. Explain that all blues progressions, regardless of key, follow this basic format.
- Help students to locate and sing the blues progression root movement in examples 15 and 16.
- Play any blues. Have the students identify the chord changes as I, IV and V. The blues form is common to all styles. Here is a brief sampling: *Pride and Joy* by Stevie Ray Vaughan, *Red House* by Jimi Hendrix, *Johnny B. Goode* by Chuck Berry, *Ain't Goin' Down* by Garth Brooks, or practically any B.B. King, Albert King, or Willie Dixon song.

**Guitar Method 1**

# Lesson 6: 3/4 Time and Repeat Signs

## New Concepts
3/4 Time Signature

### New Time Signatures

**3/4** Three Counts to a Measure
A Quarter Note Receives One Count

Songs in 3/4 receive three counts per measure.

#### Down in the Valley
*Gently*  —  Kentucky Mountain Folk Song

Down in the val - ley, val - ley so low,
Count: 1 2 3 1 2 3
hang your head o - ver, hear the wind blow.
Hear the wind blow, dear, hear the wind blow,
hang your head o - ver, hear the wind blow.

#### We Three Kings of Orient Are
*Moderately*  —  Christmas

We three kings of O - ri - ent are, bear - ing
gifts we trav - erse a - far. Field and foun - tain,
moor and moun - tain, fol - low - ing yon - der star.

*Suggested Teacher Accompaniment:*
(Moderately, with jazz waltz feel)

## Objective
- Learn the three quarter time signature
- Review dotted half notes and ties.

## Teacher Suggestions
- Have students listen to program 18 on the recording, it explains the new time signature.
- Have students count out loud while clapping the rhythm to both *Down in the Valley* and *We Three Kings*.
- Have students sing *Down in the Valley* and *We Three Kings* with the accompaniment tracks or with teacher accompaniment.
- On the recording, *Down in the Valley* is performed with a traditional, old-time bluegrass feel. This would be a good opportunity to play some early Country or Bluegrass music such as Hank Williams or the Carter family.
- *We Three Kings* is performed with a jazz feel. Contrast this version with a more traditional waltz version.

# Lesson 6: 3/4 Time and Repeat Signs

**Guitar Method 1**

## New Concepts
The repeat sign
Reinforces
Pick-up Notes
3/4
Most notes and rhythms learned so far

### Repeat Signs

Repeat signs (:||) tell us to play a section of music again. One backwards facing repeat sign means you should repeat to the beginning:

*Repeat back to the beginning.*

### Red River Valley
*Moderately* — Traditional Folk

From this val - ley they say you are go - ing. ___ I will
Come and sit by my side if you love me. ___ Do not

miss your bright eyes and sweet smile, ___ for I
hast - en to bid me a - dieu; ___ but re -

know you are tak - ing the sun - shine ___ that has
mem - ber the Red Riv - er Val - ley, ___ and the

light - ed my path - way a - while. ___
one that has loved you so true. ___

In this next song, allow each note to continue to ring for the entire measure. Keep your fingers curved while playing the fretted notes so that they do not stop the other strings from ringing. Do not lift your fingers from the notes until absolutely necessary.

### Singing Strings
*Moderately* — A.S.

hold — hold — continue simile

## Teacher Suggestions

- *Red River Valley* introduces the repeat sign. Use this song as an opportunity to review pick-up notes and ties.
- Students can sing *Red River Valley* with the accompaniment tracks or with teacher accompaniment.
- *Singing Strings* is a classical-style piece performed on the recording with guitar and strings. The melody is based on alternating Am and Em arpeggios. It is important that the notes in these measures be allowed to ring for the complete measure. Students should curve their fingers, with their finger tips perpendicular to the neck, so the fingers do not accidentally touch other strings and prevent them from ringing.
- Use the complete listening sequence described on page 19.

# Guitar Theory 1

**Theory Lesson 6: 3/4 Time**

**Reinforces**
The dotted half note
3/4

### The Dotted Half Note

A **dot** placed after a note adds one-half the value of the original note. A dotted half note (𝅗𝅥.) equals 3 counts.

Write the beats under the notes:

### New Time Signature: 3/4 Time

**3** Three Counts To A Measure
**4** A Quarter Note Receives One Count

In 3/4 time a half note receives two beats:

A quarter note receives one beat:

Write the beats under the notes. Remember, there are three beats in each measure.

Add the bar lines and name the notes of the following two musical excerpts.
End each line with a double bar.

Play the excerpts.
Use after page 16 of *Belwin's 21st Century Guitar Method 1*.

This page correlates to Method pages 16 and 17.

**Teacher Suggestions**
- On the first three fill-in examples the student is to fill in the correct count under each note.
- On the last two examples fill in the bar lines, name the notes and place a double bar at the end of each example.

# Rock Lesson 6: The Blues Progression

## Guitar Rock Shop 1

### New Concepts
The three phrases that make up a 12-bar blues progression.

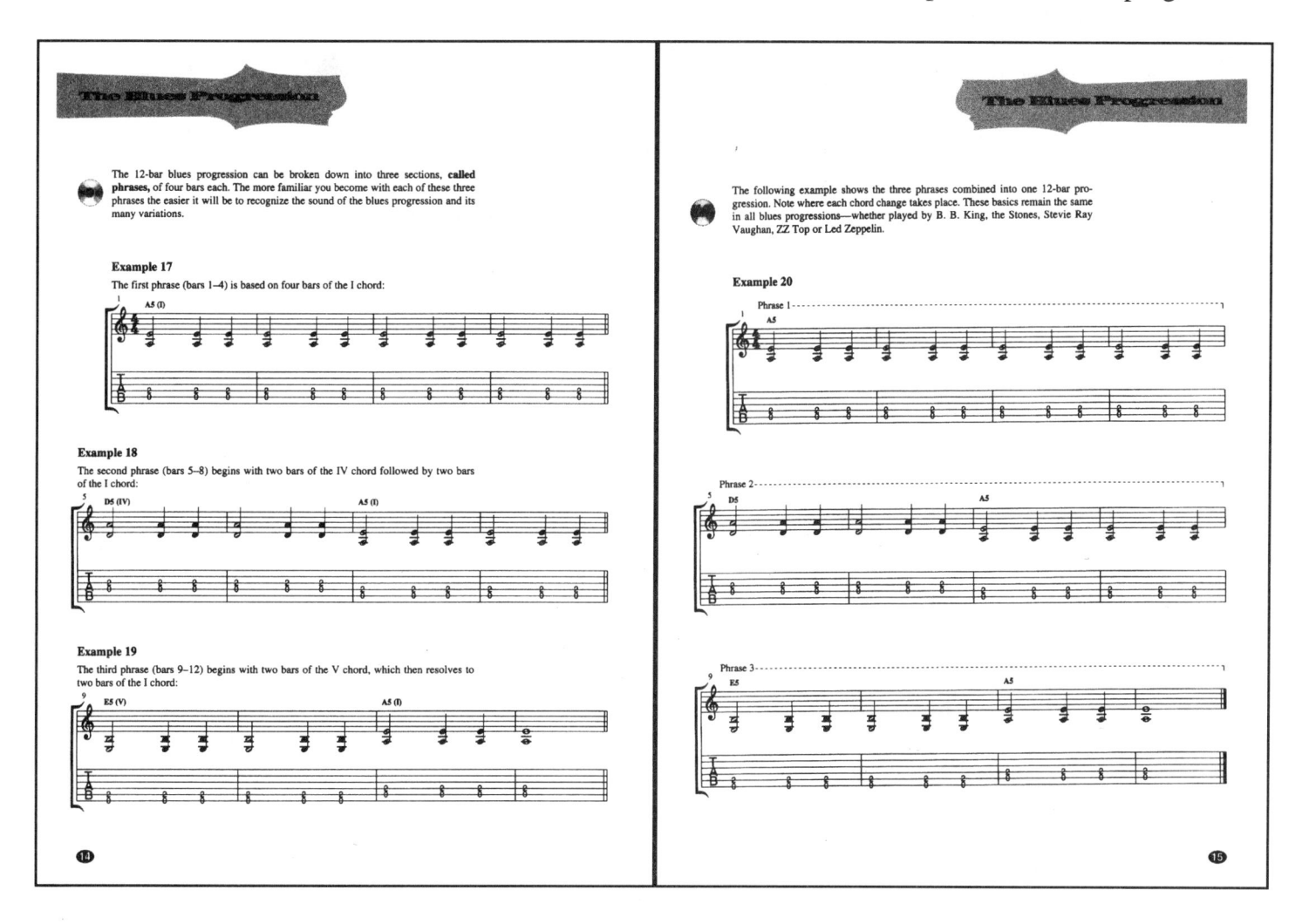

---

**The Blues Progression**

The 12-bar blues progression can be broken down into three sections, called **phrases**, of four bars each. The more familiar you become with each of these three phrases the easier it will be to recognize the sound of the blues progression and its many variations.

**Example 17**
The first phrase (bars 1–4) is based on four bars of the I chord:

**Example 18**
The second phrase (bars 5–8) begins with two bars of the IV chord followed by two bars of the I chord:

**Example 19**
The third phrase (bars 9–12) begins with two bars of the V chord, which then resolves to two bars of the I chord:

**The Blues Progression**

The following example shows the three phrases combined into one 12-bar progression. Note where each chord change takes place. These basics remain the same in all blues progressions—whether played by B. B. King, the Stones, Stevie Ray Vaughan, ZZ Top or Led Zeppelin.

**Example 20**

Phrase 1
Phrase 2
Phrase 3

---

## Objective
- By breaking the 12-bar blues progression down into its three component phrases the student will gain a greater understanding, and a better ear, for the form of the progression; enabling them to more easily recognize the blues progression and its many variations.

## Teacher Suggestions
- Play programs 9 and 10.
- Help students to locate and sing the root movements in examples 17 - 20. (Again, students can sing with the accompaniment tracks and/or with themselves as they play each example.
- At the piano or guitar or using recordings play examples of the blues progression.
- Students should play the two simple blues variations shown below. Have students identify each chord change.

|| I | ./. | ./. | ./. | IV | ./. | I | ./. | V | IV | I | ./. ||
|| I | IV | I | ./. | IV | ./. | I | ./. | V | IV | I | ./. ||

# Guitar Method 1

## Lesson 7: First String A/Review

### New Concepts
A on the first string
Ledger lines
Using the 4th finger (pinky)

**New Note: A**

A
Fourth Finger
Fifth Fret

The high A is played on the first string, at the fifth fret, with the fourth finger.

**Ledger Lines** are placed above or below the staff. The high A is placed on the first ledger line above the staff.

### Danny Boy
*Irish Folk Song*

Slowly, with feeling

Oh, Dan-ny Boy, the pipes, the pipes are call - ing... From glen to glen, and down the moun-tain side. The sum-mer's gone, and all the ros - es fall - ing... it's you, it's you must go and I must bide.

Originally a French operatic song, *Plaisir d'Amour* is so popular that it has passed on into the folk and popular music genres. The song was set to new lyrics and recorded by Elvis Presley as *Can't Help Falling In Love*. It became his 46th Top 40 hit.

### Plaisir D'Amour
*Jean-Paul Martini*

Gently

*Suggested Teacher Accompaniment:*
(Gently)

### Objective
- Learn A on the first string
- Student should be able to accurately shift the left hand 4th finger up to the 5th fret A and return to 1st position
- This lesson introduces only one new topic. The three songs serve as a review of all notes and rhythms learned so far.

### Teacher Suggestions
- Listen to program 24 which describes playing the first string A.
- Students should listen to programs 25 and 26. Using the complete listening procedure described on page 19 will make the learning process simpler, more fun and more musical.
- Students can sing *Danny Boy* with the accompaniment tracks.
- **Group Class:** On the recording, *Danny Boy* is performed with piano accompaniment and *Plaisir D'Amour* as a guitar duet using the suggested teacher accompaniment. If you have some advanced students in class, have them strum the chords while the rest of the class plays melody.

**Listening Suggestions:** *Plaisir D'Amour* is the basis for the Elvis Presley song *Can't Help Falling In Love*.

**Optional Song Book:** Students are now prepared to play *Telstar* and *In My Room* on pages 6 and 8 of *Song Trax 1*.

# Lesson 7: First String A/Review

**Guitar Method 1**

**Reinforces**
The dotted half note
Ties

*Blue Eyes Crying In The Rain* was Willie Nelson's first record to reach the Top 40. The song is a country ballad and should be played slowly, with feeling.

Note: Most printed music for rock and pop guitar includes tablature. In this book, tablature will be included with all pop songs and rock guitar examples.

## Blue Eyes Crying in the Rain

Slow country

Words and Music by Fred Rose

In the twi-light glow I see her, blue eyes cry-ing in the rain. As we kissed good-bye and part-ed, I knew we'd nev-er meet a-gain.

Suggested Teacher Accompaniment:
(Slow country)

Copyright © 1945 (renewed 1973) by MILENE MUSIC, INC.
All Rights Reserved

For more pop and rock songs, with complete play-along recordings, see the *Song Trax* books of *Belwin's 21st Century Guitar Library*.

**19**

## Teacher Suggestions

- Use the complete listening sequence described on page 19.
- **Group Class:** If you have some advanced students in class, have them strum the chords while the rest of the class plays melody.

**Listening Suggestions:** Listen to Willie Nelson's version of this song.

# Guitar Theory 1

## Theory Lesson 7: Repeat Signs, First String A

**Reinforces**
Repeat Signs
A

---

### Repeat Signs

Two dots placed before a double bar line
means go back to the beginning and play again.

This is an excerpt from a well-known song:

Write the excerpt as it would appear **without** using a repeat sign.
(Some notes are indicated as a guide.)

Play the song. Can you name it?

### New Note: A

Indicate the note A in the tablature:

Indicate the note A on the diagram:

### Country Trivia

Fill in the name of the performer and the composer.

On October 11th, 1975 _____ _____ 's recording of *Blue Eyes Crying in the Rain* climbed to #21 on the *Billboard* charts. It was recorded on the Columbia label. The music was written by _____ _____ and was first published in 1945. Its success again proves that a good song has lasting value. So, if you write one you really like, don't get discouraged if it doesn't become an overnight hit. This one reached stardom in Willie's interpretation thirty years after it was composed.

Use after page 19 of *Belwin's 21st Century Guitar Method 1*.

This page correlates to Method book pages 18 and 19.

## Teacher Suggestions

- Students should copy the music excerpt to show how it would look without a repeat sign.
- Use the tablature and fret diagram fill-in examples to develop the students ability to visualize note locations on the neck of the guitar and relate them to written music.

# Rock Lesson 7: The Blues Progression

**Guitar Rock Shop 1**

## New Concepts
Eighth notes,
Accent marks (>),
Palm mute (P.M.)

## Reinforces
A5, D5 and E5, 12-Bar Blues Progression

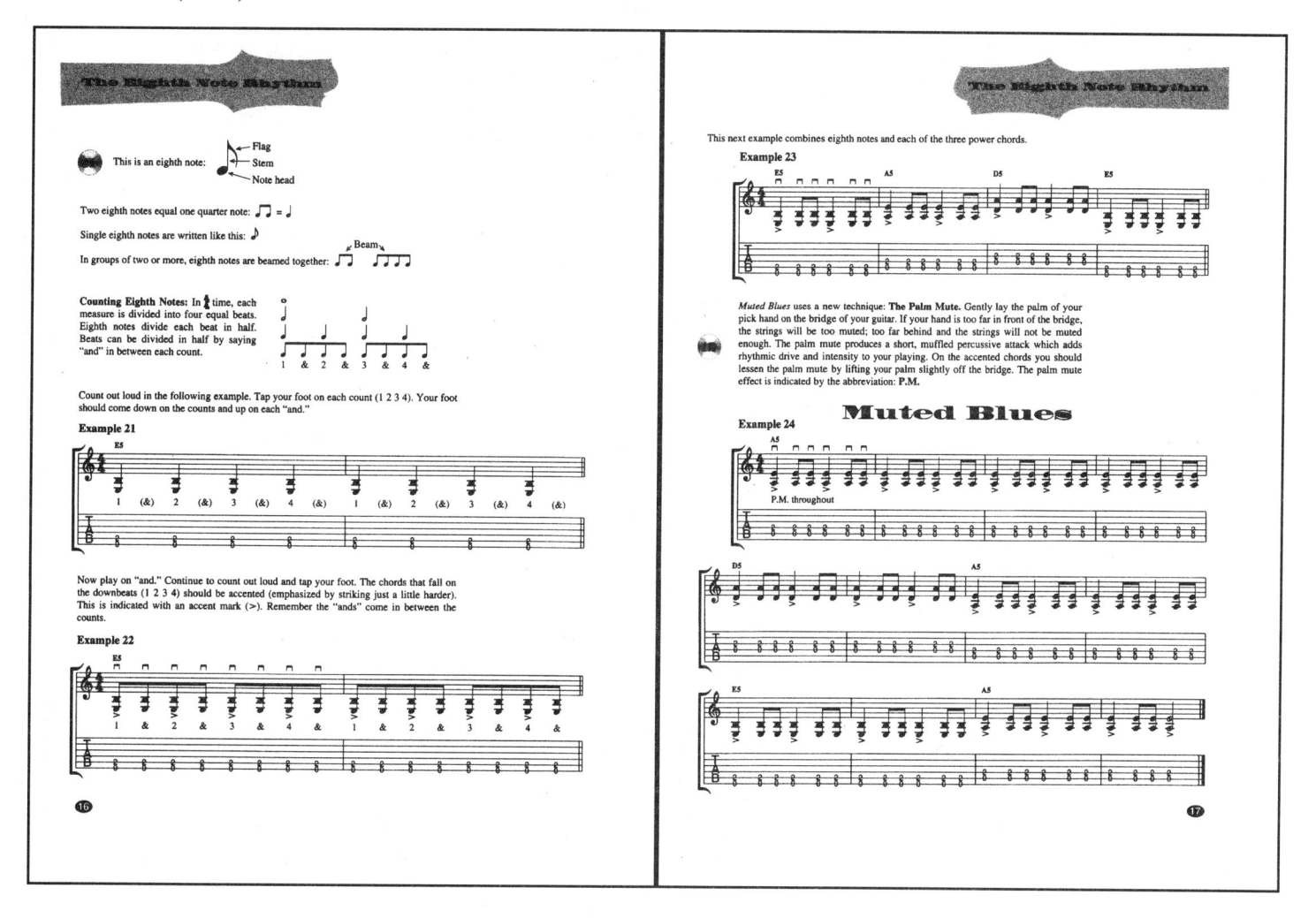

### The Eighth Note Rhythm

This is an eighth note:
- Flag
- Stem
- Note head

Two eighth notes equal one quarter note: ♪♪ = ♩

Single eighth notes are written like this: ♪

In groups of two or more, eighth notes are beamed together: ♫ ♬

**Counting Eighth Notes:** In 4/4 time, each measure is divided into four equal beats. Eighth notes divide each beat in half. Beats can be divided in half by saying "and" in between each count.

1 & 2 & 3 & 4 &

Count out loud in the following example. Tap your foot on each count (1 2 3 4). Your foot should come down on the counts and up on each "and."

**Example 21**

Now play on "and." Continue to count out loud and tap your foot. The chords that fall on the downbeats (1 2 3 4) should be accented (emphasized by striking just a little harder). This is indicated with an accent mark (>). Remember the "ands" come in between the counts.

**Example 22**

### The Eighth Note Rhythm

This next example combines eighth notes and each of the three power chords.

**Example 23**

*Muted Blues* uses a new technique: **The Palm Mute.** Gently lay the palm of your pick hand on the bridge of your guitar. If your hand is too far in front of the bridge, the strings will be too muted; too far behind and the strings will not be muted enough. The palm mute produces a short, muffled percussive attack which adds rhythmic drive and intensity to your playing. On the accented chords you should lessen the palm mute by lifting your palm slightly off the bridge. The palm mute effect is indicated by the abbreviation: **P.M.**

### Muted Blues

**Example 24**

P.M. throughout

## Objective
- Learn the eighth note rhythm
- Begin developing a rock "feel" by incorporating accenting and muting techniques

## Teacher Suggestions
- Play program 11.
- Have students count or clap alternating measures of quarter notes and eighth notes while tapping quarter notes with their feet.
- The palm mute is an important rock technique. Many rock rhythm guitar parts are very percussive and are meant to "lock in" with the drums. When done correctly the palm mute produces a short muffled attack which adds rhythmic drive and intensity to the part. Have the class listen to the explanation and example of palm muting on program 12.
- Help students to locate and sing the blues progression root movement in example 24.

# Guitar Method 1

## Lesson 8: The Notes on the Fourth String

**New Concepts**
Fourth string D, E and F

**Objective**
- Learn the fourth string D, E and F
- Be able to play the songs on Method page 21 in tempo with the recording or with the optional teacher accompaniments

**Teacher Suggestions**
- Have students play D, E and F. Show how the notes they are playing relate to the drawing, notation and tab.
- Review all the notes learned so far (4th string D through 1st string A). Draw these notes on the music staff and have students play them. Playing scales like this reinforces that the guitar neck is logical and that the note locations are sequential.
- Listen to program 28 on recording.

**Optional Ensemble Book:** Students are now prepared to play *Down In The Valley* on page 11 of *Guitar Ensemble 1*.

# Lesson 8: The Notes on the Fourth String

**Guitar Method 1**

## Reinforces
Fourth string D, E and F

## Teacher Suggestions
- Use the complete listening sequence described on page 19.
- The suggested teacher accompaniment to *House Of The Rising Sun* superimposes the open E string over every chord, adding interesting color tones to the chords. As on all songs in the book you can, of course, derive your own accompaniment parts from the basic chord symbols indicated above the melody.
- Students can sing *Amazing Grace*.
- **Group Class:** When ready, have students perform the songs in unison, playing with the accompaniment tracks. If you have some advanced students in class, have them strum the chords while the rest of the class plays melody.

# Guitar Theory 1

## Theory Lesson 8: The Notes on the Fourth String

**Reinforces**
Fourth string D, E and F

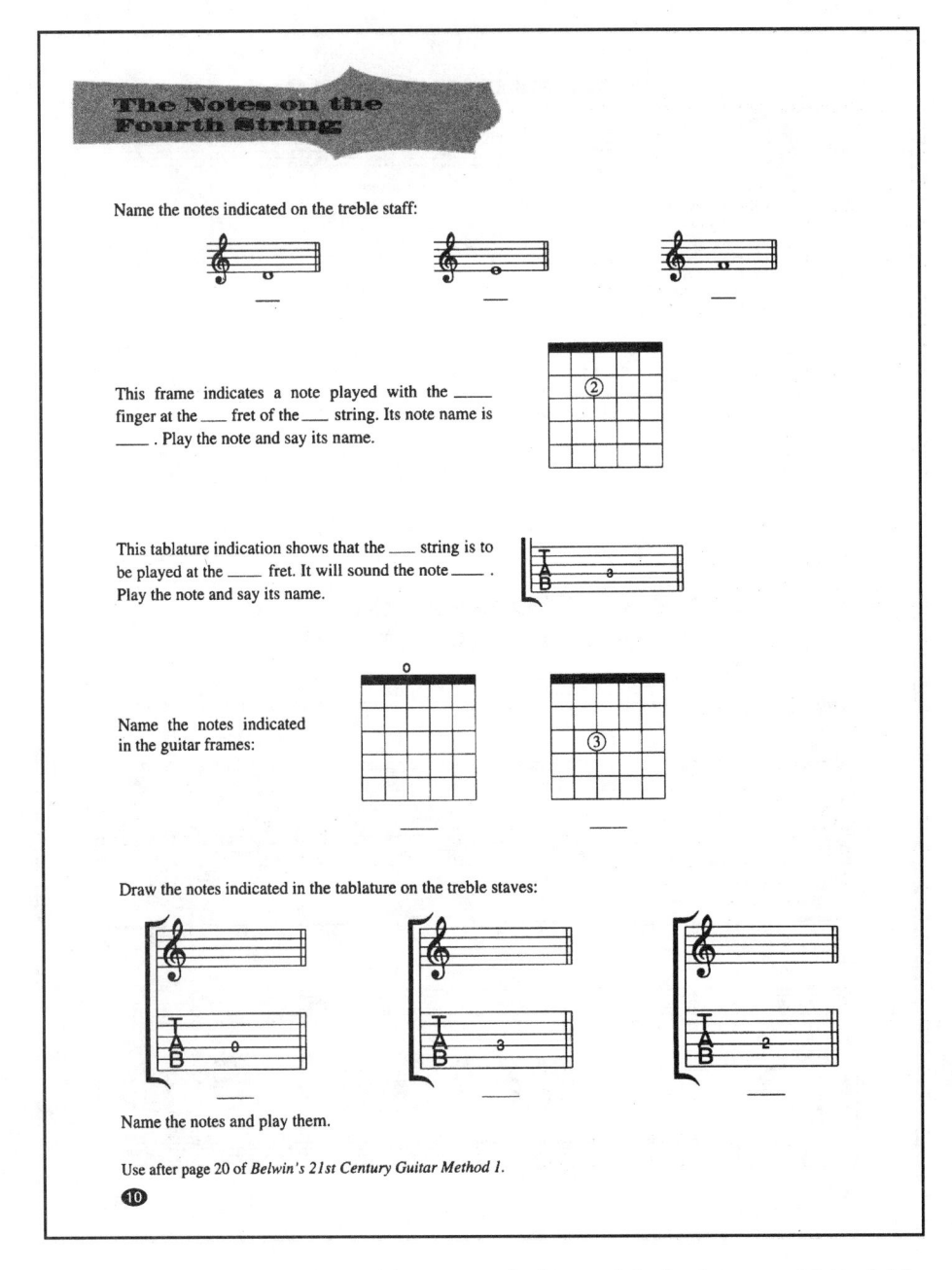

### The Notes on the Fourth String

Name the notes indicated on the treble staff:

This frame indicates a note played with the ____ finger at the ____ fret of the ____ string. Its note name is ____ . Play the note and say its name.

This tablature indication shows that the ____ string is to be played at the ____ fret. It will sound the note ____ . Play the note and say its name.

Name the notes indicated in the guitar frames:

Draw the notes indicated in the tablature on the treble staves:

Name the notes and play them.

Use after page 20 of *Belwin's 21st Century Guitar Method 1*.

This page reinforces Method pages 20 and 21.

## Objective
- Develop the students ability to understand and visualize note locations on the neck of the guitar.

## Teacher Suggestions
- Explain each fill-in example.
- Do part of each example with students.
- Have students complete the examples on their own or as homework assignments.
- **Reminder:** If students are having trouble relating the tab and guitar frame diagrams to the neck of the guitar, lay a guitar flat, horizontally on a table or desk top in front of the student. Tablature is a horizontal diagram of the neck. Now hold the guitar vertically. Guitar frames are a vertical diagram of the neck.

# Rock Lesson 8: Three Note Power Chords

**Guitar Rock Shop 1**

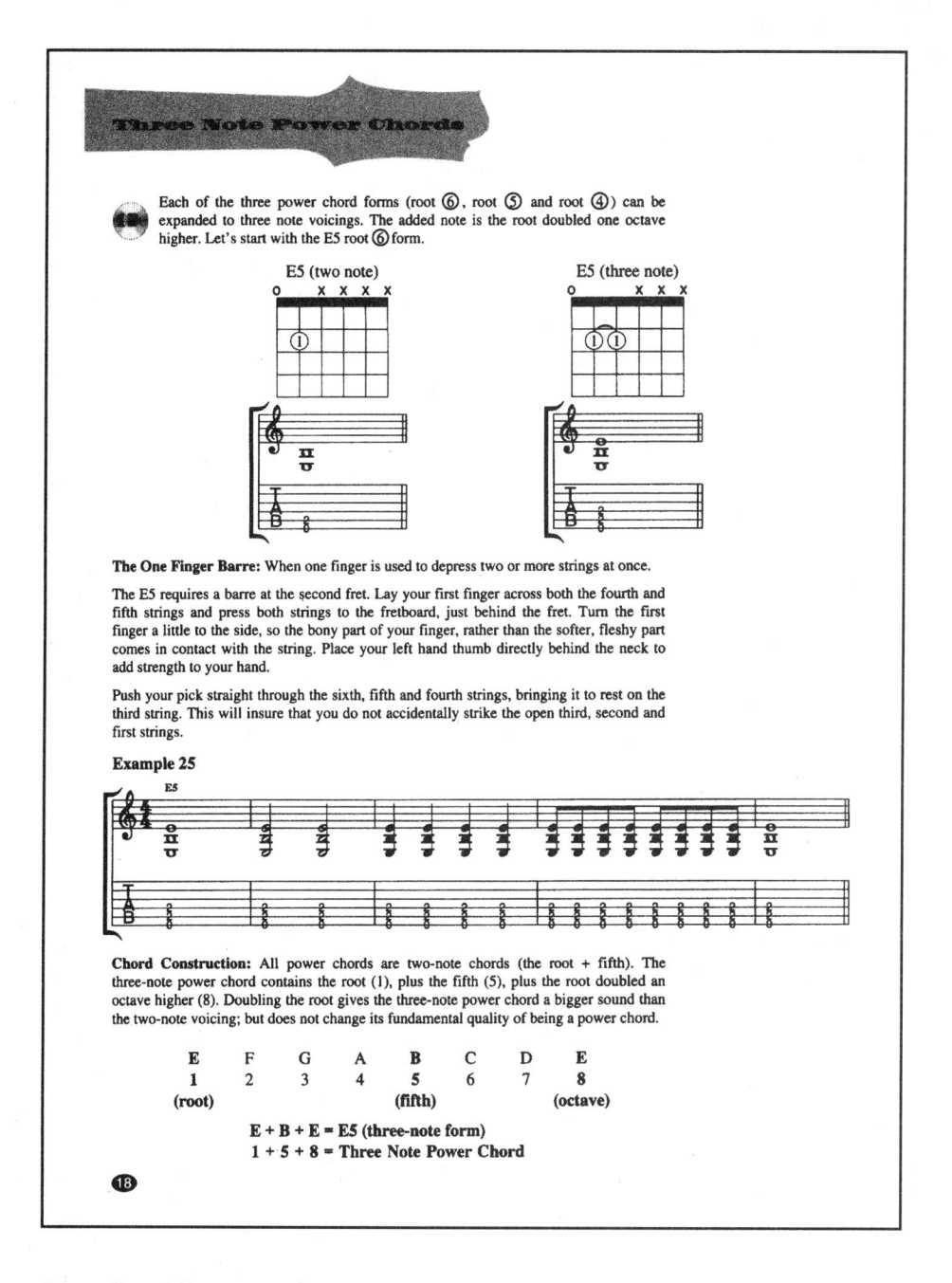

## Three Note Power Chords

Each of the three power chord forms (root ⑥, root ⑤ and root ④) can be expanded to three note voicings. The added note is the root doubled one octave higher. Let's start with the E5 root ⑥ form.

**The One Finger Barre:** When one finger is used to depress two or more strings at once.

The E5 requires a barre at the second fret. Lay your first finger across both the fourth and fifth strings and press both strings to the fretboard, just behind the fret. Turn the first finger a little to the side, so the bony part of your finger, rather than the softer, fleshy part comes in contact with the string. Place your left hand thumb directly behind the neck to add strength to your hand.

Push your pick straight through the sixth, fifth and fourth strings, bringing it to rest on the third string. This will insure that you do not accidentally strike the open third, second and first strings.

**Example 25**

**Chord Construction:** All power chords are two-note chords (the root + fifth). The three-note power chord contains the root (1), plus the fifth (5), plus the root doubled an octave higher (8). Doubling the root gives the three-note power chord a bigger sound than the two-note voicing; but does not change its fundamental quality of being a power chord.

| E | F | G | A | B | C | D | E |
|---|---|---|---|---|---|---|---|
| 1 | 2 | 3 | 4 | 5 | 6 | 7 | 8 |
| (root) | | | | (fifth) | | | (octave) |

E + B + E = E5 (three-note form)
1 + 5 + 8 = Three Note Power Chord

## New Concepts

Three-note E5 power chord
One finger barre

## Objective

- Learn the three-note form of the E5 power chord
- Understand its chord construction (root/5th/octave)
- Be able to locate the root (E on the sixth string)

## Teacher Suggestions

- Listen to program 13 on the recording, it describes the three-note power chord form and its relationship to the two-note form.
- Explain the construction of the three-note form (root/fifth/octave) and compare it to the construction of the two-note form (root/fifth).
- Point out the resemblance between the "shape" of the two-note form and that of the three-note form. The concept of similar "shapes" is an important one. Soon many chords, scales and patterns will be derived from these basic shapes. Each of these will be transposable to any key/any position on the neck simply by shifting the pattern to the correct root.

**Technique:** The E5 is played with a 1st finger "barre" across the 4th and 5th strings. A "barre" is when the side of the finger is laid flat against the neck and used to hold more than one note. Turn the finger slightly to the side so that the "bony" side of the finger rather than the softer fleshy part contacts the strings. Place the left-hand thumb behind the barre. Flatten the tip of the 1st finger across the 4th and 5th strings at the 2nd fret.

# Guitar Rock Shop 1

## Rock Lesson 8: Three Note Power Chords

**New Concepts**

Three-note A5 power chord

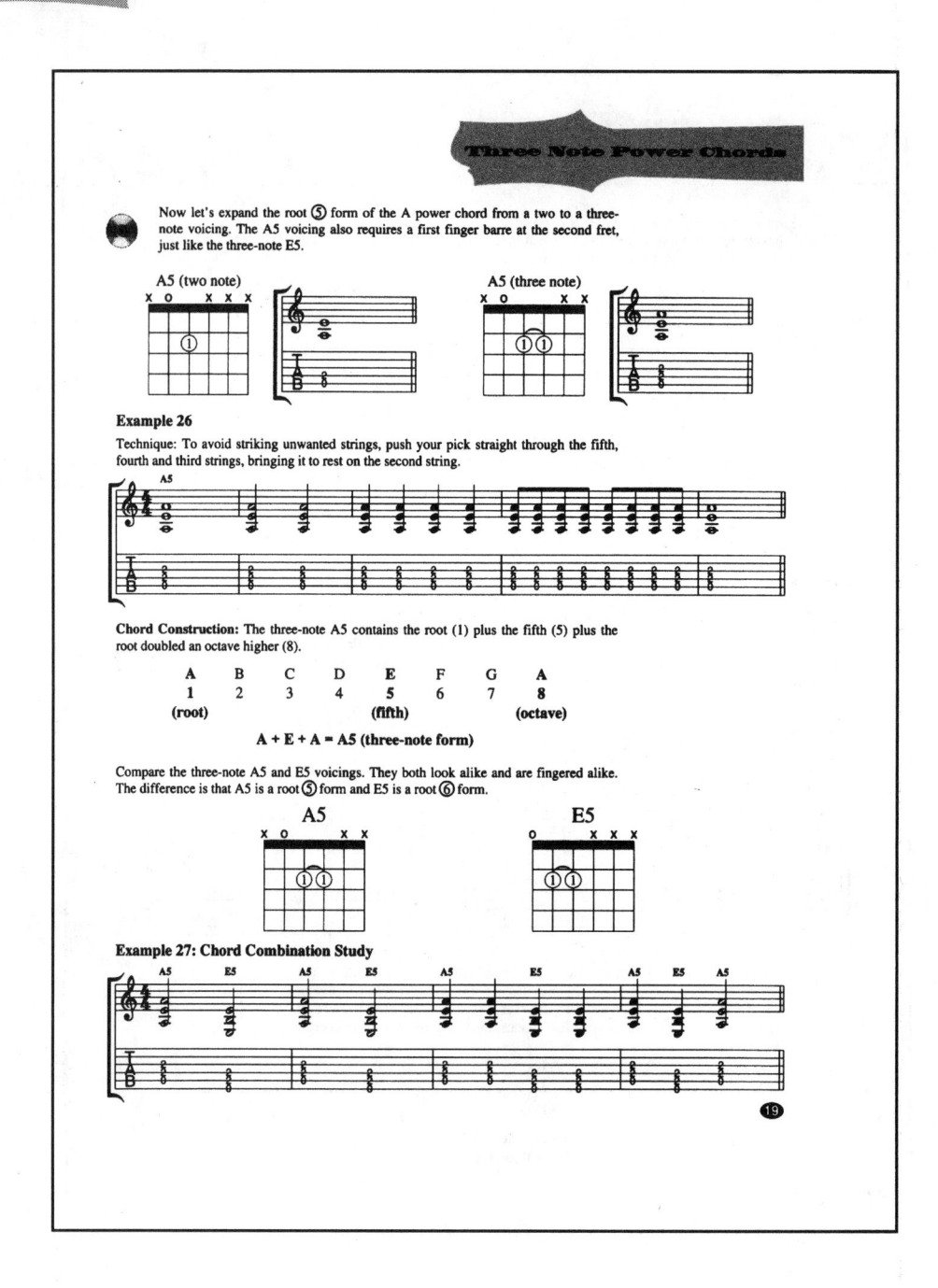

---

Now let's expand the root ⑤ form of the A power chord from a two to a three-note voicing. The A5 voicing also requires a first finger barre at the second fret, just like the three-note E5.

A5 (two note)    A5 (three note)

**Example 26**

Technique: To avoid striking unwanted strings, push your pick straight through the fifth, fourth and third strings, bringing it to rest on the second string.

**Chord Construction:** The three-note A5 contains the root (1) plus the fifth (5) plus the root doubled an octave higher (8).

| A | B | C | D | E | F | G | A |
|---|---|---|---|---|---|---|---|
| 1 | 2 | 3 | 4 | 5 | 6 | 7 | 8 |
| (root) | | | | (fifth) | | | (octave) |

A + E + A = A5 (three-note form)

Compare the three-note A5 and E5 voicings. They both look alike and are fingered alike. The difference is that A5 is a root ⑤ form and E5 is a root ⑥ form.

A5        E5

**Example 27: Chord Combination Study**

---

## Objective

- Learn the three-note form of the A5 power chord
- Understand its chord construction (root/5th/octave)
- Be able to locate the root (A on the fifth string)

## Teacher Suggestions

- Listen to program 14 on the recording, it describes the three-note A5 power chord form.
- Explain the construction of the three-note form (root/fifth/octave) and compare it to the construction of the two-note form (root/fifth).
- Point out the resemblance between the "shape" of the Root ⑤ two- and three-note forms and the Root ⑥ two- and three-note forms.
- Students should sing the root movement in example 27.

# Rock Lesson 8: Three Note Power Chords

**Guitar Rock Shop 1**

## New Concepts
Three-note D5 power chord

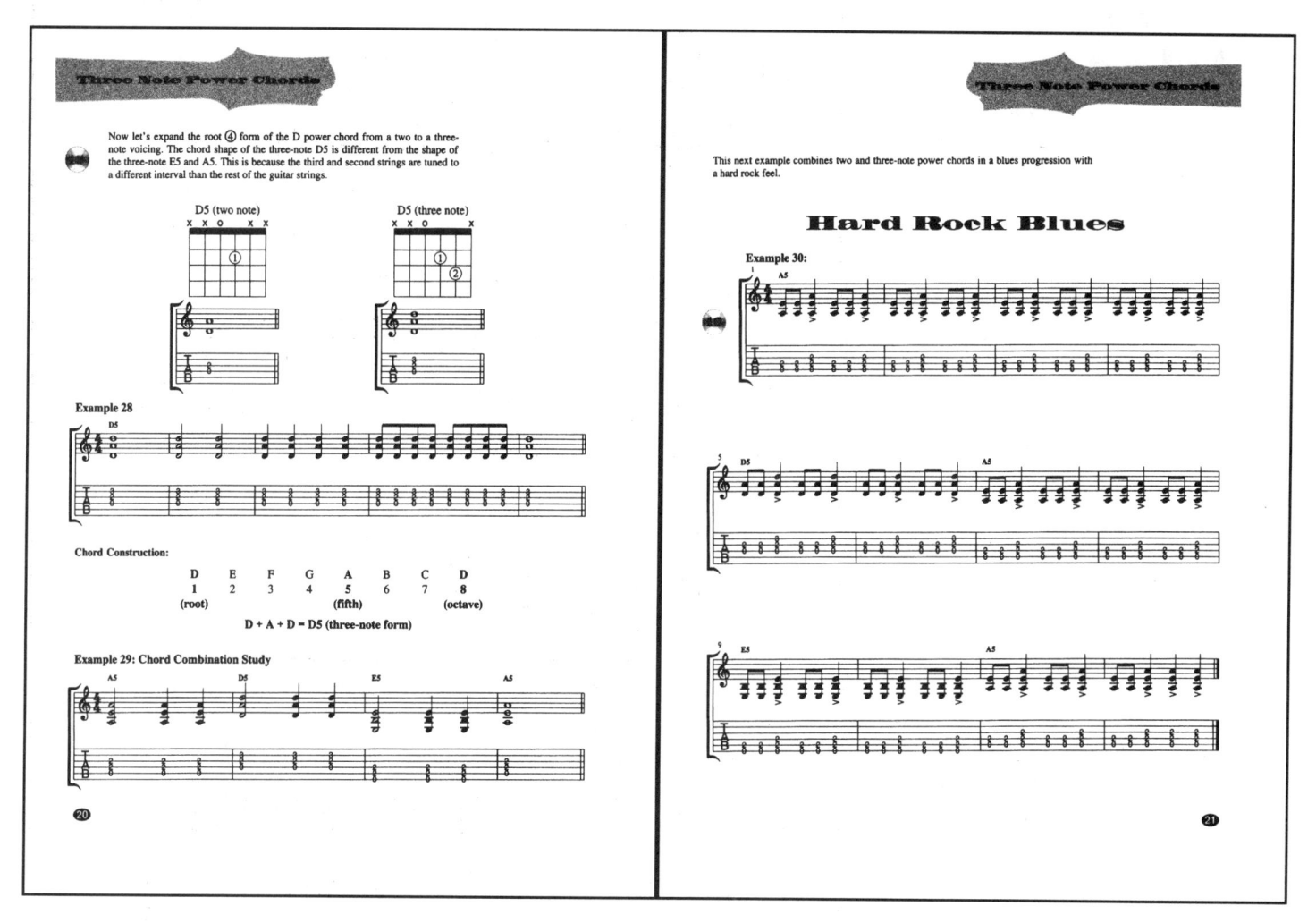

## Objective
- Learn the three-note form of the D5 power chord
- Understand its chord construction (root/5th/octave)
- Be able to locate the root (D on the fifth string)

## Teacher Suggestions
- Listen to program 15 on the recording, it describes the three-note D5 power chord form.
- Explain the construction of the three-note form (root/fifth/octave) and compare it to the construction of the two-note form (root/fifth).
- Notice the difference in shape between the three-note D5 and the three-note E5 and A5. This is because the third and second strings are tuned to a major third apart (G - B) rather than a perfect fourth like the rest of the strings (E - A, A - D, D - G, B - E).
- *Hard Rock Blues* combines two- and three-note power chords with a 12-bar blues progression in A.
- Help students locate and sing the root movements in examples 28 - 30.

# Guitar Method 1

## Lesson 9: Eighth Notes

**New Concepts**
Eighth notes
Flags and beams
Alternate picking

### Eighth Notes

This is an eighth note.
Two eighth notes equal one quarter note.

Single eighth notes are written like this.
In groups of two or more, eighth notes are beamed together.

**Counting Eighth Notes:** In 4/4 time, each measure is divided into four equal beats. Eighth notes divide each beat in half. A beat can be divided in half by saying "and" in between each count.

**The Down-Upstroke:** The down-upstroke is one continuous movement—a note is played with a downstroke, then the next note is played with an upstroke *as the pick returns to playing position*. The pick hand should swing freely from the wrist in a slight arc.

Eighth notes are played with alternating down-upstrokes. Down on the counts (1 2 3 4) and up on "and."

Downstroke: ⊓
Upstroke: V

This next study is based on the rhythm to *Ten Little Indians*. Practice this until you feel comfortable with both the counting and down/up picking.

Eighth Note Picking Study:

### Ten Little Indians
Folk Song

One lit-tle, two lit-tle, three lit-tle In-d'ans; four lit-tle, five lit-tle, six lit-tle In-d'ans; sev-en lit-tle, eight lit-tle, nine lit-tle In-d'ans; ten lit-tle In-di-an boys.

### Spy to Spy
A.S.

**Teacher Note:** If you are using the *Rock Shop* book the students will already have been introduced to eighth notes.

### Objective
- Learn the eighth note rhythm
- Develop a smooth down-upstroke

### Teacher Suggestions
- Play program 31.
- Students should count alternating measures of quarter notes and eighth notes while tapping quarter notes with their feet. Then clap alternating measures of quarter notes and eighth notes while tapping quarter notes with their feet.
- Play the *Eighth Note Picking Study* with all downstrokes. Then play it with alternate (down-up) picking.
- Play programs 32 and 33. Use the complete listening procedure described on page 19. Although this may seem time consuming, the students will learn each new song and concept faster if encouraged to use their ears.

**Technique:** Hold the pick loosely between the thumb and index fingers. If the pick is held to tightly the alternate picking motion will not be smooth.

**Optional Ensemble Book:** Students are now prepared to play *Variations On Old Saint Nick* on page 15 of *Guitar Ensemble 1*.

# Lesson 9: Eighth Notes/More Repeat Signs

## Guitar Method 1

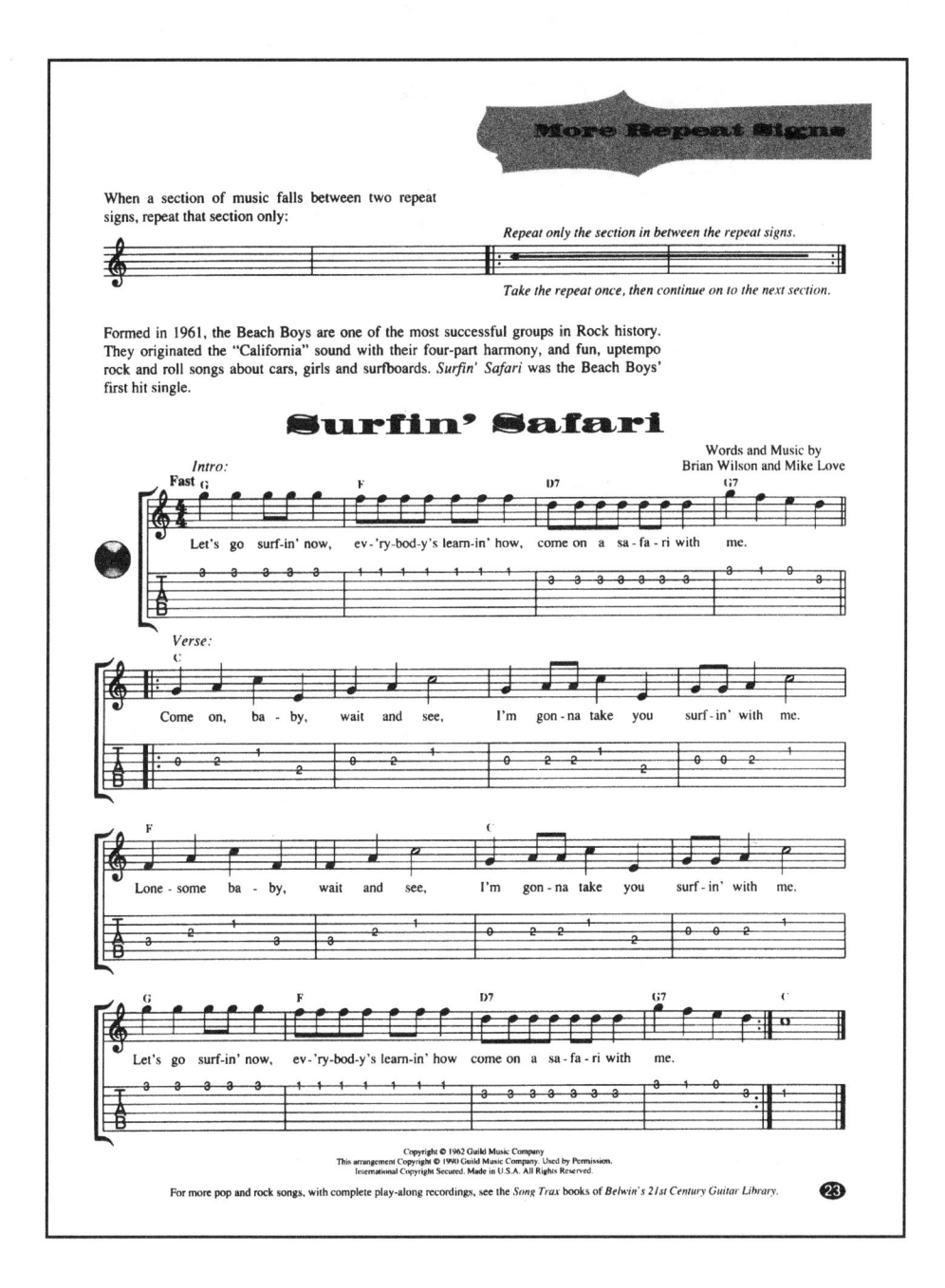

### New Concepts
Eighth notes
Facing repeat signs

## Teacher Suggestions
- Use the complete listening sequence described on page 19.
- Have students perform *Surfin' Safari* with the accompaniment tracks.
- **Group Class:** Have students perform *Surfin' Safari* in unison with the accompaniment tracks. If you have some advanced students, have them strum the chords while the rest of the class plays melody.

**Optional Song Book:** Students are now prepared to play *Green Onions* on page 10 of *Song Trax 1*.

# Guitar Theory 1

## Theory Lesson 9: Eighth Notes/More Repeat Signs

**Reinforces**

Eighth notes and repeat signs.

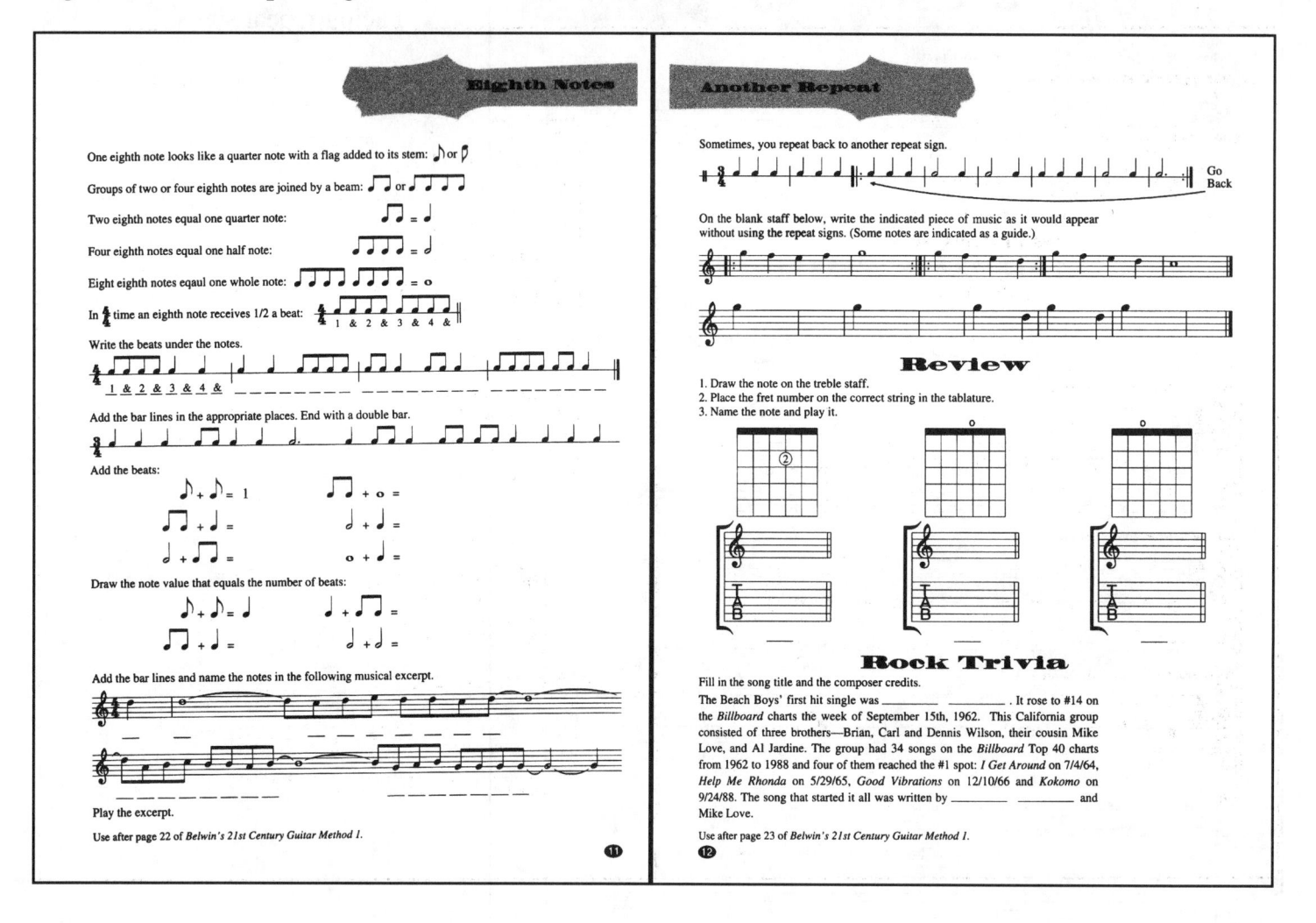

### Eighth Notes

One eighth note looks like a quarter note with a flag added to its stem: ♪ or ♪

Groups of two or four eighth notes are joined by a beam: ♫ or ♫♫

Two eighth notes equal one quarter note: ♫ = ♩

Four eighth notes equal one half note: ♫♫ = ♩

Eight eighth notes equal one whole note: ♫♫♫♫ = o

In 4/4 time an eighth note receives 1/2 a beat:

Write the beats under the notes.

Add the bar lines in the appropriate places. End with a double bar.

Add the beats:

♪ + ♪ = 1     ♫ + o =
♫ + ♩ =       ♩ + ♫ =
♩ + ♫ =       o + ♩ =

Draw the note value that equals the number of beats:

♪ + ♪ = ♩     ♩ + ♫ =
♫ + ♩ =       ♩ + ♩ =

Add the bar lines and name the notes in the following musical excerpt.

Play the excerpt.

Use after page 22 of *Belwin's 21st Century Guitar Method 1*.

### Another Repeat

Sometimes, you repeat back to another repeat sign.

Go Back

On the blank staff below, write the indicated piece of music as it would appear without using the repeat signs. (Some notes are indicated as a guide.)

### Review

1. Draw the note on the treble staff.
2. Place the fret number on the correct string in the tablature.
3. Name the note and play it.

### Rock Trivia

Fill in the song title and the composer credits.

The Beach Boys' first hit single was _____ _____. It rose to #14 on the *Billboard* charts the week of September 15th, 1962. This California group consisted of three brothers—Brian, Carl and Dennis Wilson, their cousin Mike Love, and Al Jardine. The group had 34 songs on the *Billboard* Top 40 charts from 1962 to 1988 and four of them reached the #1 spot: *I Get Around* on 7/4/64, *Help Me Rhonda* on 5/29/65, *Good Vibrations* on 12/10/66 and *Kokomo* on 9/24/88. The song that started it all was written by _____ _____ and Mike Love.

Use after page 23 of *Belwin's 21st Century Guitar Method 1*.

These pages correlate to Method book pages 22 and 23.

**Teacher Suggestions**
- Explain each fill-in example.
- Do part of each example with students.
- Have students complete the examples on their own or as homework assignments.
- The Trivia questions are intended to expose students to pop music history.

# Rock Lesson 9: Single-Note Studies

## Guitar Rock Shop 1

### New Concepts
All the natural notes in first position

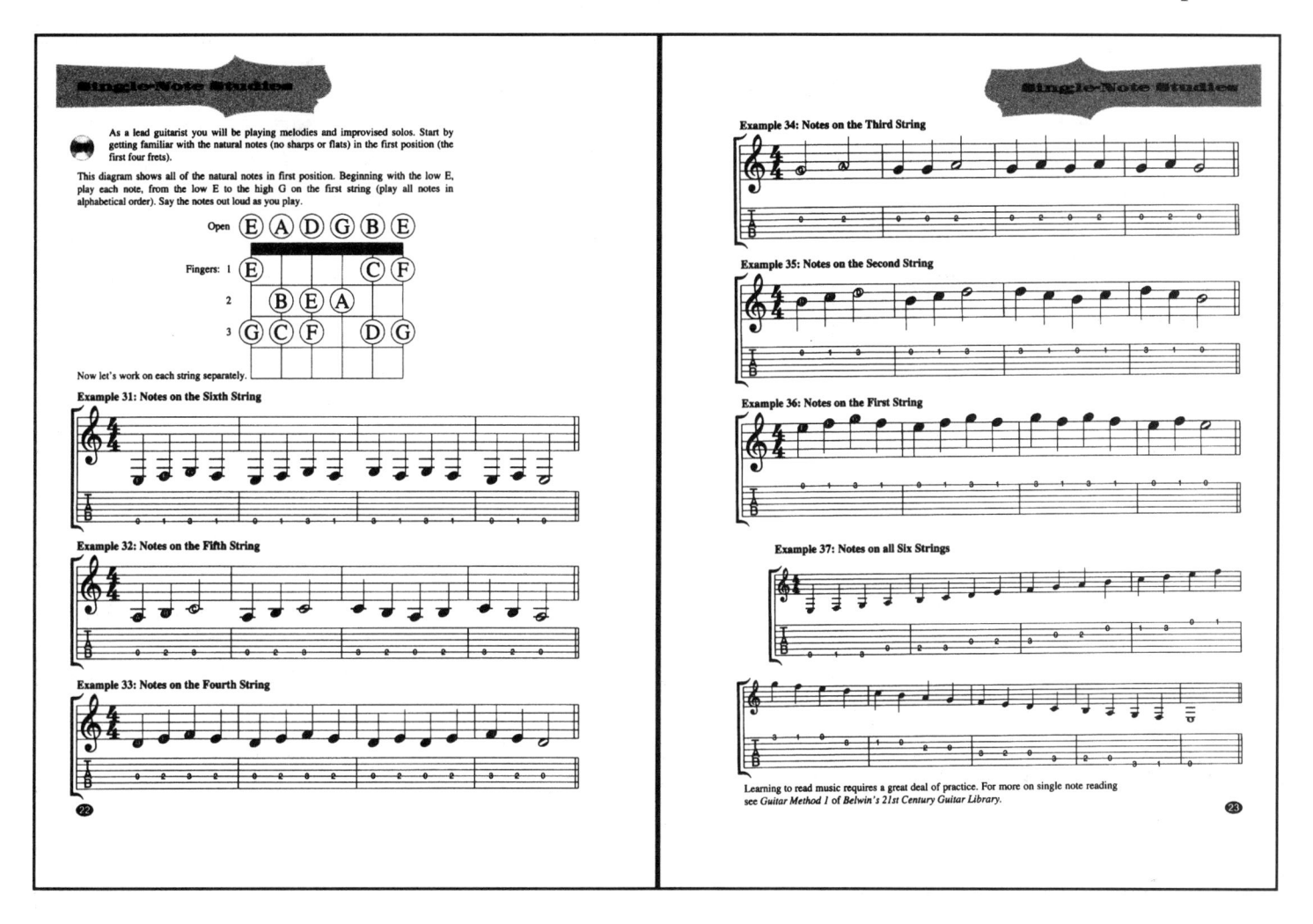

## Objective
- For students who have not been using the *Guitar Method* book, these pages are intended as a quick note-reading primer for the upcoming single-note riff sections of the book.

## Teacher Suggestions
- Have the students play examples 31 - 36.
- Now have them play from the 6th string E to the 1st string G and back, reading from the fretboard diagram at the top of page 22. This will reinforce their understanding of fretboard diagrams.
- Have them play Example 37.
- Compare the notation and tablature in Example 37 (all natural notes in first position) to the diagram at the top of page 22 (all natural notes in first position).

# Guitar Method 1

## Lesson 10: Sharp Signs and Key Signatures

**New Concepts**
The sharp sign
F#

---

### The Sharp Sign

A sharp sign (#) raises the pitch of a note one-half step, a distance of one fret. When a sharp sign is indicated before a note, that note remains sharp for the rest of the measure. The sharp sign is cancelled at the bar line, unless tied.

**F#** Fourth Finger Fourth Fret — F# (4th Fret)

**F#** Second Finger Second Fret — F# (2nd Fret)

Earlier, on page 11, we played the first half of *Aura Lee*. Here is the complete version, placed in a different key.

Written in 1861, *Aura Lee* became a favorite of soldiers during the Civil War. The song has such a beautiful melody that, like *Plaisir d'Amour*, it was adapted and recorded by Elvis Presley. This new version of *Aura Lee* became the title song from Elvis' first movie—*Love Me Tender*.

#### Aura Lee
*Civil War Era Folk Song*

Slowly

As the black-bird in the spring, 'neath the wil-low tree. Sat and piped I heard him sing, sing of Au-ra Lee. Au-ra Lee, Au-ra Lee, maid of gold-en hair; sun-shine came a-long with thee and swal-lows in the air.

*Suggested Teacher Accompaniment:* (Slowly)

---

## Objective
- Learn the sharp sign
- Be able to locate F# on the 4th and 1st strings

## Teacher Suggestions
- Play program 35.
- Describe the function of a sharp sign.
- Have students play F and then F# on both the 4th and 1st strings.
- Contrast this arrangement of *Aura Lee* with that on page 11. This version contains both the Verse and Chorus, and is played in the key of G.
- Have students sing *Aura Lee* with either the accompaniment tracks or teacher accompaniment.

# Lesson 10: Sharp Signs and Key Signatures

## Guitar Method 1

### New Concepts
Key signature
Reinforces
Sharp signs
F#
Repeat signs

### Objective
- Students should learn that they should check the key signature before playing any song

### Teacher Suggestions
- Use the complete listening sequence described on page 19.
- Have students sing *Simple Gifts* with either the accompaniment tracks or teacher accompaniment.
- **Group classes:** Have students perform each song in unison, playing with the accompaniment tracks. If you have some advanced students in class, have them strum the chords while the rest of the class plays melody.

### Listening Suggestions
- Christopher Parkening plays a beautiful classical guitar version of *Simple Gifts* on the album *Sacred Music*. There is also a version of *Simple Gifts* during the finale of Aaron Copland's *Hoedown*.

**Optional Song Book:** Students are now prepared to play *I'm A Traveling Man* on page 12 of *Song Trax 1*.

**Optional Ensemble Book:** Students are now prepared to play *Dona Nobis Pacem* on page 18 of *Guitar Ensemble 1*.

53

# Guitar Theory 1

## Theory Lesson 10: Sharp Signs and Key Signatures

**Reinforces**
Sharp signs
Key signatures
Rhythm notation

### Sharp Signs

A **sharp** sign (#) raises the pitch of a note a half step.

When saying a sharp note's name, we say the letter name first and the sharp next—F sharp. When we write it on the music, the sharp sign comes first.

To draw a sharp, draw two vertical lines:

Then add the slanted lines:

Draw sharps before both F's:

Name the indicated notes:

Draw the indicated notes:
G  F#  A  F#  B  C
   (low)  (high)

### Key Signature

When the F# is indicated at the beginning of the piece of music, it means every F in the piece is played F#.

The key of G contains 1 sharp

Write the key signature for the key of G:

Name the notes:

### Rhythm Review

Fill in the missing beats with the appropriate notes. Each measure should contain 4 counts:

Fill in the missing beats with the appropriate notes. Each measure should contain 3 counts:

Use after page 25 of *Belwin's 21st Century Guitar Method 1*.

This page correlates to Method pages 24 and 25.

**Teacher Suggestions**
- Explain each fill-in example.
- Do part of each example with students.
- Have students complete the examples on their own or as homework assignments.

54

# Rock Lesson 10: Rhythm Riffs and Patterns

**Guitar Rock Shop 1**

## New Concepts
The E minor pentatonic scale, Alternate picking

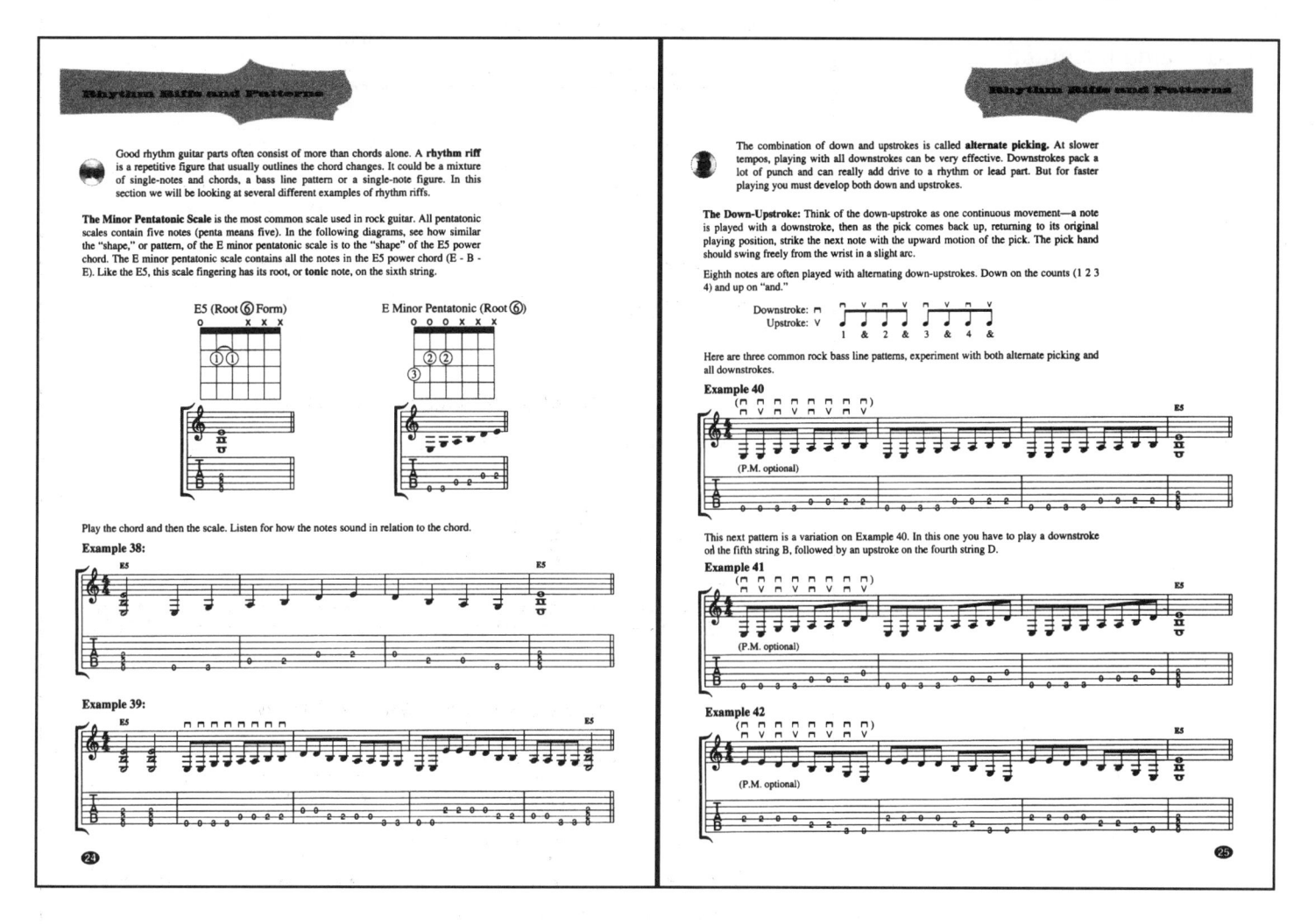

## Objective
- Learn the one octave E minor pentatonic scale
- Demonstrate the similarities (same root, similar "shape" or pattern) between the E5 power chord and the E minor pentatonic scale
- Begin to develop alternate picking for fast passages

## Teacher Suggestions
- Play programs 18 and 19.
- Point out the similarity in shape of the E5 power chord to that of the E minor pentatonic scale.
- Examples 39 - 42 are common rhythm guitar riffs based on the E minor pentatonic scale.
- Experiment with both alternate picking and all downstrokes. Alternate picking is good for fast passages but downstrokes have more rhythmic impact. Neither is right or wrong. Always choose whichever is appropriate for the situation.
- Help students to sing the E minor pentatonic scale along with example 38.
- **Group Class:** Have half the class play an E5 chord in half-note rhythm while the rest play each examples 40 - 42, then reverse.

55

# Guitar Method 1

## Lesson 11: The C, G and G7 Chords

**New Concepts**
C Chord
G Chord
G7 Chord
Chord Frame Diagrams

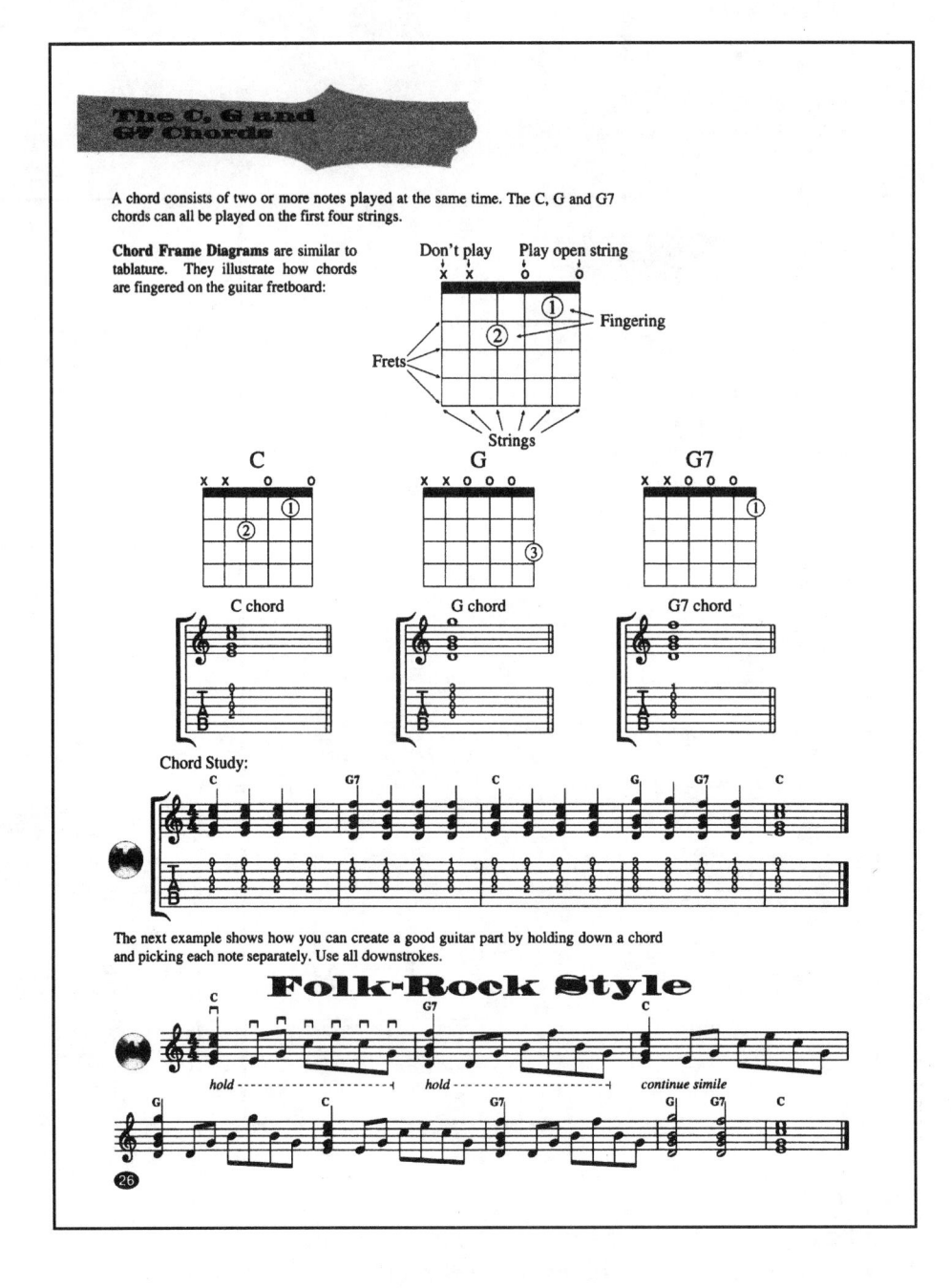

### The C, G and G7 Chords

A chord consists of two or more notes played at the same time. The C, G and G7 chords can all be played on the first four strings.

**Chord Frame Diagrams** are similar to tablature. They illustrate how chords are fingered on the guitar fretboard.

The next example shows how you can create a good guitar part by holding down a chord and picking each note separately. Use all downstrokes.

**Folk-Rock Style**

**Objective**
- Learn the three new chords
- Move from chord to chord smoothly, in rhythm

**Teacher Suggestions**
- Draw a chord frame diagram and explain its relationship to the guitar neck. If you hold a guitar vertically in front of you, the chord frame diagram shows the guitar neck from the nut to the 4th fret. (Note: Students who have been using either the *Rock Shop*, *Theory* or *Song Trax* books have already been exposed to these types of diagrams.)
- Listen to programs 40 and 41.
- Students should practice the *Chord Study* until they can change chords smoothly without breaking rhythm.
- Before playing *Folk-Rock Style* explain that the single-notes are just arpeggiated chords. The chord played on the first beat should be held for the entire measure.
- Help students to sing the root and then the arpeggio of each chord. Since these chords are not in root position play the root for the students on either the guitar or piano.
- Teacher Note: For more practice on the C, G and G7 chords have the students go back and play the chords to *Ten Little Indians* (page 22), *Blue Eyes Crying in the Rain* (page 19), *Down in The Valley* (page 16), and *Mary Ann* (page 12).

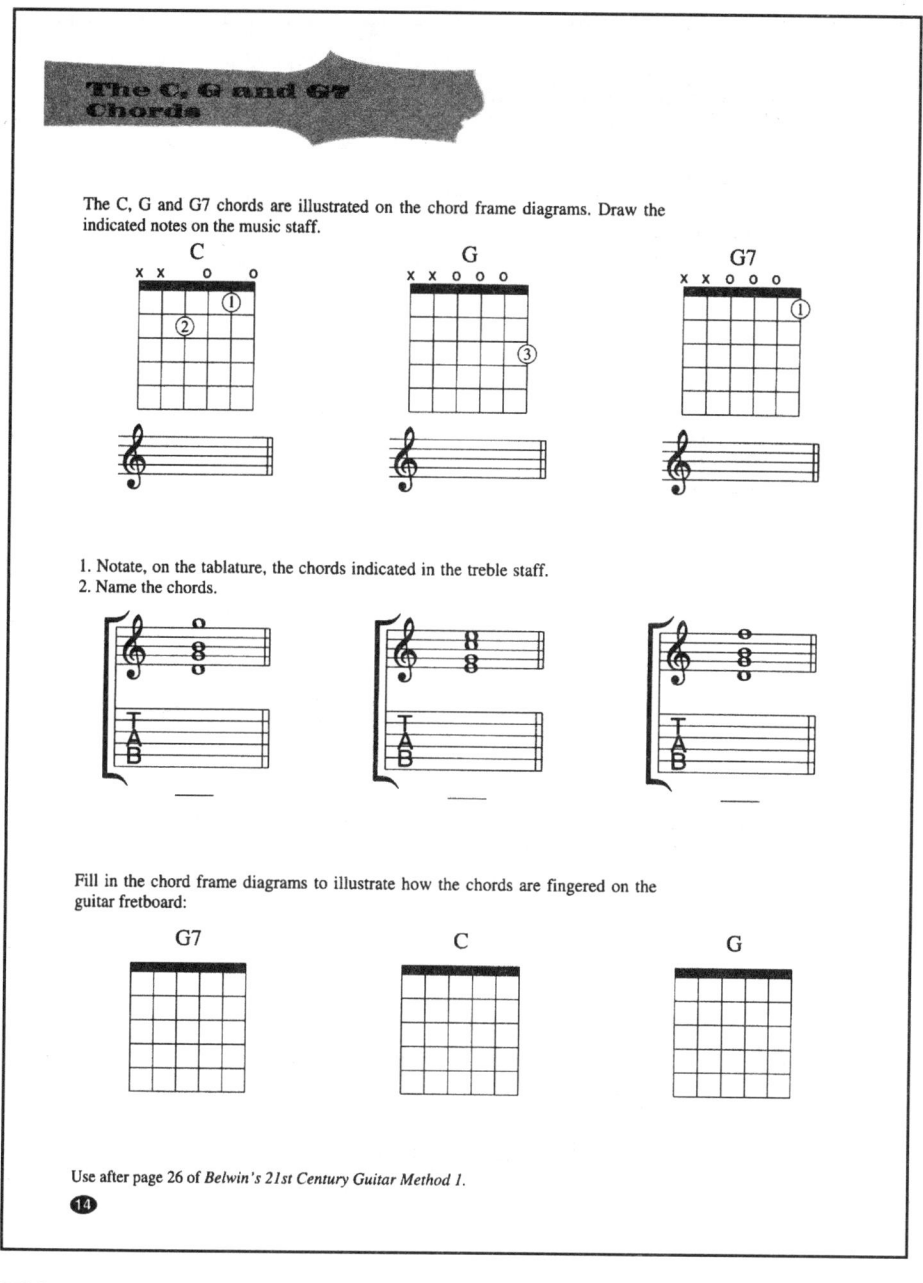

# Theory Lesson 11: The C, G and G7 Chords

**Guitar Theory 1**

## Reinforces
C Chord
G Chord
G7 Chord
Chord Frame Diagrams

This page correlates to Method book page 26.

## Objective
- Develop the students ability to understand and visualize note locations on the neck of the guitar

## Teacher Suggestions
- Explain each fill-in example.
- Do part of each example with students.
- Have students complete the examples on their own or as homework assignments.

**Teacher Note:** As suggested earlier, if students are having trouble relating the tab and guitar frame diagrams to the neck of the guitar, lay a guitar flat, horizontally on a table or desk top in front of the student. Tablature is a horizontal diagram of the neck. Now hold the guitar vertically. Guitar frames are a vertical diagram of the neck.

57

# Guitar Rock Shop 1 — Rock Lesson 11: Rhythm Riffs and Patterns

**New Concepts**
The A minor pentatonic scale

**Reinforces**
Alternate picking
Moveable Shape Concept

### Rhythm Riffs and Patterns

Now let's take the E minor pentatonic scale and transpose it to A. The A minor pentatonic is played on the fifth, fourth, and third strings. Notice that the basic shape of the A minor pentatonic scale is exactly the same as the E minor pentatonic, except the root of the scale is on the fifth string.

A5 (Root ⑤ Form)   A Minor Pentatonic (Root ⑤)

Play the chord and then the scale. Listen for how the notes sound in relation to the chord.

**Example 43**

**Example 44**
(Example 40 transposed to A)
(P.M. optional)

**Example 45**
(Example 41 transposed to A)
(P.M. optional)

**Example 46**
(Example 42 transposed to A)
(P.M. optional)

**Objective**
- Learn the one octave A minor pentatonic scale
- Demonstrate the similarities (same root, similar "shape" or pattern) between the A5 power chord and the A minor pentatonic scale
- Reinforce moveable shape concept

**Teacher Suggestions**
- Play program 20.
- Point out the similarity in shape of the A5 power chord to that of the A minor pentatonic scale.
- Point out the similarity in shape of the A minor pentatonic scale to that of the E minor pentatonic scale (same pattern/shape played on a different set of strings).
- Explain that examples 44 - 46 are the same as examples 40 - 42, only transposed to A. On the guitar, any pattern, scale or chord can be transposed by shifting it to the correct root location.
- Have students sing the A minor pentatonic scale with example 43.

# Rock Lesson 11: Rhythm Riffs and Patterns

**Guitar Rock Shop 1**

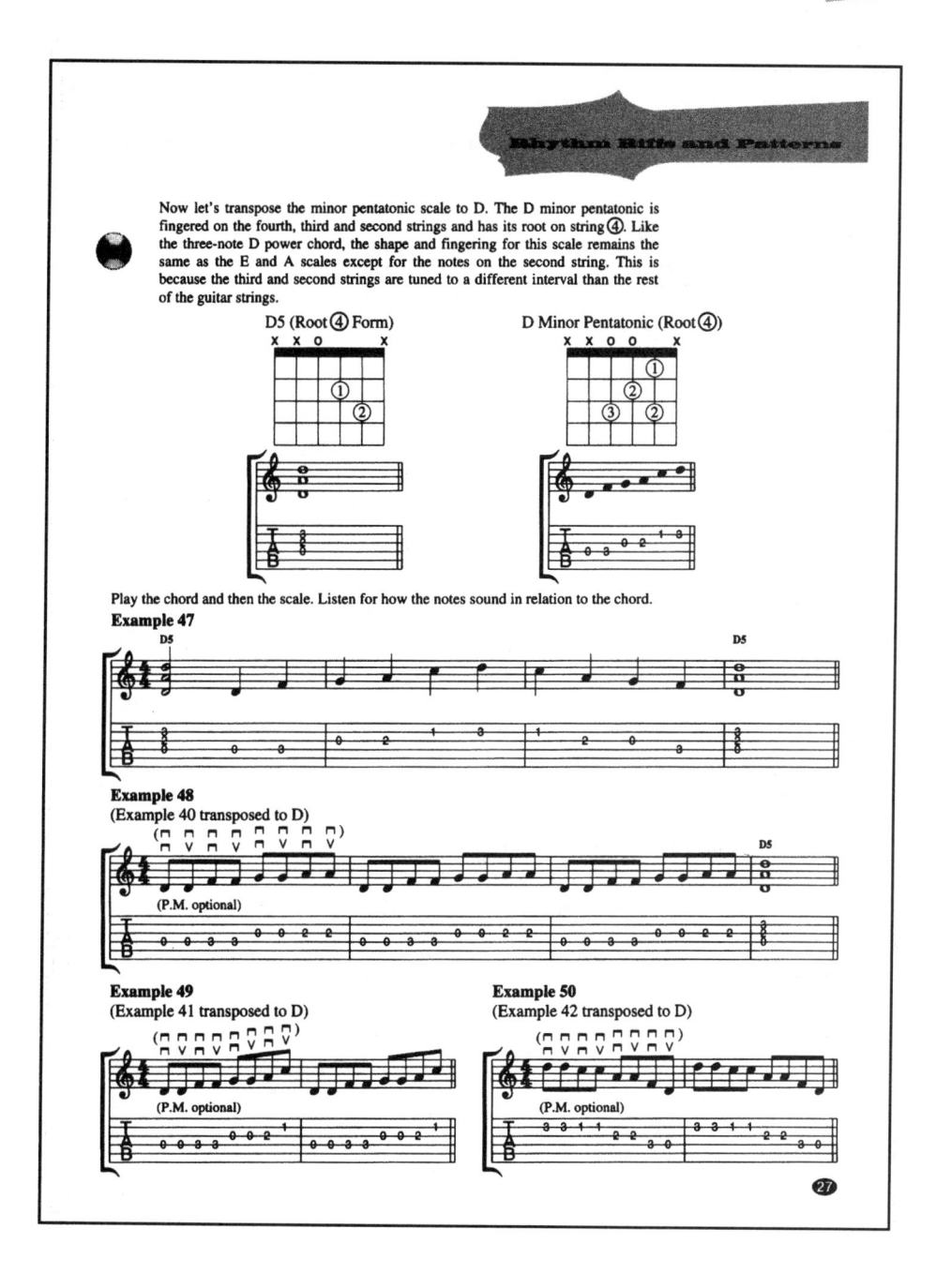

### Rhythm Riffs and Patterns

Now let's transpose the minor pentatonic scale to D. The D minor pentatonic is fingered on the fourth, third and second strings and has its root on string ④. Like the three-note D power chord, the shape and fingering for this scale remains the same as the E and A scales except for the notes on the second string. This is because the third and second strings are tuned to a different interval than the rest of the guitar strings.

D5 (Root ④ Form)   D Minor Pentatonic (Root ④)

Play the chord and then the scale. Listen for how the notes sound in relation to the chord.

**Example 47**

**Example 48**
(Example 40 transposed to D)
(P.M. optional)

**Example 49**
(Example 41 transposed to D)
(P.M. optional)

**Example 50**
(Example 42 transposed to D)
(P.M. optional)

## New Concepts
The D minor pentatonic scale

## Reinforces
Alternate picking
Moveable Shape Concept

## Objective
- Learn the one octave D minor pentatonic scale
- Demonstrate the similarities (same root, similar "shape" or pattern) between the D5 power chord and the D minor pentatonic scale
- Reinforce moveable shape concept

## Teacher Suggestions
- Play program 21.
- Point out the similarity in shape of the D5 power chord to that of the D minor pentatonic scale.
- Point out that the reason the three-note D5 and the D minor pentatonic scale don't share the exact same shape as their counterparts in A and E is because the 2nd and 3rd strings are tuned a different distance apart (major 3rd, G - B) than the rest of the guitar (in perfect 4ths, E - A, A - D, D - G, B - E). This is the reason that the highest notes in the D patterns (on the 2nd string) are one fret higher than the highest notes in the A (on the 3rd string) and E (on the 4th string) patterns.
- Have students sing the D minor pentatonic scale with example 47.

# Guitar Method 1

## Lesson 12: The D and D7 Chords

**New Concepts**
D chord
D7 chord
Rhythm slashes
Fermata

**Reinforces**
The G and C Chords

**Objective**
- Learn the two new chords
- Move from chord to chord smoothly, in rhythm

**Teacher Suggestions**
- Listen to programs 42 and 43.
- Students should practice the *Chord Study* until they can change chords smoothly without breaking rhythm.
- Help students to sing the root and then the arpeggio of each chord. Since these chords are not in root position play the root for the students on either the guitar or piano.
- Before playing *New River Train* explain rhythm slash notation.
- **Group Class:** Have half the class play the melody to *New River Train* while the rest play the accompaniment, then reverse. (Note the fermata sign at the end.)

**Teacher Note:** For more practice on the D, C, and G chords have the students go back and play the chords to *Amazing Grace* (page 21).

# Theory Lesson 12: The D and D7 Chords

**Guitar Theory 1**

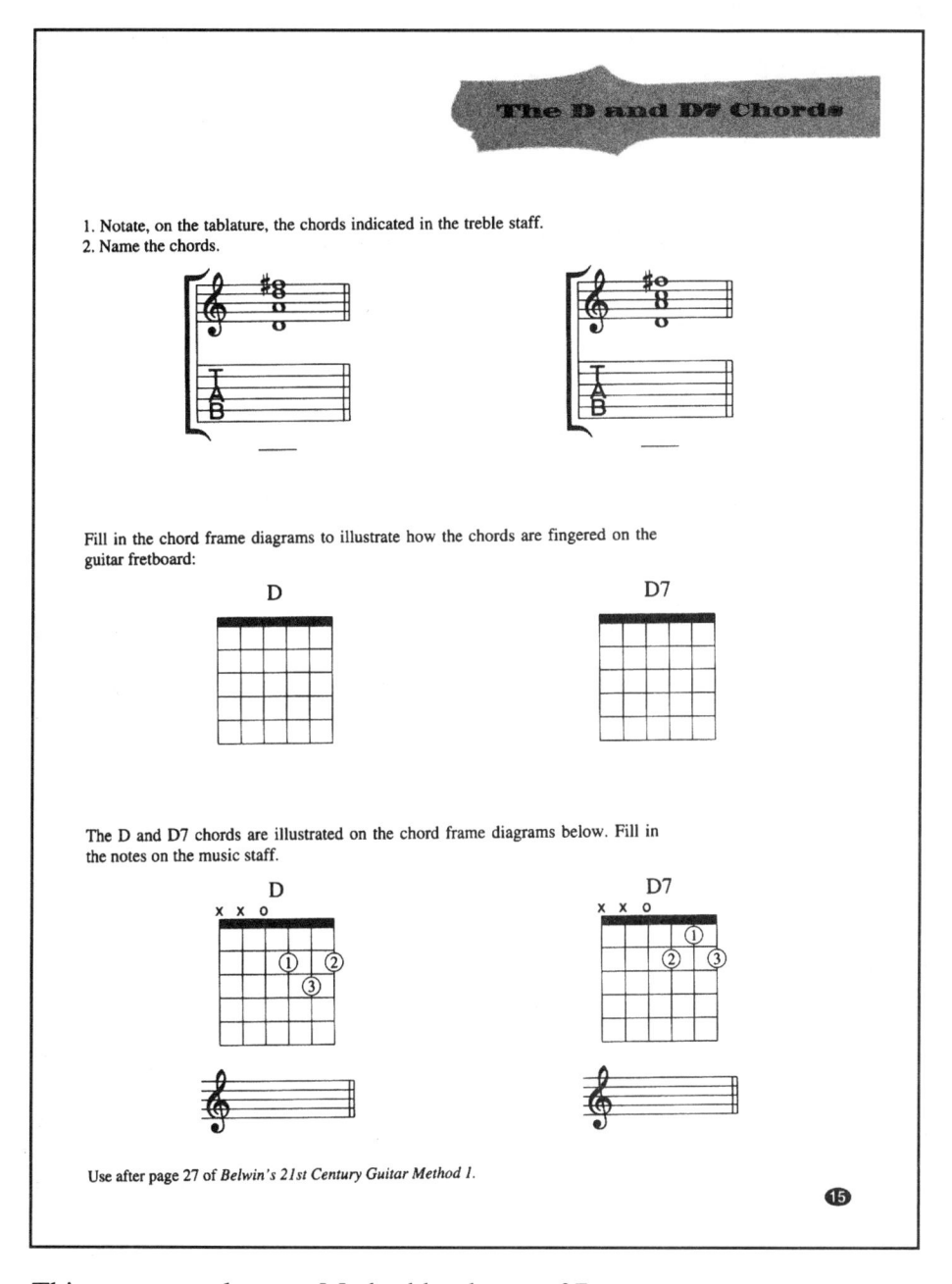

### Reinforces
D Chord
D7 Chord
Chord Frame Diagrams

This page correlates to Method book page 27.

## Objective
• Develop the students ability to understand and visualize note locations on the neck of the guitar

## Teacher Suggestions
• Explain each fill-in example.
• Do part of each example with students.
• Have students complete the examples on their own or as homework assignments.

**Teacher Note:** Again, If students are having trouble relating the tab and guitar frame diagrams to the neck of the guitar, lay a guitar flat, horizontally on a table or desk top in front of the student. Tablature is a horizontal diagram of the neck. Now hold the guitar vertically. Guitar frames are a vertical diagram of the neck.

# Guitar Rock Shop 1 — Rock Lesson 12: Rhythm Riffs and Patterns

## New Concepts
Riffs

## Reinforces
Moveable shape concept

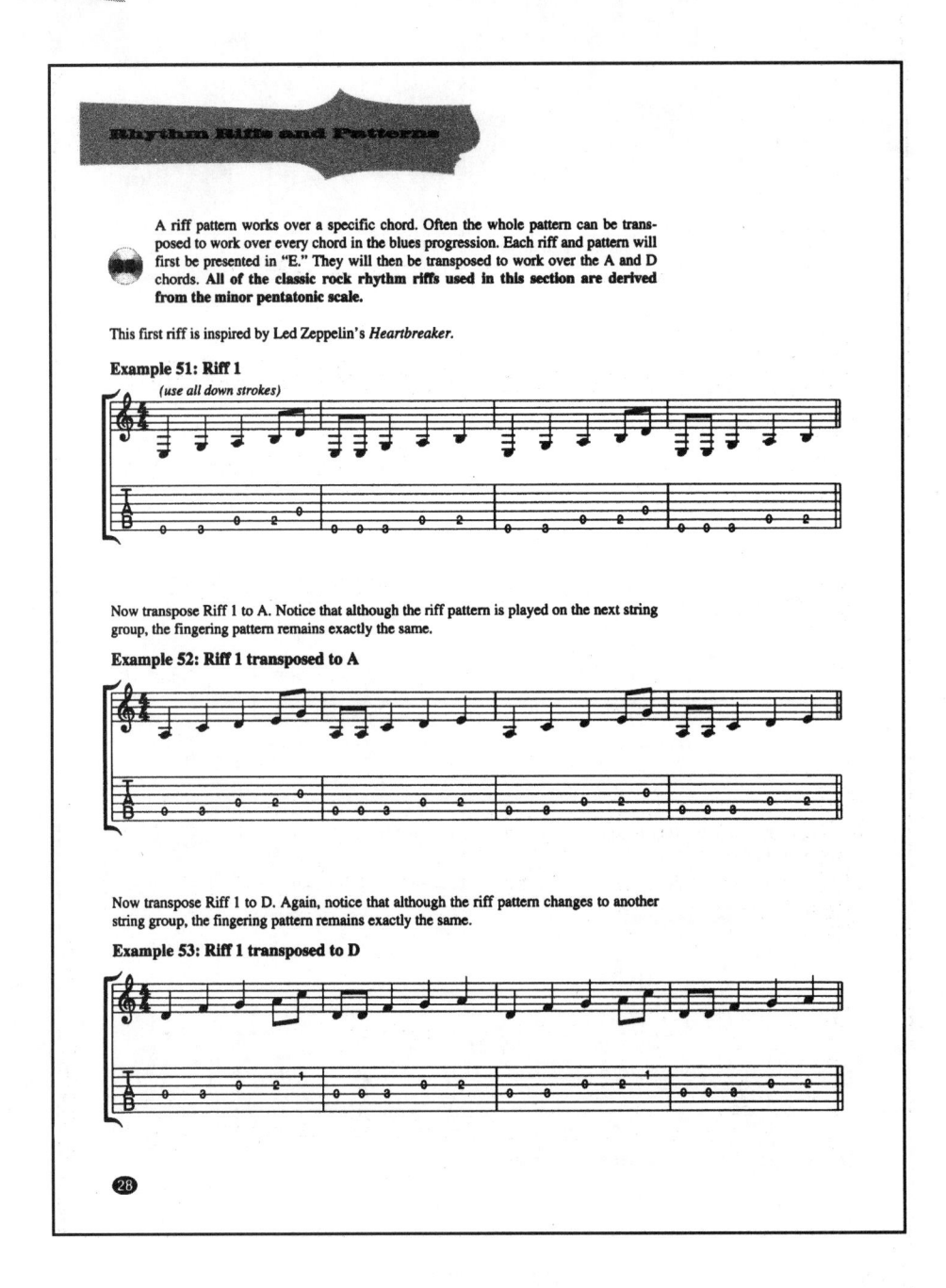

---

### Rhythm Riffs and Patterns

A riff pattern works over a specific chord. Often the whole pattern can be transposed to work over every chord in the blues progression. Each riff and pattern will first be presented in "E." They will then be transposed to work over the A and D chords. All of the classic rock rhythm riffs used in this section are derived from the minor pentatonic scale.

This first riff is inspired by Led Zeppelin's *Heartbreaker*.

**Example 51: Riff 1**
*(use all down strokes)*

Now transpose Riff 1 to A. Notice that although the riff pattern is played on the next string group, the fingering pattern remains exactly the same.

**Example 52: Riff 1 transposed to A**

Now transpose Riff 1 to D. Again, notice that although the riff pattern changes to another string group, the fingering pattern remains exactly the same.

**Example 53: Riff 1 transposed to D**

㉘

---

## Objective
- Learn a basic riff in E, derived from the E minor pentatonic scale
- Transpose the riff to A and D

## Teacher Suggestions
- Play program 22
- Riff 1 is loosely based on Led Zeppelin's *Heartbreaker*.
- Demonstrate that Riff 1 uses every note of the minor pentatonic scale fingering (except the octave).
- Show that as the riff is transposed from E to A and D the shape of the pattern remains the same (except of course for the highest notes in the D pattern which are one fret higher than in the E and A patterns).

# Rock Lesson 12: Rhythm Riffs and Patterns

## Guitar Rock Shop 1

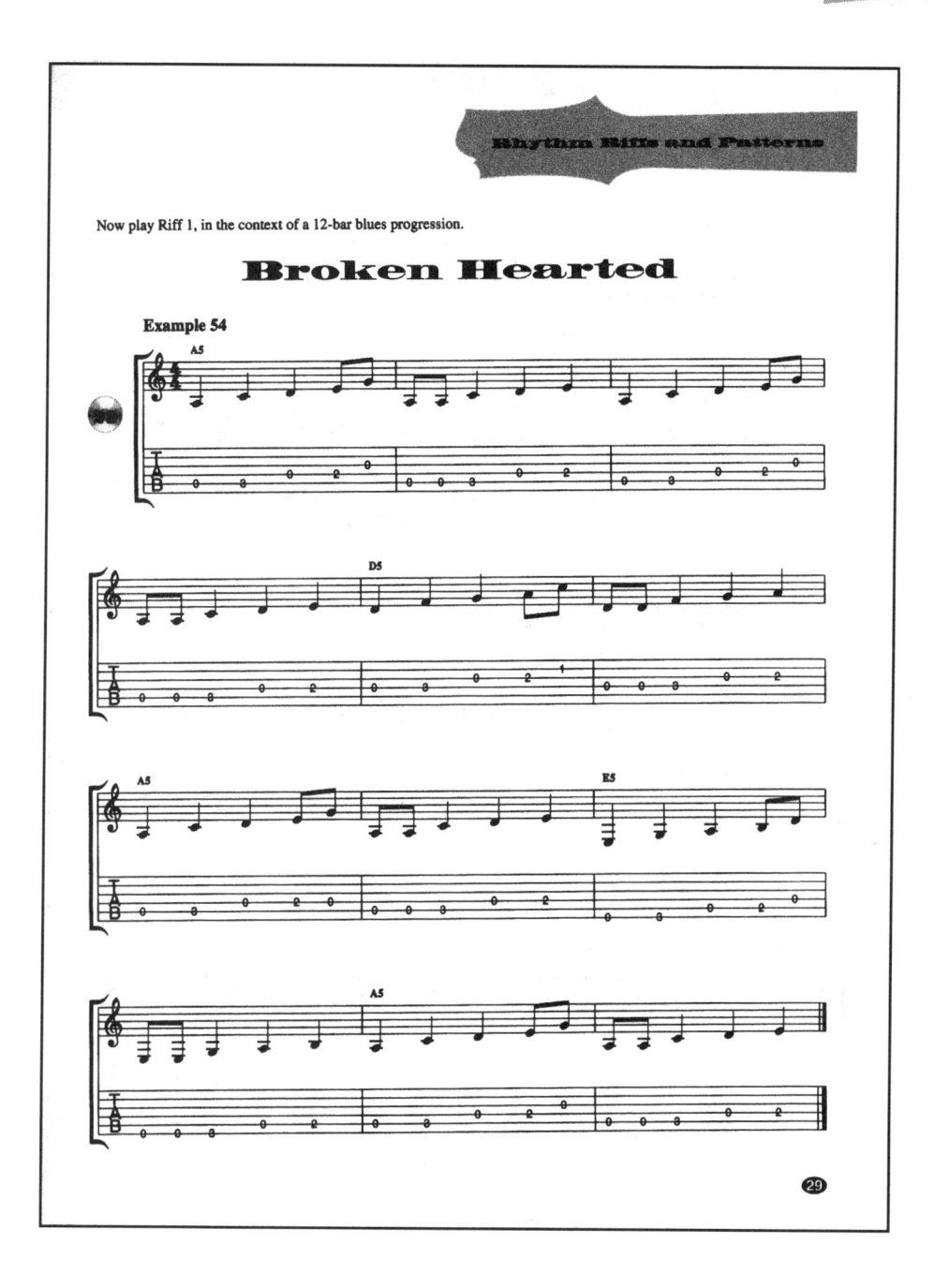

**Reinforces**
The blues progression
Riffs 1, 2 and 3
Moveable shape concept
A5, D5 and E5

Now play Riff 1, in the context of a 12-bar blues progression.

### Broken Hearted

**Example 54**

## Objective
- Play Riff 1 in the context of a 12-bar blues form

## Teacher Suggestions
- Play program 23.
- Have students play along with the recording.
- Have students sing the blues progression root movement with example 54 (just roots, not the entire rhythm figure).
- **Group Class:** Have some students play power chords, in eighth notes (muted), while the rest play the riff.

**Suggested Listening:** Led Zeppelin's *Heartbreaker* from the album *Led Zeppelin II*. Note: *Heartbreaker* is a blues in A. See if anyone can figure out the exact guitar part.

**Guitar Method 1**

**Lesson 13: Rock Workshop 101**
**The Blues Progression**

**New Concepts**
The Blues Progression,
I, IV and V

**Reinforces**
G, G7, C and D7 Chords

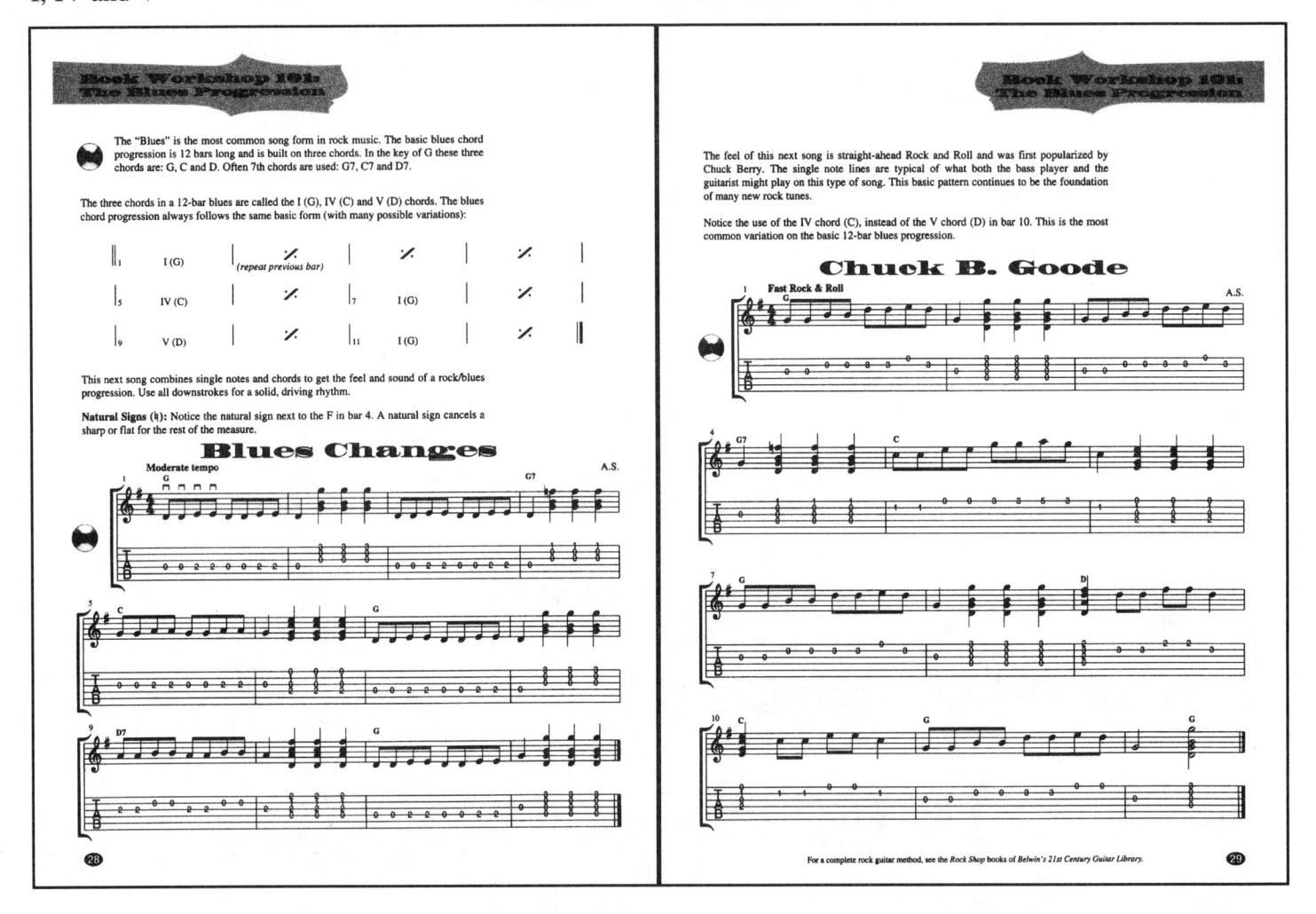

**Teacher Note:** Students using the Rock Shop book have already been introduced to the blues.

## Objective
- Learn the Blues Progression

## Teacher Suggestions
- Use the complete listening sequence described on page 19.
- At the piano or guitar or using recordings play examples of the blues progression. Have the students identify by ear the three phrases of the blues progression and the I, IV and V chords.
- Have students sing the blues progression root movements with programs 45 and 46.
- Experiment with identifying simple variations on the basic progression, like those shown below.

$$\| \text{I} \mid \text{/.} \mid \text{/.} \mid \text{/.} \mid \text{IV} \mid \text{/.} \mid \text{I} \mid \text{/.} \mid \text{V} \mid \text{IV} \mid \text{I} \mid \text{V} \|$$
$$\| \text{I} \mid \text{IV} \mid \text{I} \mid \text{/.} \mid \text{IV} \mid \text{/.} \mid \text{I} \mid \text{/.} \mid \text{V} \mid \text{IV} \mid \text{I} \mid \text{I} \|$$

**Group Class:** Have half the class play the written part to *Blues Changes* while the rest play a chord accompaniment, then reverse.

# Theory Lesson 13: The Blues

## Guitar Theory 1

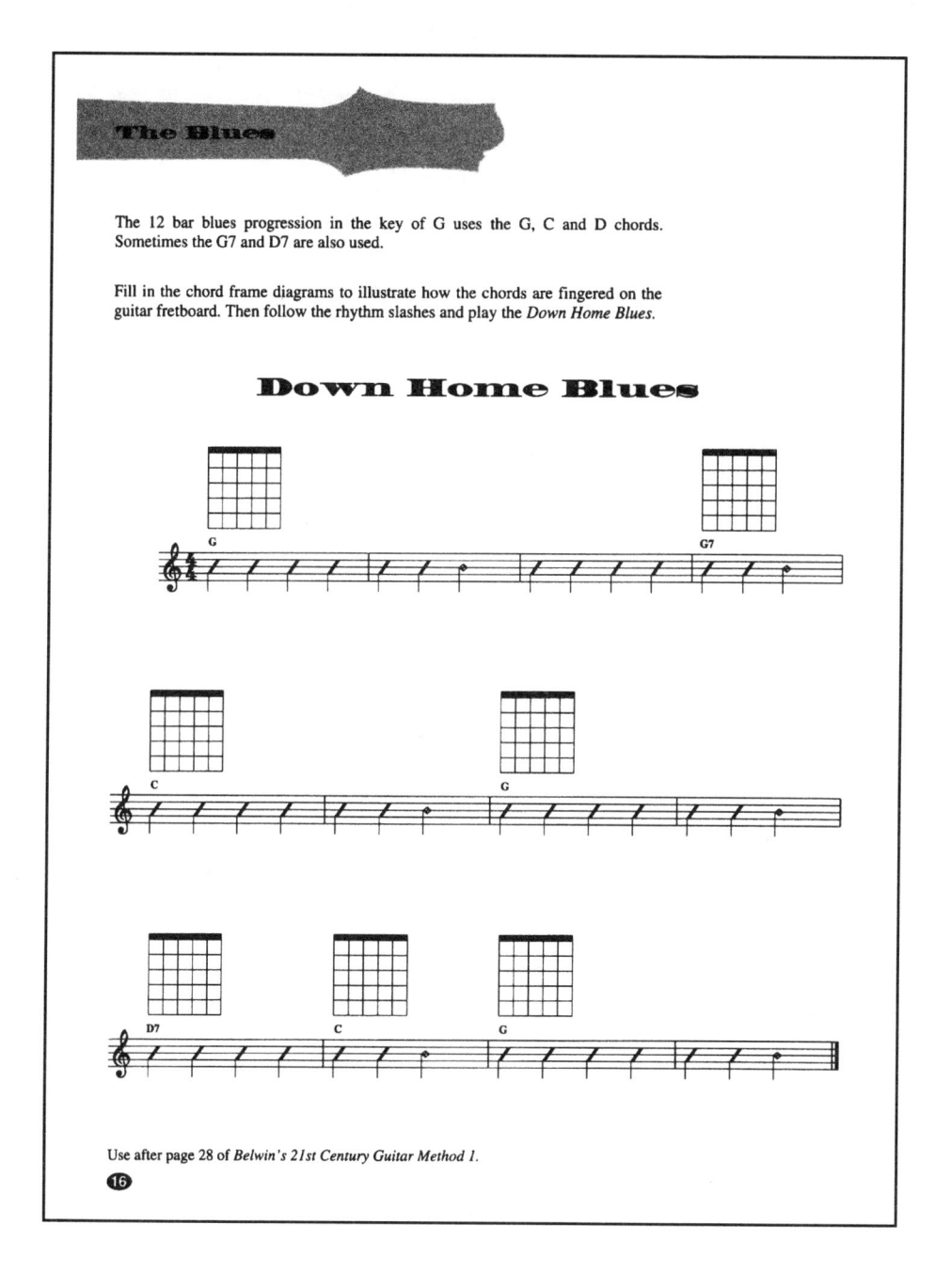

> The 12 bar blues progression in the key of G uses the G, C and D chords. Sometimes the G7 and D7 are also used.
>
> Fill in the chord frame diagrams to illustrate how the chords are fingered on the guitar fretboard. Then follow the rhythm slashes and play the *Down Home Blues*.
>
> **Down Home Blues**
>
> Use after page 28 of *Belwin's 21st Century Guitar Method 1*.

### Reinforces
The Blues Progression
G, G7, C and D7
Chord Frame Diagrams

This page correlates to Method book pages 28 and 29.

## Objective
- Develop the students ability to understand and visualize note locations and chord fingerings on the neck of the guitar.

## Teacher Suggestions
- **Group Class:** Have half the class play *Down Home Blues* while the other half plays *Chuck B. Goode*, (page 28 of *Guitar Method 1*.)

# Guitar Rock Shop 1 — Rock Lesson 13: Rhythm Riffs and Patterns

## Objective
- Learn a basic riff in E (Riff 2), derived from the E minor pentatonic scale
- Transpose the riff to A and D

## Teacher Suggestions
- Play programs 24 - 25.
- Riff 2 is based on Eric Clapton's version of *Crossroads*.
- Demonstrate that as the riff is transposed from E to A and D, the shape of the pattern remains the same (except of course for the highest notes in the D pattern which are one fret higher than in the E and A patterns).
- *Georgia Roads* places Riff 2 in the context of a 12-bar blues. Have students sing the blues progression root movement with program 25 (*Georgia Roads*).

**Suggested Listening:** *Crossroads* as performed by Cream (with Eric Clapton) and the original Robert Johnson version.

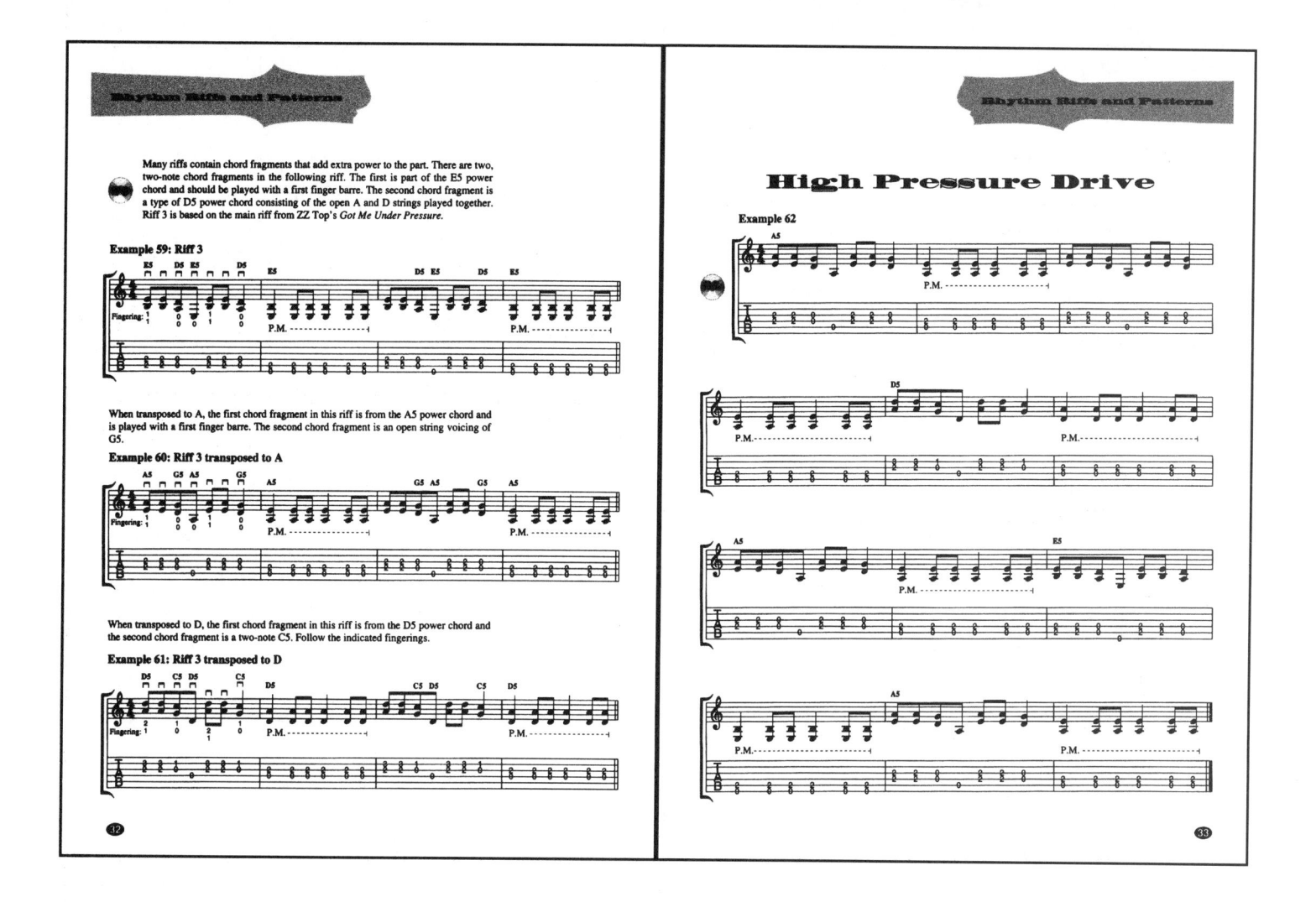

# Rock Lesson 13: Rhythm Riffs and Patterns

## Objective
- Learn a basic riff in E (Riff 3) and transpose that riff to A and D

## Teacher Suggestions
- Play programs 26 - 27.
- Riff 3 is based on ZZ Top's *Got Me Under Pressure*.
- Show that as the riff is transposed from E to A and D, the shape of the pattern remains the same (except of course for the highest notes in the D pattern which are one fret higher than in the E and A patterns).
- *High Pressure Drive* places Riff 3 in the context of a 12-bar blues. Have students sing the blues progression root movement with program 46 (*High Pressure Drive*).

## Suggested Listening: *Got Me Under Pressure* by ZZ Top.

# Guitar Method 1

## Lesson 14: The Notes on the Fifth String

**New Concepts:**

Fifth String A, B and C

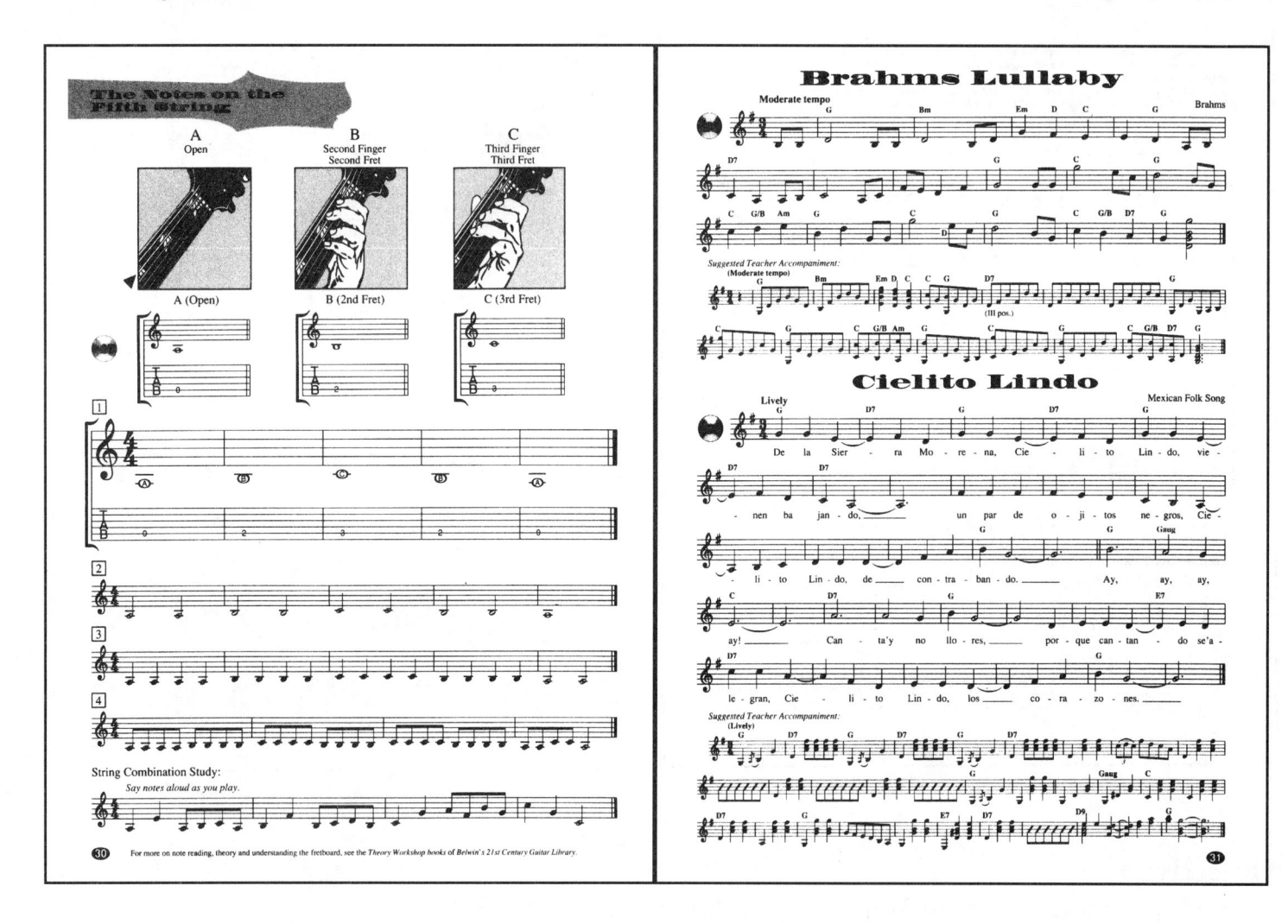

## Objective
- Learn the second string A, B and C
- Be able to play the songs on method book page 31 in tempo with the recording or with the optional teacher accompaniments

## Teacher Suggestions
- Have students play A, B and C. Show how the notes they are playing relate to the drawing, notation and tab.
- Have students play a two-octave scale, low A to high A. This reinforces the logical, linear layout of the guitar.
- Have students listen to program 47 - 49 on recording.
- Use the complete listening sequence described on page 19.

**Optional Song Book:** Students are now prepared to play *Over The Rainbow* on page 16 of Song Trax 1.

**Optional Ensemble Book:** Students are now prepared to play *Blue Rock* on page 21 of *Guitar Ensemble 1*.

# Theory Lesson 14: The Notes on the 5th String

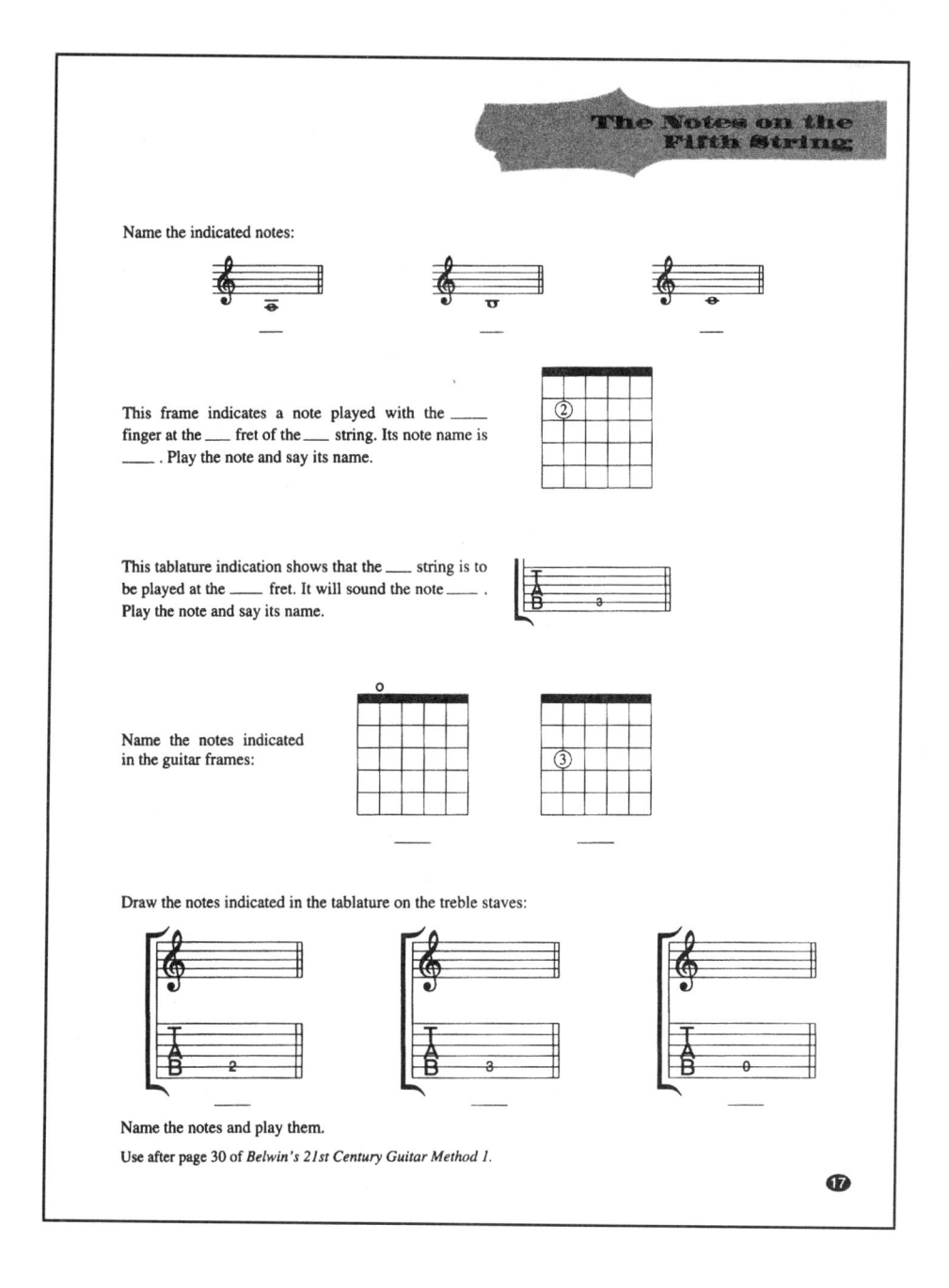

## Guitar Theory 1

**Reinforces**
A, B and C

---

### The Notes on the Fifth String

Name the indicated notes:

[three treble clef staves with single whole notes]

___  ___  ___

This frame indicates a note played with the ___ finger at the ___ fret of the ___ string. Its note name is ___ . Play the note and say its name.

[guitar frame with ② on 2nd fret]

This tablature indication shows that the ___ string is to be played at the ___ fret. It will sound the note ___ . Play the note and say its name.

[tablature showing 3]

Name the notes indicated in the guitar frames:

[two guitar frames: one with open string "o", one with ③]

___  ___

Draw the notes indicated in the tablature on the treble staves:

[three treble staves with tablature showing 2, 3, 0]

Name the notes and play them.

Use after page 30 of *Belwin's 21st Century Guitar Method 1*.

⓱

---

This page correlates to Method book pages 30 and 31.

## Objective
- Develop the students ability to understand and visualize note locations and chord fingerings on the neck of the guitar.

# Guitar Rock Shop 1

## Rock Lesson 14: Rhythm Riffs and Patterns

## Objective
- Learn a basic riff (Riff 4) derived from the E minor pentatonic scale
- Transpose the riff to A and D

## Teacher Suggestions
- Play programs 28 - 29.
- Riff 4 is based on *Jumpin' Jack Flash* by The Rolling Stones.
- Show that as the riff is transposed from E to A and D that the shape of the pattern remains the same (except of course for the highest notes in the D pattern which are one fret higher than in the E and A patterns).
- The Jack Flash Riff places Riff 4 in the context of a 12-bar blues. Have students sing the blues progression root movement with program 29 (The Jack Flash Riff).

**Suggested Listening:** *Jumpin' Jack Flash* by The Rolling Stones.

# Rock Lesson 14: Rhythm Riffs and Patterns

## Guitar Rock Shop 1

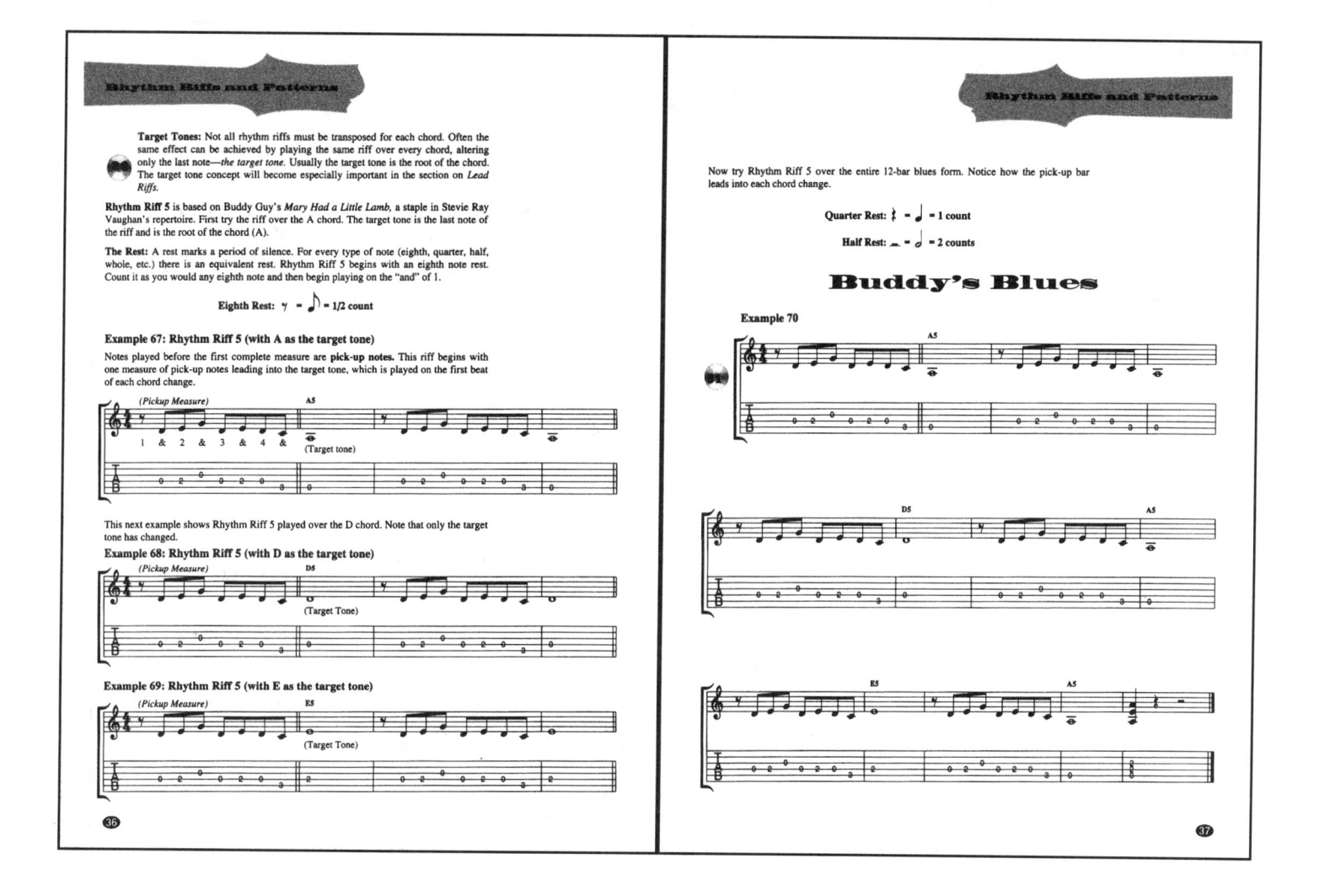

## Objective
- Learn a basic riff in E (Riff 5) and transpose that riff to A and D

## Teacher Suggestions
- Play programs 30 - 31.
- Riff 5 is based on Buddy Guy's *Mary Had a Little Lamb*.
- Show that as the riff is transposed from E to A and D, the shape of the pattern remains the same (except of course for the highest notes in the D pattern which are one fret higher than in the E and A patterns).
- *Buddy's Blues* places Riff 5 in the context of a 12-bar blues. Have students sing the blues progression root movement with program 31 (*Buddy's Blues*).

## Suggested Listening:
Listen to both Buddy Guy's and Stevie Ray Vaughan's versions of *Mary Had a Little Lamb*.

## Guitar Method 1

## Lesson 15: The C, Am, and Dm Chords

**New Concepts**
C
Am
Dm

> ### The C, A Minor and D Minor Chords
>
> So far you have been playing the C chord on four strings. Here is the full five string form of the C chord. The A minor chord is also a five-string chord form. The D minor chord uses four strings.
>
> C     Am     Dm
>
> C Chord     Am Chord     Dm Chord
>
> **Fingering Tip:** When moving from C to Am, keep your first and second fingers in place. Just shift your third finger. When moving from Dm to G7, keep your first finger in place and lift your second and third fingers.
>
> Chord Study:
>
> *The Roots of Rock* consists mostly of chords played one note at a time. This is called "arpeggio style." Hold each chord down for a full measure. Do not finger each note separately.
>
> **Glide Picking:** Instead of alternate picking, allow the pick to glide from string to string as shown (all down strokes). For guitar parts like this, glide picking is easier and sounds smoother than alternate picking.
>
> ### The Roots of Rock

## Objective
- Learn the three new chords
- Move from chord to chord smoothly, in rhythm

## Teacher Suggestions
- Listen to programs 50 and 51 with the class.
- Students should practice the *Chord Study* until they can change chords smoothly without breaking rhythm.
- Use the suggested fingerings, they will make changing from one chord to the next easier, smoother and faster.
- Help students to locate and sing the root and arpeggio of each chord. (Students should sing simple, root position chords in 3rds, not the exact inversions being played on the guitar.)
- Before playing *The Roots of Rock* explain that the single-notes are just arpeggiated chords. Hold the indicated chords for the full measure.

**Optional Song Book:** Students are now prepared to play *I Will Always Love You* on page 18 of *Song Trax 1*.

# Theory Lesson 15: The C, Am, and Dm Chords

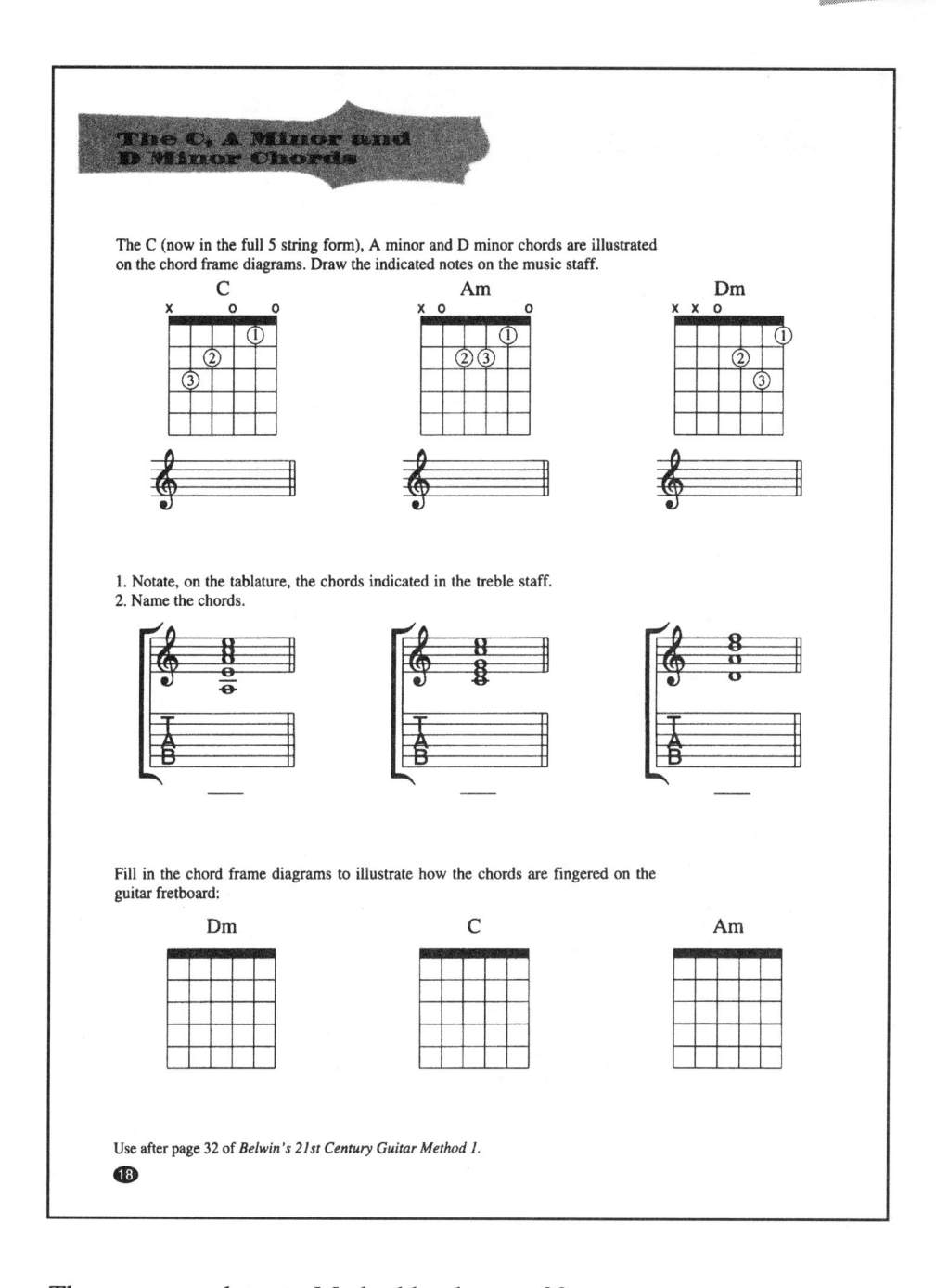

## Guitar Theory 1

**Reinforces**
C
Am
Dm

The page correlates to Method book page 32.

## Objective
- Develop the students ability to understand and visualize note locations and chord fingerings on the neck of the guitar.

# Guitar Rock Shop 1

## Rock Lesson 15: The Major Scale

**New Concepts**
Major scale construction

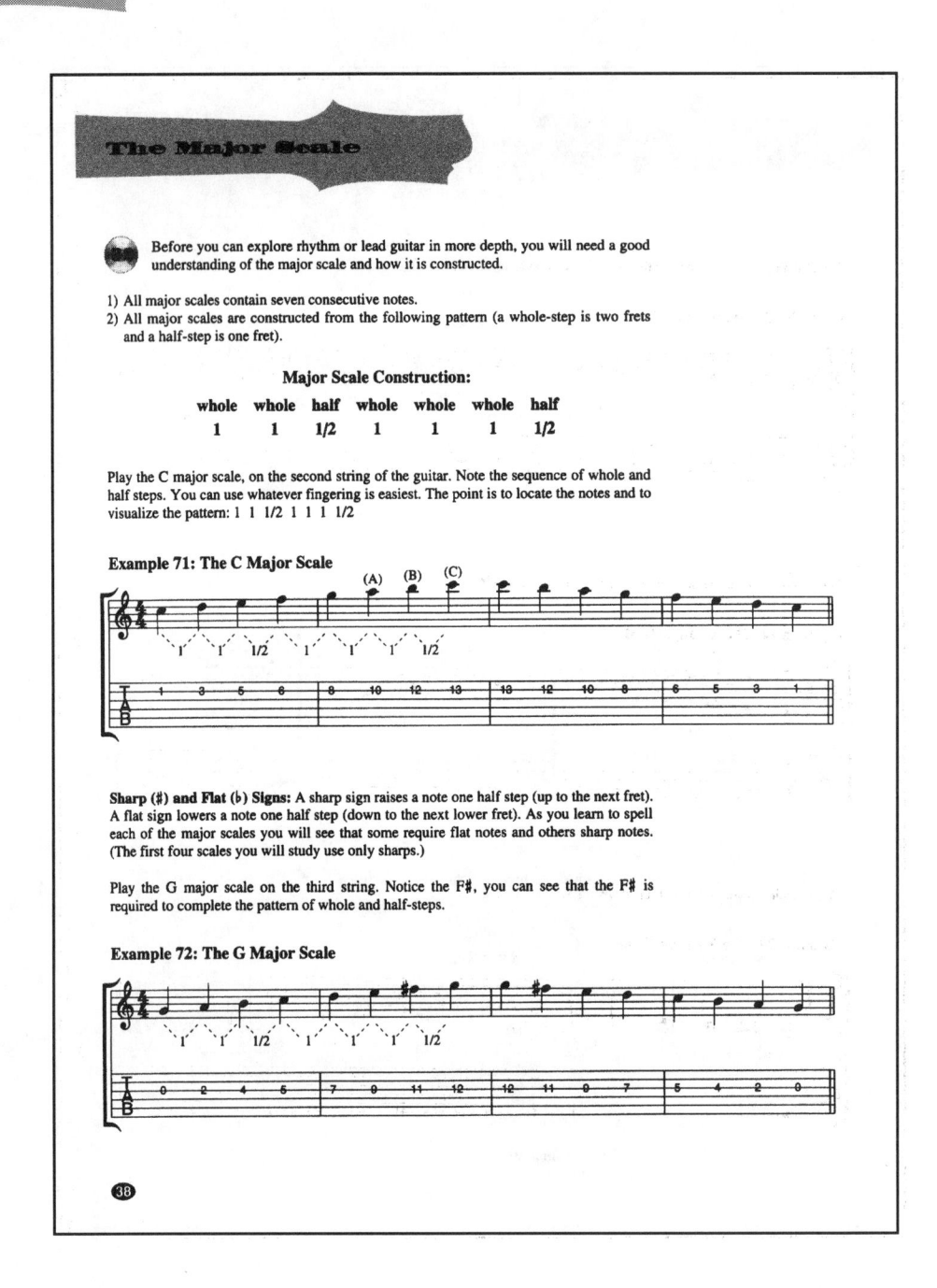

---

### The Major Scale

Before you can explore rhythm or lead guitar in more depth, you will need a good understanding of the major scale and how it is constructed.

1) All major scales contain seven consecutive notes.
2) All major scales are constructed from the following pattern (a whole-step is two frets and a half-step is one fret).

**Major Scale Construction:**

| whole | whole | half | whole | whole | whole | half |
|-------|-------|------|-------|-------|-------|------|
| 1     | 1     | 1/2  | 1     | 1     | 1     | 1/2  |

Play the C major scale, on the second string of the guitar. Note the sequence of whole and half steps. You can use whatever fingering is easiest. The point is to locate the notes and to visualize the pattern: 1 1 1/2 1 1 1 1/2

**Example 71: The C Major Scale**

**Sharp (#) and Flat (♭) Signs:** A sharp sign raises a note one half step (up to the next fret). A flat sign lowers a note one half step (down to the next lower fret). As you learn to spell each of the major scales you will see that some require flat notes and others sharp notes. (The first four scales you will study use only sharps.)

Play the G major scale on the third string. Notice the F#, you can see that the F# is required to complete the pattern of whole and half-steps.

**Example 72: The G Major Scale**

---

## Objective
- Learn the basic major scale pattern of whole and half steps

## Teacher Suggestions
- Play program 32.
- Explain that all major scales contain seven different notes and that all are built from the pattern: 1 1 1/2 1 1 1 1/2.
- Draw the C major scale and indicate the whole and half steps.
- Have students play Example 71, the C major scale played on the 2nd string, paying special attention to the pattern of whole and half steps.
- Do the same with Example 72, the G major scale played on the 3rd string.
- Have students sing the C and G major scales. Use letter names or solfege.

# Rock Lesson 15: The Major Scale

**Guitar Rock Shop 1**

## Reinforces
Major scale construction

---

### The Major Scale

The D major scale contains both F# and C#. Play it on the fourth string.

**Example 73: The D Major Scale**

The A major scale contains three sharps: F#, C# and G#.

**Example 74: The A Major Scale**

The E major scale contains four sharps: F#, C#, G# and D#.

**Example 75: The E Major Scale**

㊴

---

## Teacher Suggestions
- Have students play Example 73, the D major scale played on the 4th string, paying special attention to the pattern of whole and half steps.
- Do the same with Examples 74 and 75, the A and E major scales.
- Have students sing the D, A and E major scales. Use letter names or solfege.
- Pick random starting tones and have the students play a major scale from that tone entirely on one string.

# Guitar Method 1

## Lesson 16: Eighth Note Strumming

**New Concepts**
Down-up strumming

### Eighth Note Strumming

This next song uses an eighth note rhythm to make the strum pattern more interesting. Use an upstroke to strum on "and."

**Important Tip:** When strumming up and down, always swing your pick hand loosely from the wrist. The pick should pivot in a semi-circle, so that on the up stroke, the top three strings (E, B and G) are accentuated.

### Wrist Rock

### Battle of Aughrim
Irish

## Objective
- Begin to play more sophisticated strum pattern

## Teacher Suggestions
- Listen to programs 52–53.
- Have students hold the pick loosely and strum from the wrist. On the upstroke, the pick should travel in a semi-circular motion striking only the top strings.
- Students should strum the chords to *Wrist Rock* and *Battle of Aughrim* along with the recordings.
- **Group Class**: Have half the class play the melody to *Battle of Aughrim* while the rest play the accompaniment part. Then reverse.

# Rock Lesson 16: The Boogie Pattern

**Guitar Rock Shop 1**

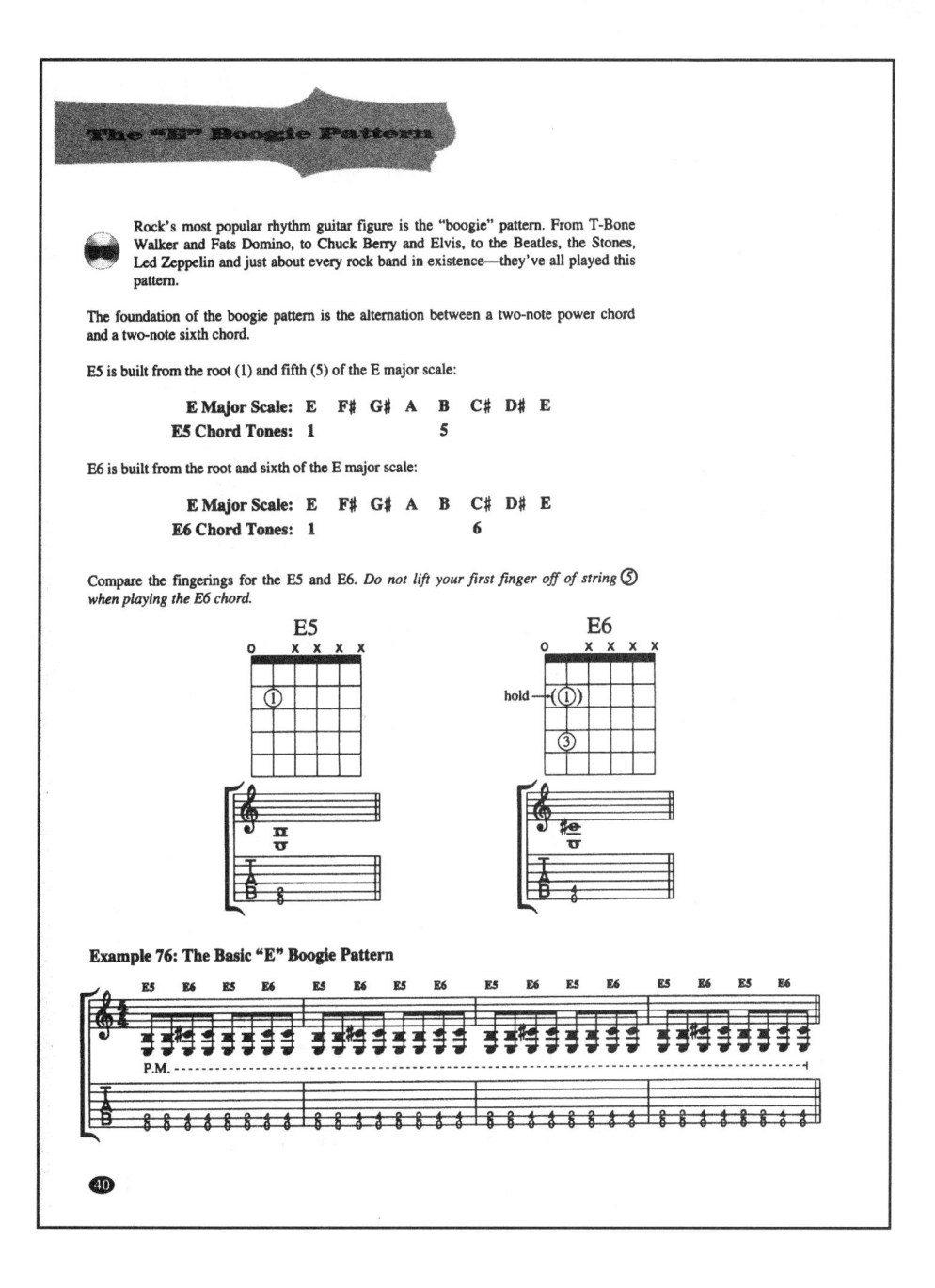

## The "E" Boogie Pattern

Rock's most popular rhythm guitar figure is the "boogie" pattern. From T-Bone Walker and Fats Domino, to Chuck Berry and Elvis, to the Beatles, the Stones, Led Zeppelin and just about every rock band in existence—they've all played this pattern.

The foundation of the boogie pattern is the alternation between a two-note power chord and a two-note sixth chord.

E5 is built from the root (1) and fifth (5) of the E major scale:

| E Major Scale: | E | F# | G# | A | B | C# | D# | E |
|---|---|---|---|---|---|---|---|---|
| E5 Chord Tones: | 1 | | | | 5 | | | |

E6 is built from the root and sixth of the E major scale:

| E Major Scale: | E | F# | G# | A | B | C# | D# | E |
|---|---|---|---|---|---|---|---|---|
| E6 Chord Tones: | 1 | | | | | | 6 | |

Compare the fingerings for the E5 and E6. *Do not lift your first finger off of string ⑤ when playing the E6 chord.*

**Example 76: The Basic "E" Boogie Pattern**

## New Concepts
Two-note E6 chord
Boogie progression

## Objective
- Learn the basic E boogie pattern (alternating power 5th and 6th chords)

## Teacher Suggestions
- Play program 33.
- Explain the derivation of E5 and E6 from the E major scale (root/5th and root/6th).
- Students should play example 76 with the recording.

77

# Guitar Rock Shop 1

## Rock Lesson 16: The Boogie Pattern

### New Concepts
Two-note A6 chord (power 6th)

---

**The "A" Boogie Pattern**

Now we will transpose the boogie pattern to the root ⑤ A chord.

A5 is built from the root and fifth of the A major scale:

| A Major Scale: | A | B | C# | D | E | F# | G# | A |
|---|---|---|---|---|---|---|---|---|
| A5 Chord Tones: | 1 | | | | 5 | | | |

A6 is built from the root and sixth of the A major scale:

| A Major Scale: | A | B | C# | D | E | F# | G# | A |
|---|---|---|---|---|---|---|---|---|
| A6 Chord Tones: | 1 | | | | | 6 | | |

Compare the fingerings for A5 and A6. *Do not lift your first finger off of string ④ when playing the A6 chord.*

**Example 77: The Basic "A" Boogie Pattern**

The next example combines the E and A boogie patterns.

**Example 78**

---

### Objective
- Learn the basic A boogie pattern (alternating power 5th and 6th chords)

### Teacher Suggestions
- Play program 34.
- Explain the derivation of A5 and A6 from the A major scale (root/5**th** and root/6**th**).
- Demonstrate that the A boogie pattern is exactly the same as the E boogie pattern only transposed to a different set of strings.
- Have students play examples 77 - 78 with the recordings.

# Rock Lesson 16: The Boogie Pattern

**Guitar Rock Shop 1**

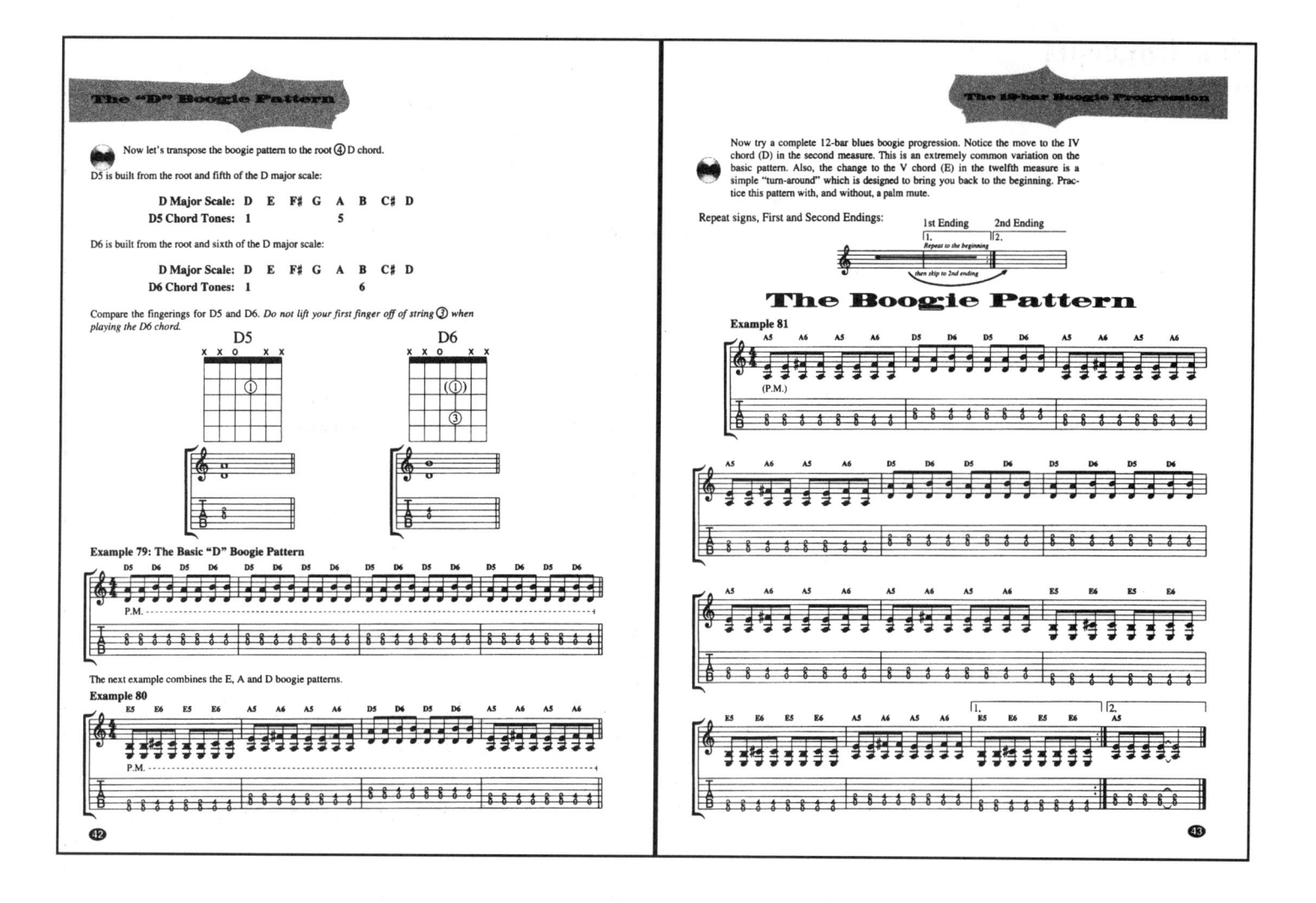

### The "D" Boogie Pattern

Now let's transpose the boogie pattern to the root ④ D chord.

D5 is built from the root and fifth of the D major scale:

| D Major Scale: | D | E | F# | G | A | B | C# | D |
| --- | --- | --- | --- | --- | --- | --- | --- | --- |
| D5 Chord Tones: | 1 | | | | 5 | | | |

D6 is built from the root and sixth of the D major scale:

| D Major Scale: | D | E | F# | G | A | B | C# | D |
| --- | --- | --- | --- | --- | --- | --- | --- | --- |
| D6 Chord Tones: | 1 | | | | | 6 | | |

Compare the fingerings for D5 and D6. *Do not lift your first finger off of string ③ when playing the D6 chord.*

**Example 79:** The Basic "D" Boogie Pattern

The next example combines the E, A and D boogie patterns.

**Example 80**

### The 12-bar Boogie Progression

Now try a complete 12-bar blues boogie progression. Notice the move to the IV chord (D) in the second measure. This is an extremely common variation on the basic pattern. Also, the change to the V chord (E) in the twelfth measure is a simple "turn-around" which is designed to bring you back to the beginning. Practice this pattern with, and without, a palm mute.

Repeat signs, First and Second Endings:

## The Boogie Pattern

**Example 81**

## Teacher Suggestions

- Play program 35 and 36.
- Explain the derivation of D5 and D6 from the D major scale.
- Demonstrate that the D boogie pattern is exactly the same as the E and A boogie patterns only transposed to a different set of strings.
- Have students play examples 79 - 80 with the recordings.
- Example 81 is a complete 12-bar blues boogie pattern in A. Have students sing the blues progression root movement with program 36 (example 81). This will help demonstrate that although the chords alternate between power 5th and 6th chords the basic root movement of the progression remains the same.

**Listening Suggestions:** Any straight-eighth rock boogie songs. Chuck Berry, Bob Seger, the Beach Boys and Stevie Ray Vaughan have all recorded many songs of this type.

# Guitar Method 1

**Lesson 17: Rock Workshop 102**
**Power Chords**

## New Concepts
Power chords
A5 and D5

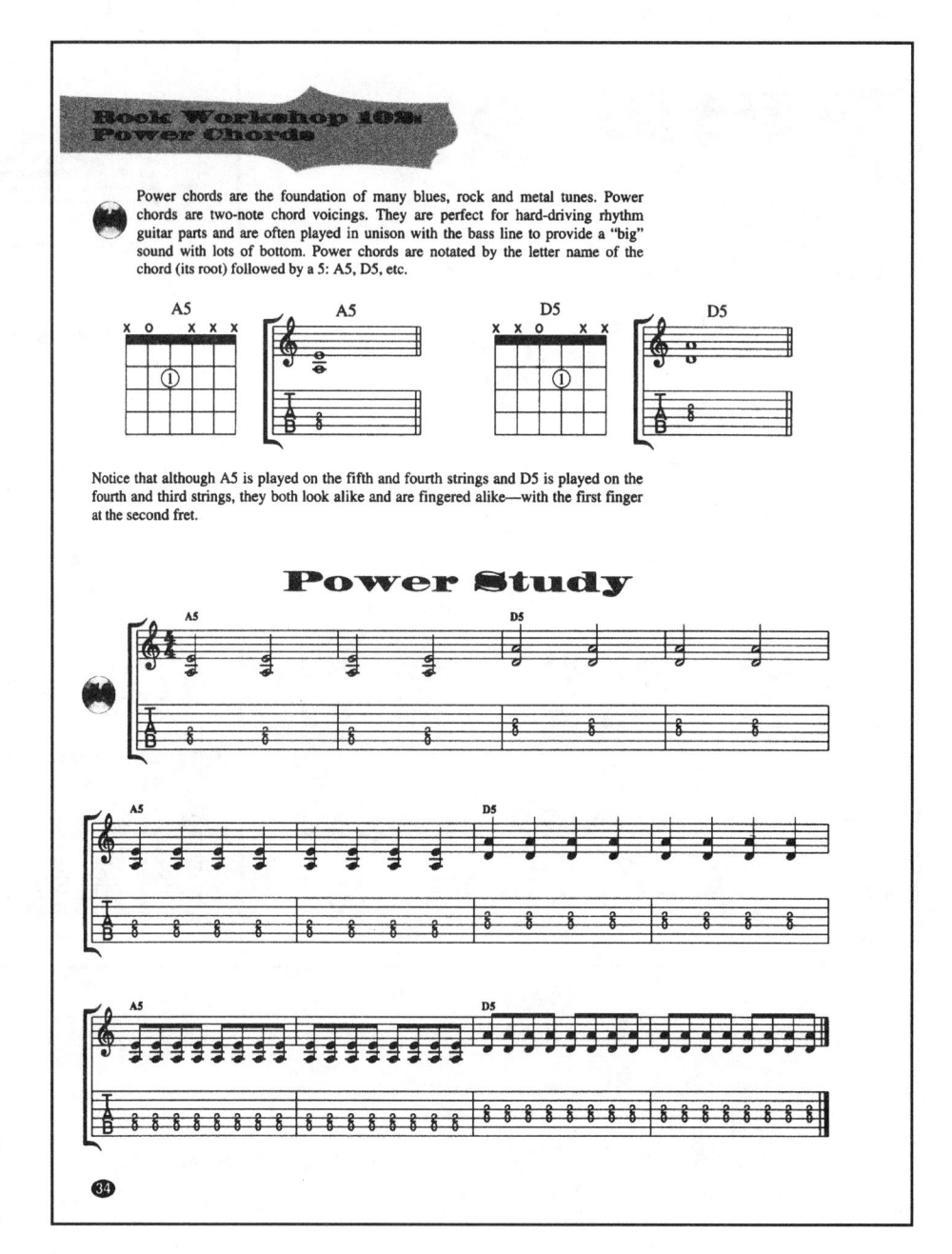

> ### Rock Workshop 102: Power Chords
>
> Power chords are the foundation of many blues, rock and metal tunes. Power chords are two-note chord voicings. They are perfect for hard-driving rhythm guitar parts and are often played in unison with the bass line to provide a "big" sound with lots of bottom. Power chords are notated by the letter name of the chord (its root) followed by a 5: A5, D5, etc.
>
> [A5 and D5 chord diagrams and notation]
>
> Notice that although A5 is played on the fifth and fourth strings and D5 is played on the fourth and third strings, they both look alike and are fingered alike—with the first finger at the second fret.
>
> ## Power Study
>
> [Musical notation and tablature for Power Study exercise]

**Teacher Note:** Students using the Rock Shop book have already learned the A5 and D5 power chords.

## Objective
- Learn the A5 and D5 power chords
- Play these new chords in the context of a 12-bar blues progression

## Teacher Suggestions
- Listen to programs 55 and 56.
- Explain that a power chord is a two-note chord voicing common to all forms of rock. Power chords are so named because they have the perfect sound for hard-driving, rhythm guitar parts. When playing a power chord rhythm-part the guitarist usually "locks in" with the bass and drums providing a very powerful rhythm section sound.
- Demonstrate that the A5 and D5 have the same shape or fingering, only played on different strings.
- Power Study uses the A5 and D5 power chords with half, quarter and eighth notes. Have students sing the blues progression root movement with program 56 (Power Study).

**Lesson 17: Rock Workshop 102**
**Power Chords**

# Guitar Method 1

## New Concepts
1st and 2nd endings

## Reinforces
A5 and D5
Blues progression

## Objective
- Play these new chords in the context of a 12-bar blues progression

## Teacher Suggestions
- Play program 57.
- Metalurgy combines power chords with a single-note riff in a 12-bar blues form. Explain the form of Metalurgy and demonstrate how the 1st and 2nd endings work.
- Have students sing the blues progression root movement with program 57 (Metalurgy).

# Guitar Theory 1

## Theory Lesson 17: Power Chords 1st and 2nd Endings

### Review
The G, C and D7 chords

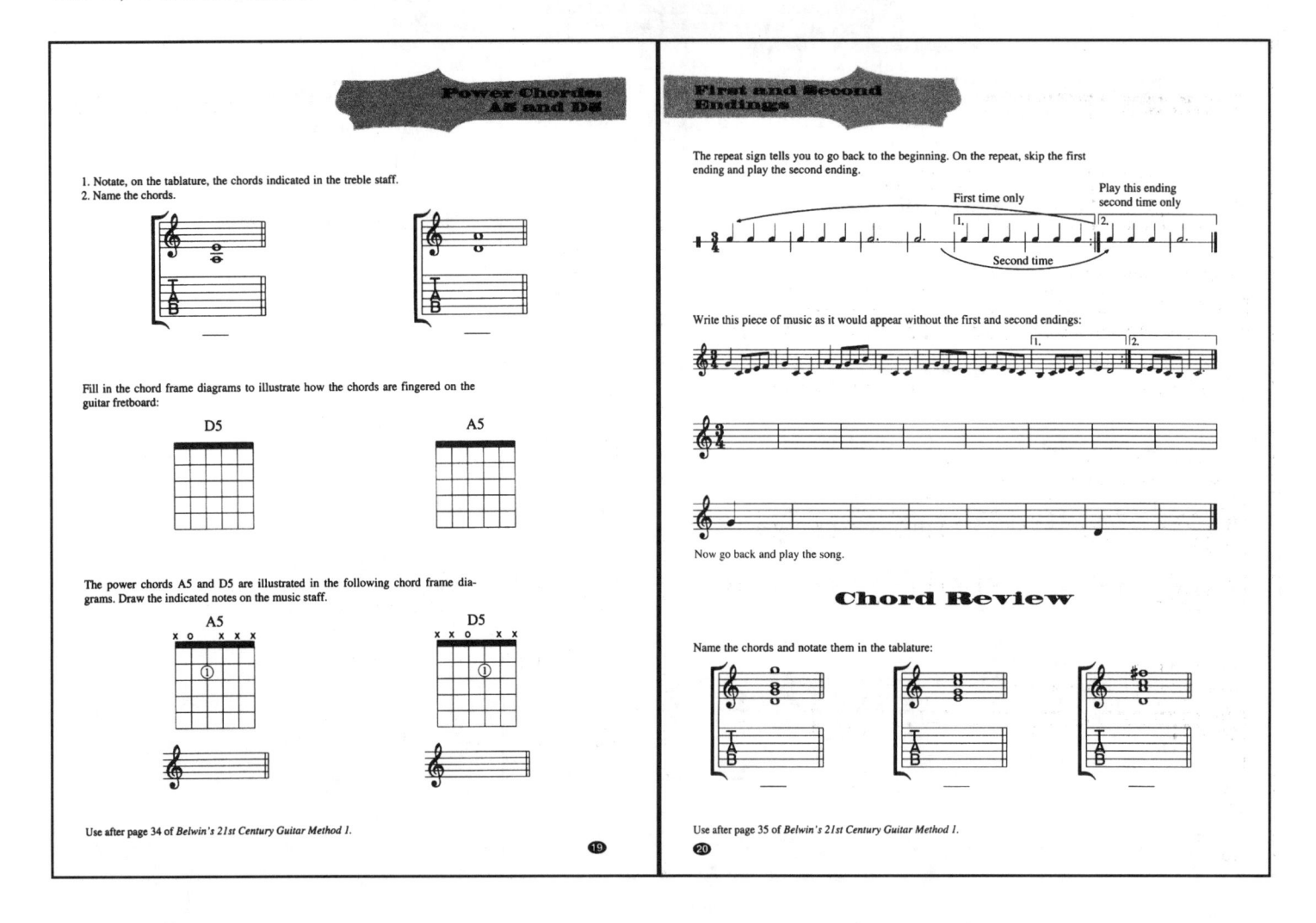

These pages correlate to Method book pages 34 and 35.

### Objective
- Develop the students ability to understand and visualize note locations and chord fingerings on the neck of the guitar.

### Teacher Suggestions
- Explain each fill-in example.
- Do part of each example with students.
- Have students complete the examples on their own or as homework assignments.

# Rock Lesson 17: Boogie Variation 1

## New Concept
Anticipation

## Objective
- Explore more sophisticated variations on the rock boogie pattern

## Teacher Suggestions
- Play program 37 and 38.
- Have students learn Example 82 (Variation 1 in E).
- Show that the A and D patterns are exactly the same only transposed to different string sets.
- Example 85 places Variation 1 in the context of a 12-bar blues progression. Have students sing the blues progression root movement with program 38 (example 85).
- Students should play examples 82 - 85 with the recordings.

# Guitar Method 1

## Lesson 18: The Notes on the Sixth String

## New Concept
Sixth string E, F, and G

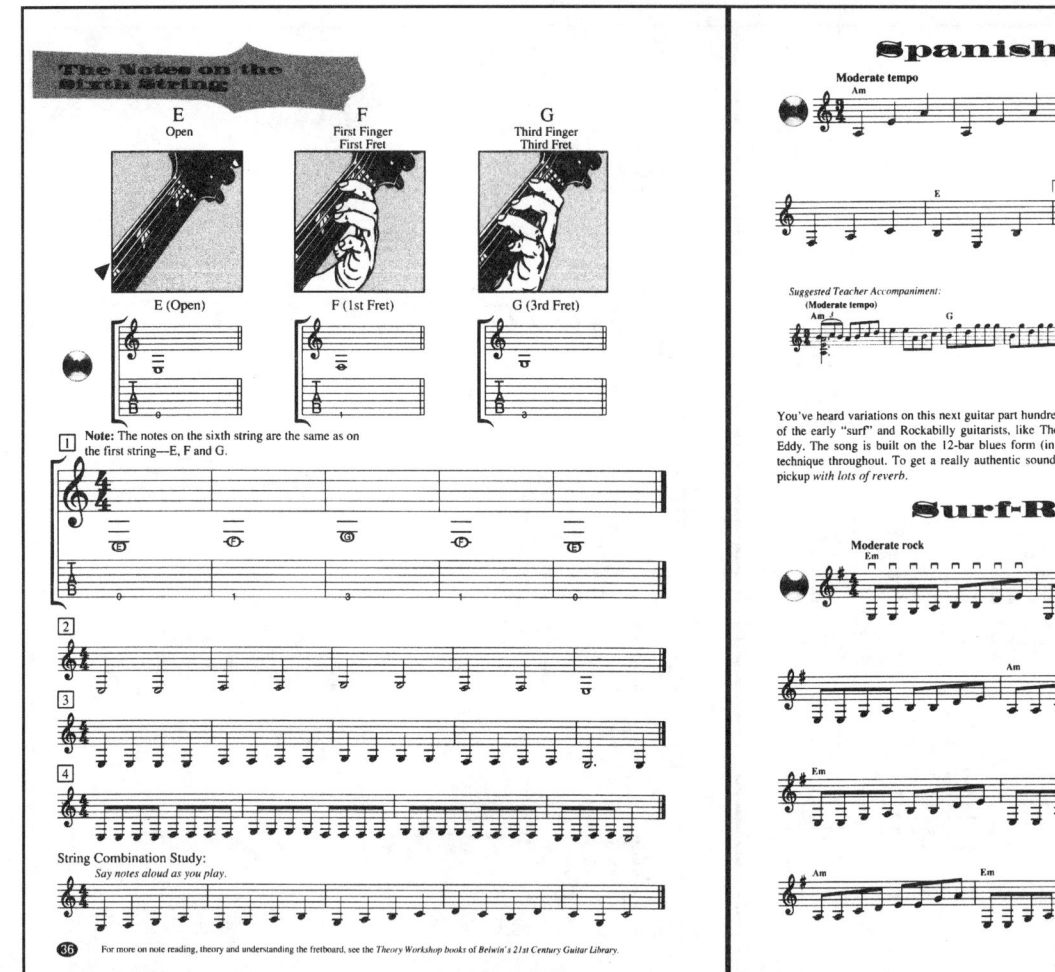

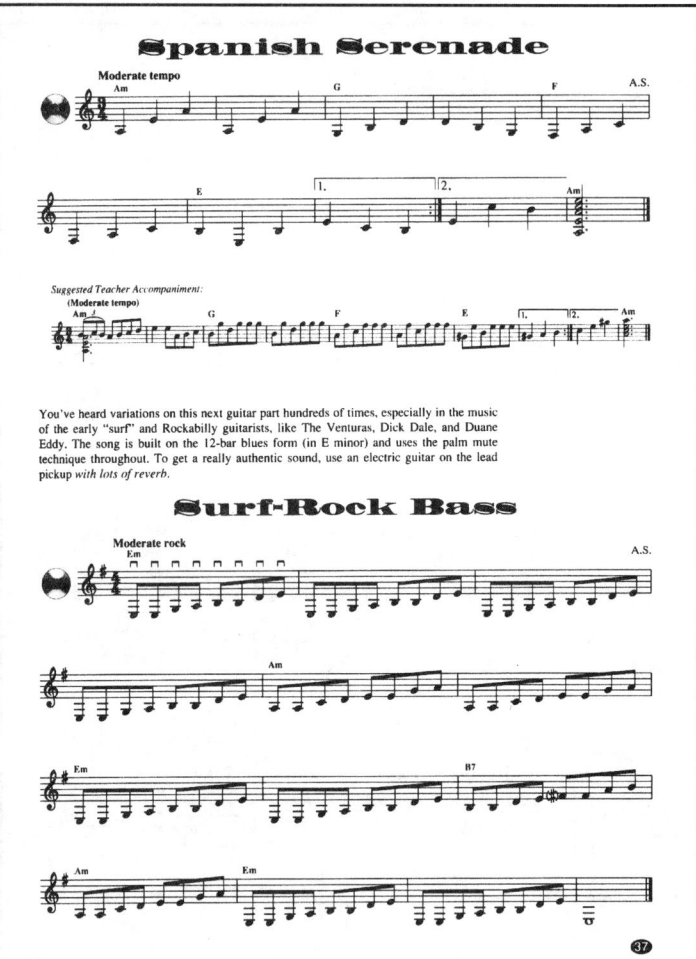

## Objective:
- Learn the sixth string D, E and F
- Be able to play the songs on Method page 37 in tempo with the recording or with the optional teacher accompaniments

## Teacher Suggestions
- Play program 58.
- Students should play E, F and G. Show how the notes they are playing relate to the drawing, notation and tab.
- Explain that the notes on the 6th string are the same as on the 1st string, only two octaves lower.
- Review all the notes learned so far (low E to A on the 1st String). Draw these notes on the music staff and have the students play them. Playing scales like this reinforces that the guitar neck is logical and the note locations are sequential.
- Play programs 59 and 60. Use the complete listening sequence describe on page 19.
- Students should play Spanish Serenade and Surf-Rock Bass with the recordings.
- Discuss stylistic differences between the various songs. For example, if both the optional song book and ensemble book are being used, this lesson goes from Spanish to surf, to rock and roll and classical.

**Listening Suggestions:** Malaguena by Ernesto Lecuna, *Wipe Out*, *Pipeline* or any early surf guitar by Dick Dale, The Surfaris, The Chantays or The Ventures.

**Optional Song Book:** Students are now prepared to play *Pretty Woman* on page 20 of *Song Trax 1*.

**Optional Ensemble Book:** Students are now prepared to play *Minuet* on page 24 of *Guitar Ensemble 1*.

# Lesson 18: The Notes on the Sixth String

**Guitar Theory 1**

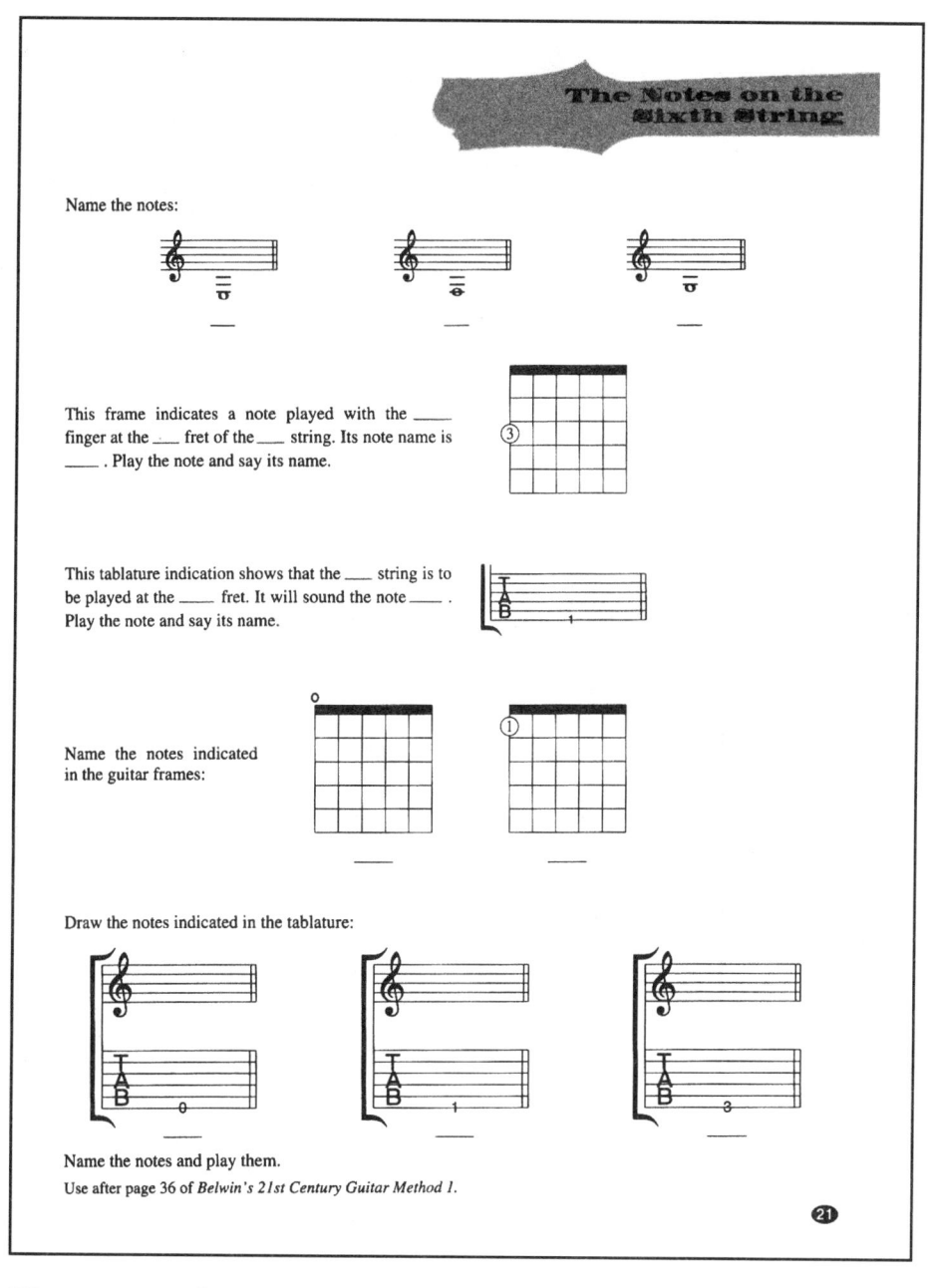

### The Notes on the Sixth String

Name the notes:

This frame indicates a note played with the ____ finger at the ____ fret of the ____ string. Its note name is ____ . Play the note and say its name.

This tablature indication shows that the ____ string is to be played at the ____ fret. It will sound the note ____ . Play the note and say its name.

Name the notes indicated in the guitar frames:

Draw the notes indicated in the tablature:

Name the notes and play them.
Use after page 36 of *Belwin's 21st Century Guitar Method 1*.

## Reinforces
Sixth string E, F and G

The page correlates to Method book page 36.

## Objective
- Develop the students ability to understand and visualize note locations and chord fingerings on the neck of the guitar

## Teacher Suggestions
- Explain each fill-in example.
- Do part of each example with students.
- Have students complete the examples on their own or as homework assignments.

# Guitar Rock Shop 1

# Rock Lesson 18: Boogie Variation 2

## New Concepts
The two-note power 7th chord

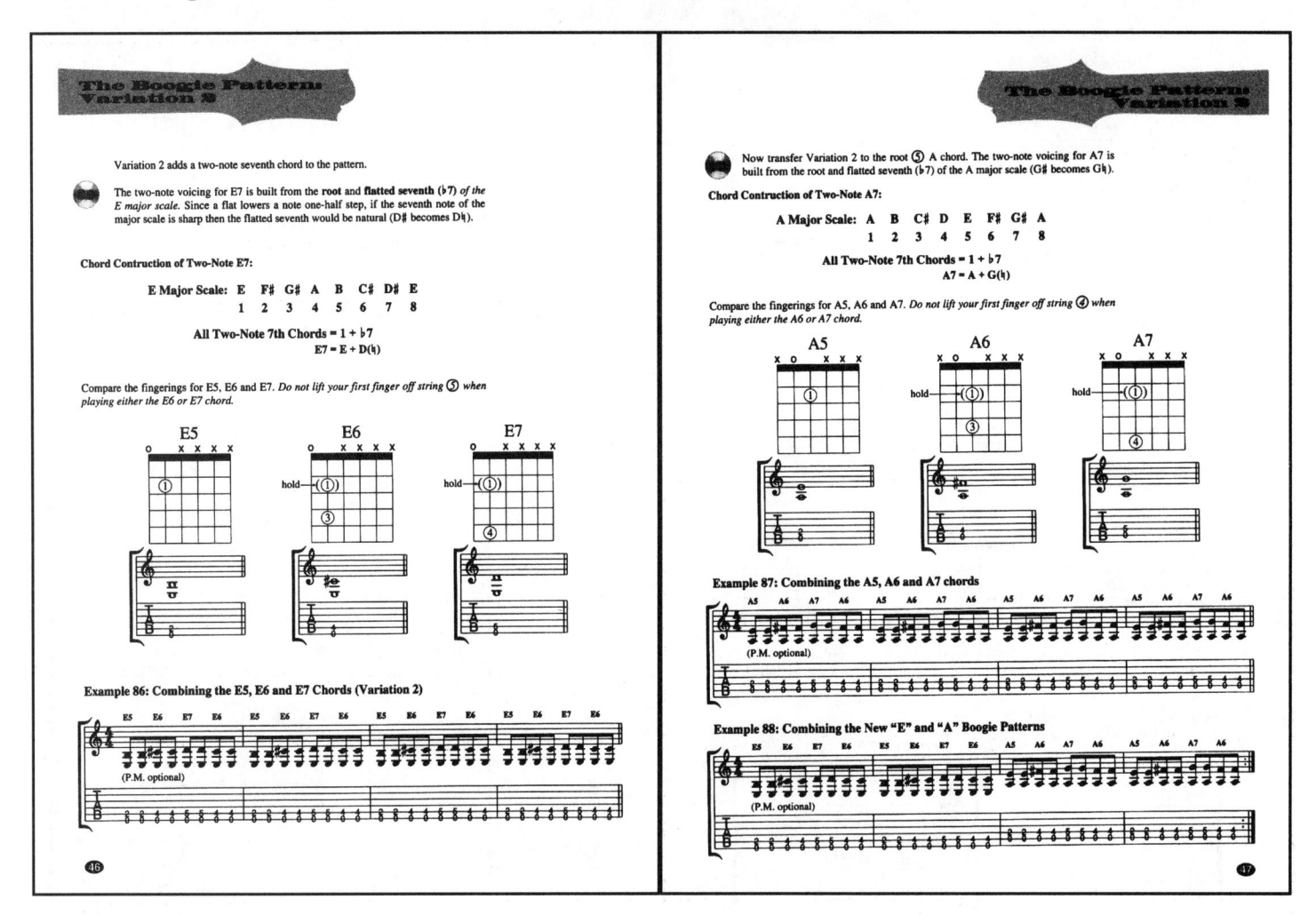

## Objective
- Explore more sophisticated variations on the rock boogie pattern

## Teacher Suggestions
- Play programs 39 and 40.
- Explain the derivation of E7 and A7 from the E and A major scales (root/b7th).
- Show that the E and A patterns (shapes) are exactly the same only transposed to different string sets.
- Students should play Examples 86 - 88 with the recordings.

# Rock Lesson 18: Boogie Variation 2

**Guitar Rock Shop 1**

## Teacher Suggestions
- Play program 41.
- Explain the derivation of the two-note D7 from the D major scale (root/b7th).
- Show that the E, A and D patterns are exactly the same only transposed to different string sets (again, the "shape" concept).
- Students should play Examples 89 and 90 with the recordings.
- Play program 42. Use the complete listening procedure described on page 19.
- Student should sing the blues progression root movement with program 42 (example 91).
- Students should play Examples 91 with the recording.
- Group Class: If you have some rock improvisers in the class, they could play solos while the class plays Example 91.

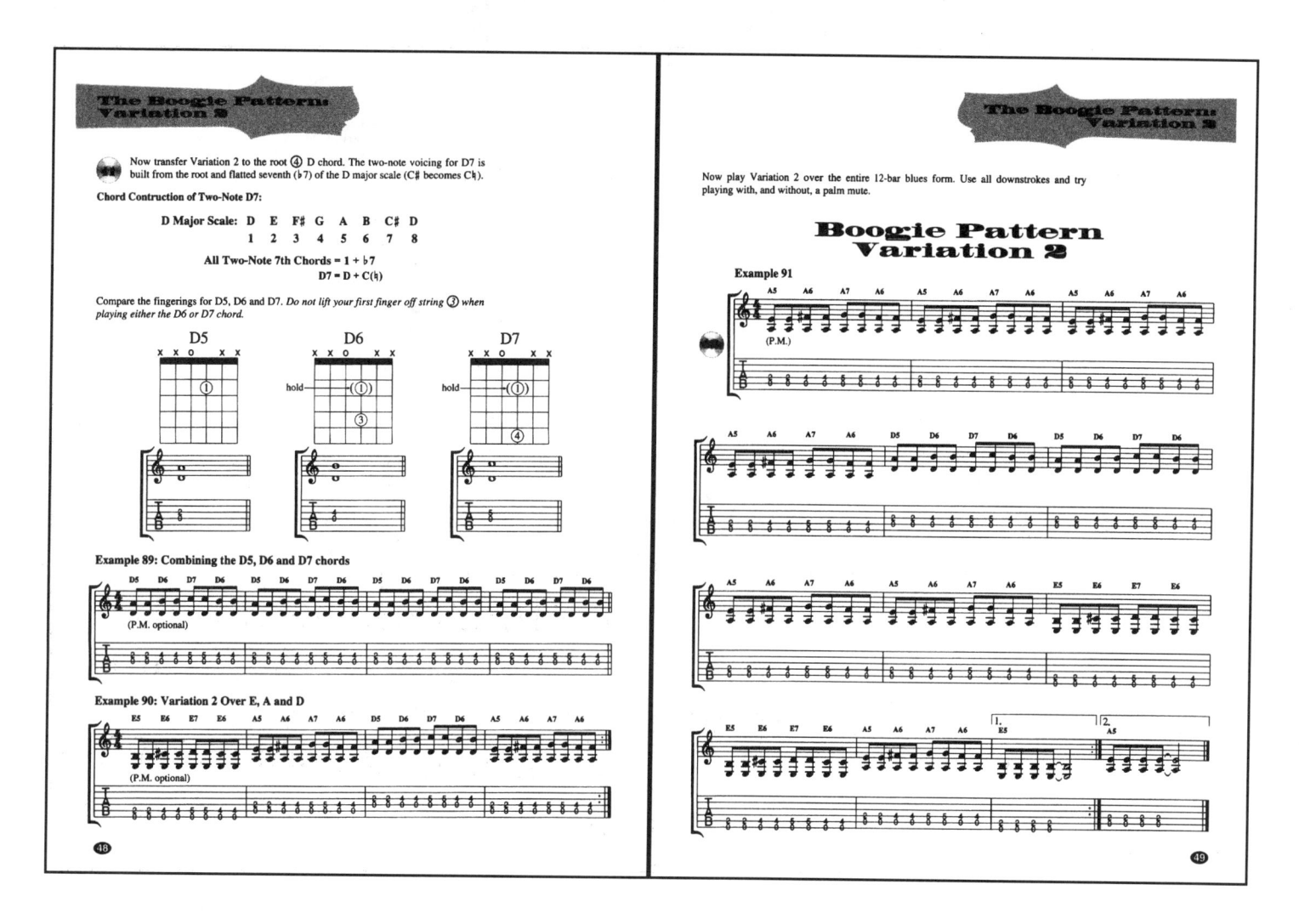

87

# Guitar Method 1

## Lesson 19: Rock Workshop 103
## Getting the Feel

**New Concepts**
E5
Palm Mute
Accents

### Rock Workshop 103: Getting the Feel

Getting the right "feel" is everything when playing rock guitar. Two techniques that will help you get that feel are: **Accents** and **Palm Muting**.

**Palm Mute:** Gently lay the palm of your pick hand on the bridge of your guitar. If your hand is too far in front of the bridge, the strings will be too muted and not produce any tone at all. If your hand is too far behind the bridge, the strings will not be muted enough. The palm mute produces a short, muffled, percussive attack which greatly adds to the rhythmic drive and intensity of your playing.

The palm mute is indicated by the abbreviation: **P.M.**

**The E5 Power Chord** has its *root* on the sixth string. Notice that although each of the three power chords (E5, A5 and D5) are played on different string groups, they all look alike and are fingered alike—with the first finger at the second fret.

In the following three examples, work on getting a short, percussive attack on the muted chords. Note the contrast between the muted and unmuted sections.

**Teacher Note:** Students using the Rock Shop book have already learned the E5 power chords and palm mute technique.

## Objective
- Learn the E5 power chord
- Demonstrate the relationship of E5, A5 and D5
- Develop a more rhythmic feel by incorporating the palm muting technique and accents
- Play these new chords in the context of a 12-bar blues progression

## Teacher Suggestions
- Listen to program 61.
- Demonstrate that the E5, A5 and D5 have the same shape or fingering, only played on different strings.
- Students should play examples 1 - 4 using enough of a palm mute to produced a percussive, muffled attack (example 4 is shown on the next page).

88

# Lesson 19: Rock Workshop 102
## Getting the Feel

**Guitar Method 1**

**Reinforces**

E5, A5 and D5
Blues progression

## Objective
- Play these new techniques in the context of a 12-bar blues progression

## Teacher Suggestions
- Play program 62. Use the complete listening sequence described on page 19.
- Rock Steady combines power chords and a single-note riff with the palm mute and accents in a 12-bar blues form.
- Students should play Rock Steady with the recording.
- Students should sing the blues progression root movement with program 62 (Rock Steady).
- If the palm mute is being done properly the part will have a very driving, percussive feel, but the notes should still be clearly audible.

# Guitar Theory 1

## Theory Lesson 19: E5/Palm Mute/Accents

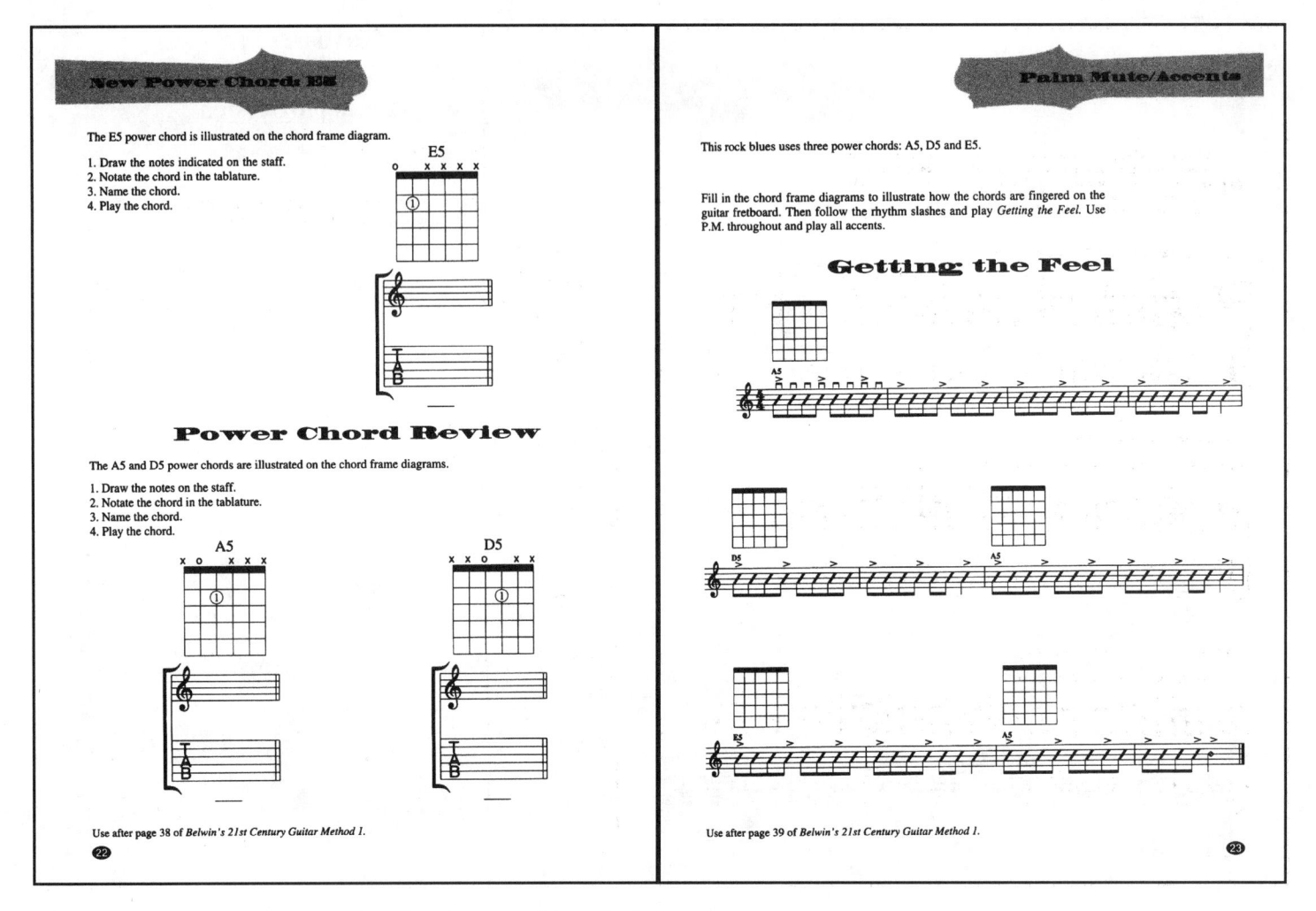

These pages correlate to Method book pages 38 and 39.

## Objective
- Develop the students ability to understand and visualize note locations and chord fingerings on the neck of the guitar

## Teacher Suggestions
- Explain each fill-in example.
- Have students complete the examples on their own or as homework assignments.
- After filling in the chord frame diagrams on page 23 students should play the song.

# Rock Lesson 19: Boogie Variation 3

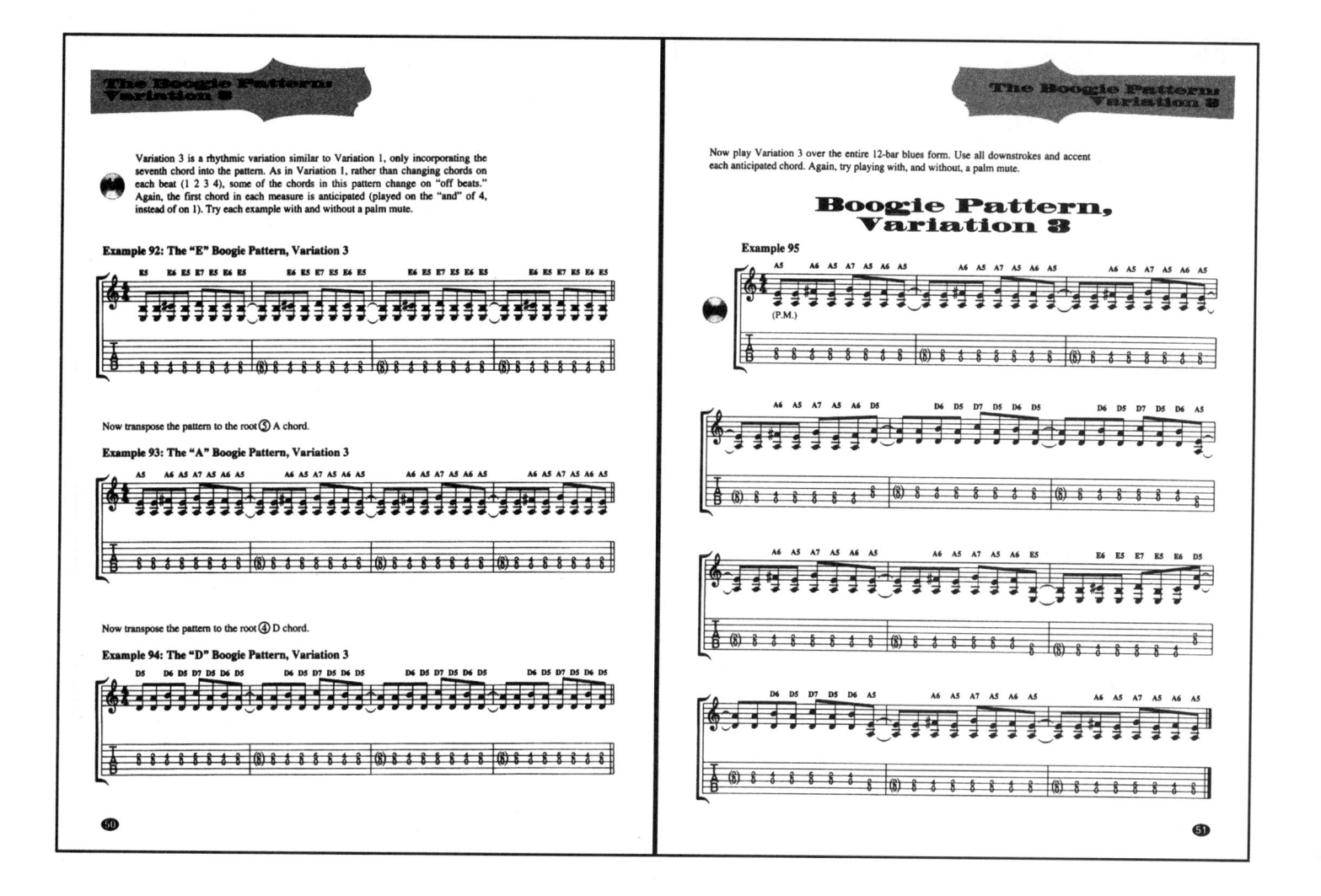

## Objective
- Explore more sophisticated variations on the rock boogie pattern

## Teacher Suggestions
- Play program 43.
- Variation 3 combines the three power chord types (power 5th, 6th and 7th chords) with an off-beat rhythm variation similar to Variation 1.
- Students learn Example 92 (Variation 3 in E).
- Show that the A and D patterns are exactly the same only transposed to different string sets.
- Students should play examples 92 - 94 with the recordings.
- Example 95 places Variation 3 in the context of a 12-bar blues progression. Play program 44 using the complete listening sequence described on page 19.
- Students should sing the blues progression root movement with program 44 (example 95).
- Students should play example 95 with the recording.

# Guitar Method 1 — Lesson 20: The Full G, G7 and Em Chords

**New Concepts**
Six string G, G7 and Em

## The Full G, G7 and E Minor Chords

Here are the complete, six string chord forms for G and G7, along with a new chord: E minor.

G    G7    Em

G Chord    G7 Chord    Em Chord

Notice how similar the G7 chord shape is to the C chord shape. To change between C and G7, simply move each finger to the next string.

To change between the G and D7 chords, slide your third finger along the first string while shifting your first and second fingers.

Chord Study 1:  G  G7  C  G7  C

Chord Study 2:  G  D7  G  D7  G

### Loch Lomond
*Scottish*
Medium tempo

By yon bon-nie banks, and by yon bon-nie braes, where the
sun shines bright on Loch Lo-mond, where me and my true love were
ev-er want to gae, on the bon-nie, bon-nie banks of Loch Lo-mond.

**Objective**
- Learn the three new chords
- Move from chord to chord smoothly, in rhythm

**Teacher Suggestions**
- Listen to program 63.
- Students should practice the Chord Studies until they can change chords smoothly without breaking rhythm.
- Use the suggested fingerings, they will make changing from one chord to the next easier, smoother and faster.
- Help students to locate and sing the root and arpeggio of each chord. (Students should sing simple, root position chords in 3rds, not the exact inversions being played on the guitar.)
- Play program 64.
- **Group Class**: Half the class should play the melody to *Loch Lomond* while the rest play the accompaniment part (indicated with rhythm slashes), then reverse.

**Optional Song Book:** Students are now prepared to play *My Girl* on page 22 of *Song Trax 1*.
**Optional Ensemble Book:** Students are now prepared to play *Blue Moon* on page 40 of *Guitar Ensemble 1*.

# Lesson 20: The Full G, G7 and Em Chords

**Guitar Method 1**

## New Concepts
6th String F#
ABA Form

## Reinforces
G, G7 and Em
C, D and D7

## Objective
- Utilize all chords learned so far
- Move from chord to chord smoothly, in rhythm

## Teacher Suggestions
- Listen to programs 65 and 66.
- *Rock Ballad* is written like a rhythm chart, moving from fully notated to slash notation. The song is written in ABA form. Describe this song form and explain that most pop songs follow it.
- Emphasize that the A section consists of arpeggios. Students should hold the full chord, keeping their fingers down while picking out the arpeggio pattern.
- See if the students can make up their own arpeggio style parts based on the chord progression in Rock Ballad. Making up simple accompaniments is a good way to begin developing creativity, independence and improvisational skills.

**Optional Song Book:** Students are now prepared to play Riders On The Storm on page 24 of Song Trax 1.

# Guitar Theory 1

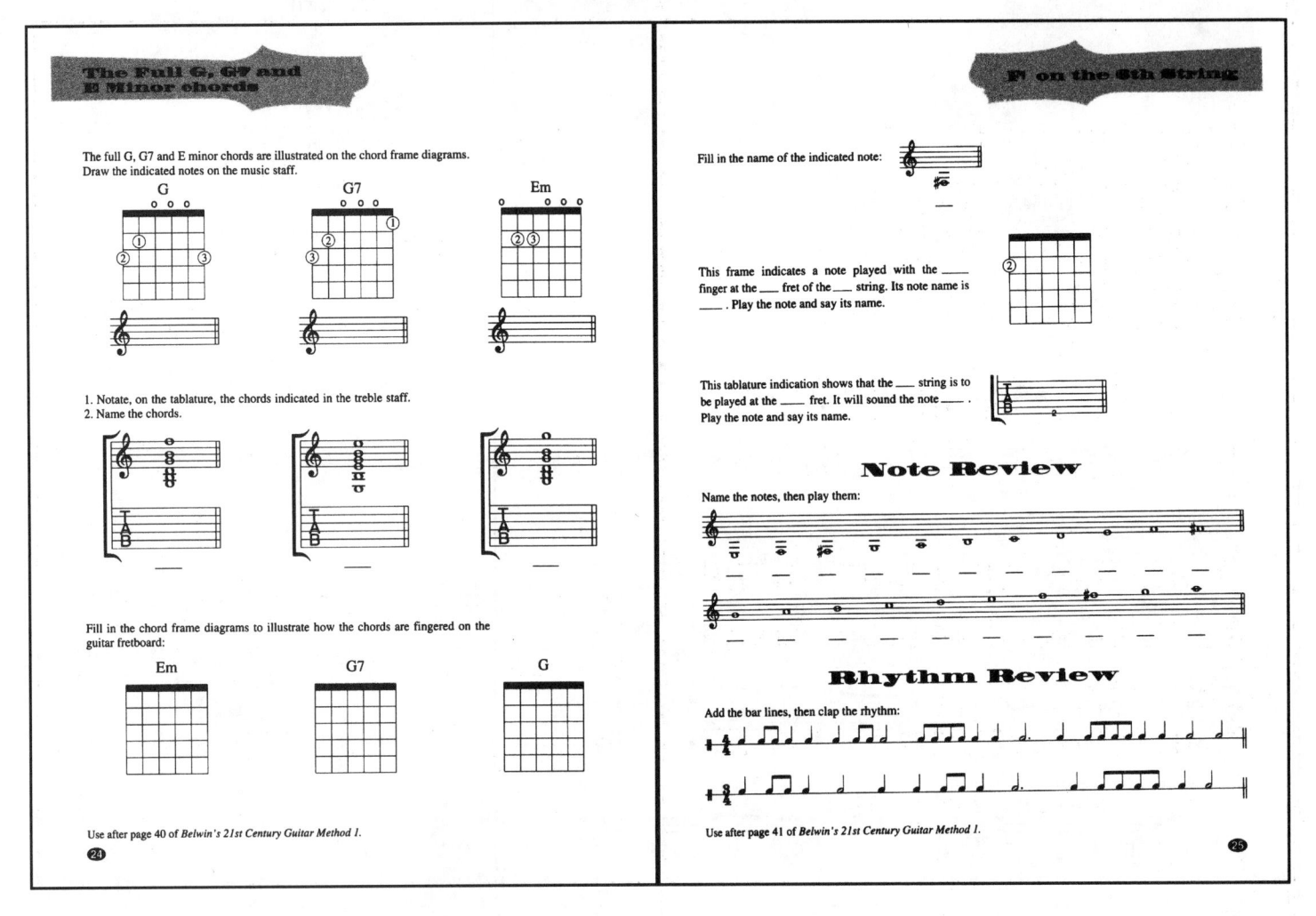

## Theory Lesson 20: G, G7 and Em and 6th String F#

These pages correlates to Method book pages 40 and 41.

## Objective
- Develop the students ability to understand and visualize note locations and chord fingerings on the neck of the guitar.
- Review notes and rhythms

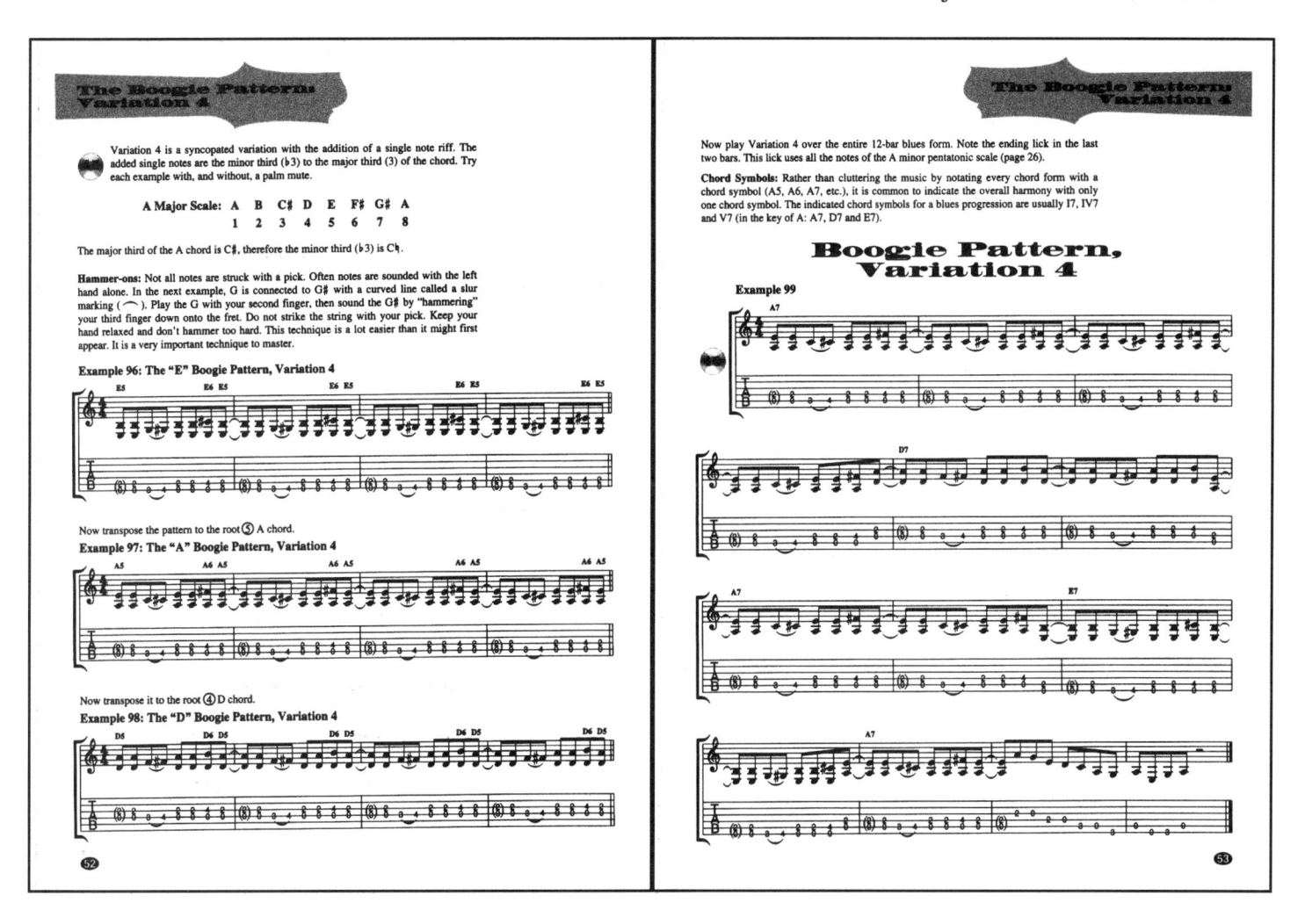

# Rock Lesson 20: Boogie Variation 4

## Objective
- Learn the hammer-on technique (an upward slur)

## Teacher Suggestions
- Play program 45.
- Variation 4 combines a rhythmic approach similar to Variations 1 and 3 with a common blues riff: the minor 3rd slurred into the major 3rd.
- Show that the E, A and D patterns are exactly the same only transposed to different string sets.
- Write out the E, A and D major scales and demonstrate the minor and major 3rd of each.
- Students should play examples 96 - 98 with the recordings.
- Example 99 places Variation 4 in the context of a 12-bar blues progression. Play program 46 using the complete listening sequence described on page 19.
- Students should sing the blues progression root movement with program 46 (example 99).
- Students should play example 99 with the recording.

# Guitar Method 1

## Lesson 21: Scarbororough Fair/Cloud Nine

**Reinforces**
All chords learned so far

**Objective**
- Review notes and chords learned so far

**Teacher Suggestions**
- Listen to programs 67 and 68.
- Students should learn both the melody and chords to *Scarborough Fair*. Students should improvise simple accompaniment patterns—both strumming and arpeggio style as shown in the following two examples.
- Have students sing the melody to *Scarborough Fair* with the accompaniment tracks or with teacher accompaniment.
- *On Cloud Nine* is a pop-style arpeggio study. The progression uses some more sophisticated chords like Em9, G/B and D/F#. Demonstrate how chords with alternate bass notes, like G/B and D/F#, are used to create smooth bass-lines. (The letter after the slash indicates the bass note. For example: G/B = a G chord with B in the bass.)

96

# Theory Lesson 21: Chord Review

## Guitar Theory 1

### Reinforces
ABA Form, Power Chords, G, Em, Am and D7

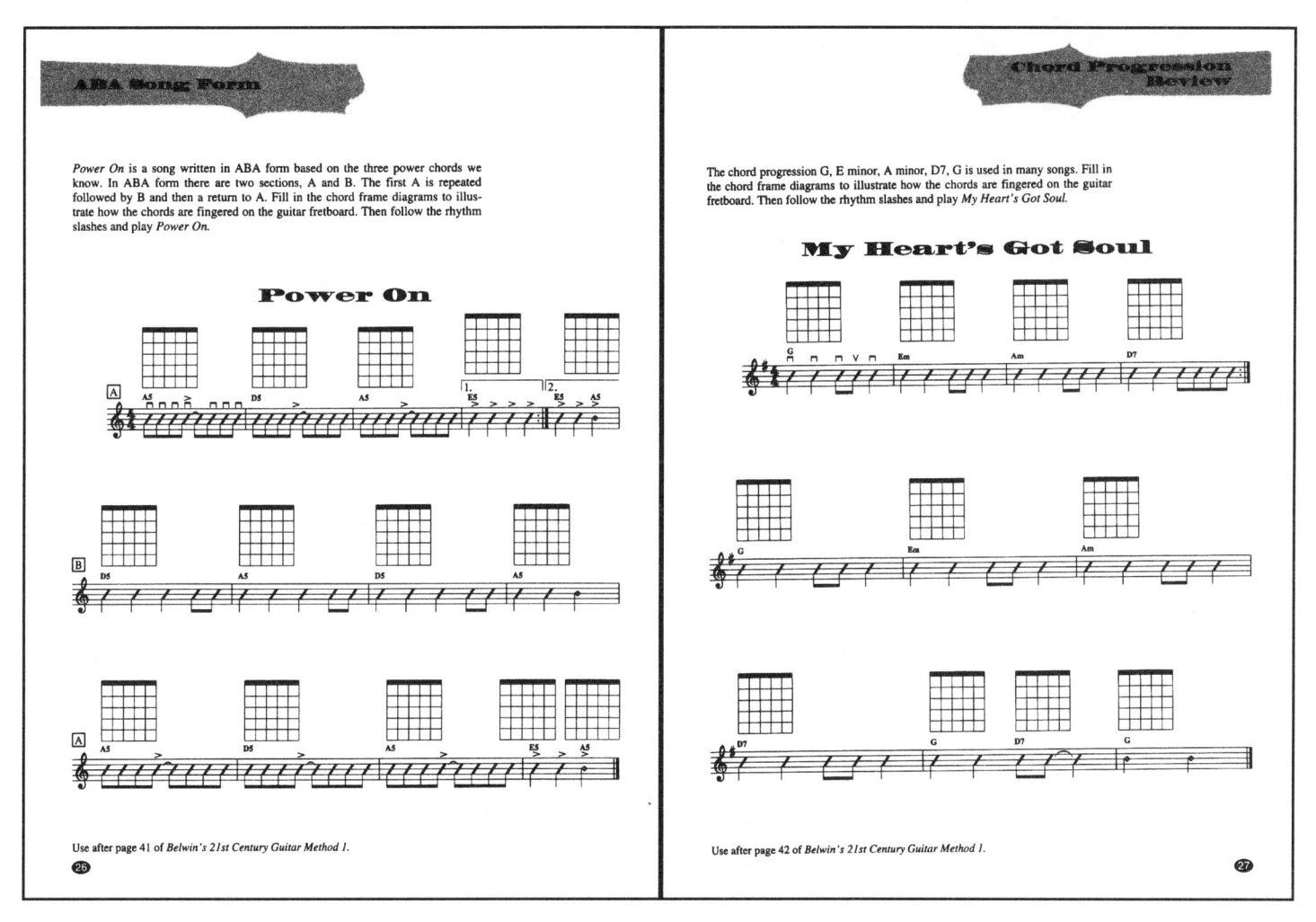

These pages correlate to Method book pages 41 and 42.

## Teacher Suggestions
- ABA form is taught on page 41 of the *Guitar Method*.
- Fill in the chord frame diagrams.
- Play Power On.
- *My Heart's Got Soul* is a play on *Heart and Soul*.
- Fill in the chord frame diagrams.
- Play *My Heart's Got Soul*.

97

**Guitar Rock Shop 1**

Rock Lesson 21: Boogie Variation 5

## New Concepts
The natural sign

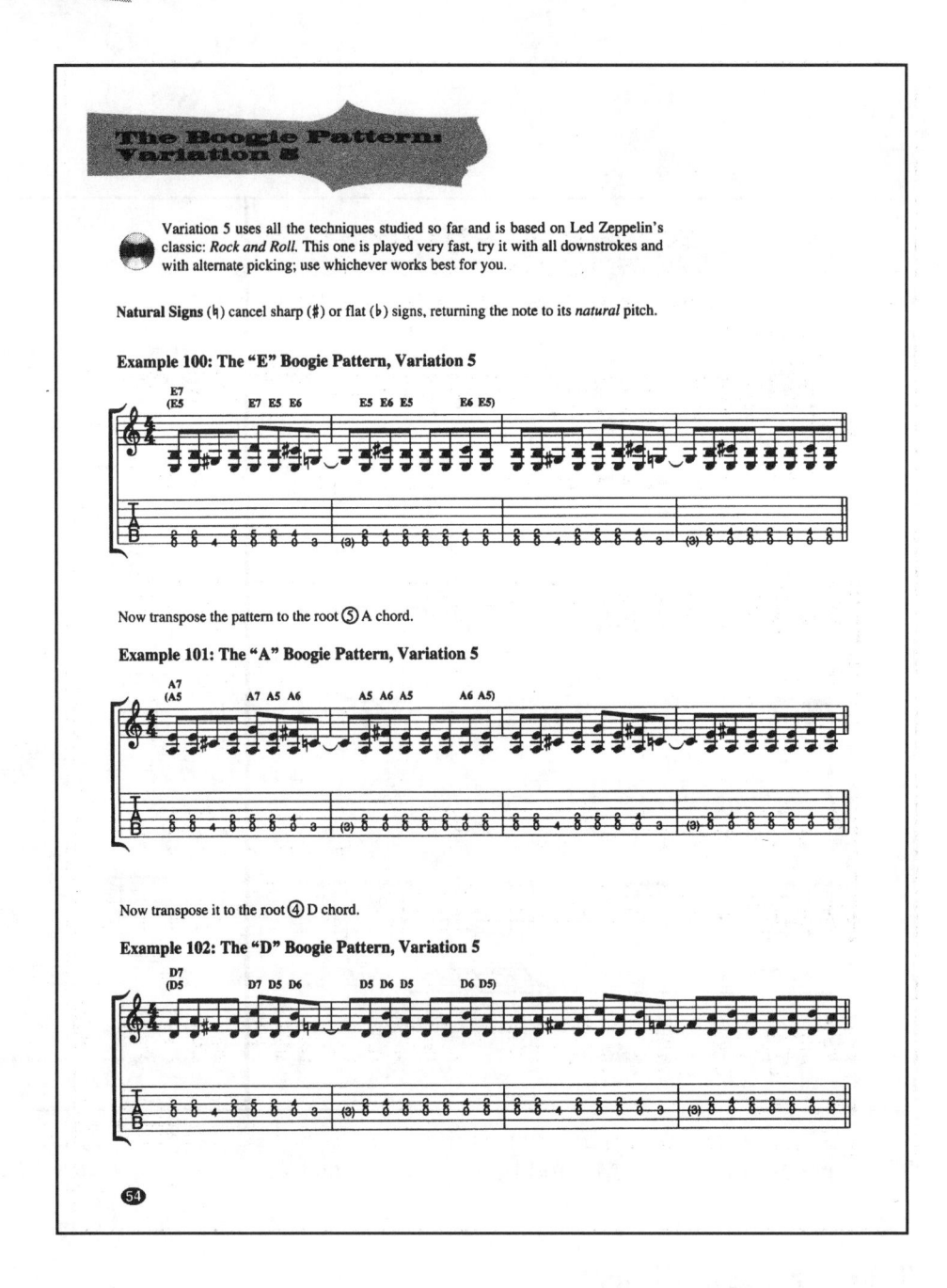

### The Boogie Pattern: Variation 5

Variation 5 uses all the techniques studied so far and is based on Led Zeppelin's classic: *Rock and Roll*. This one is played very fast, try it with all downstrokes and with alternate picking; use whichever works best for you.

**Natural Signs** (♮) cancel sharp (♯) or flat (♭) signs, returning the note to its *natural* pitch.

**Example 100: The "E" Boogie Pattern, Variation 5**

Now transpose the pattern to the root ⑤ A chord.

**Example 101: The "A" Boogie Pattern, Variation 5**

Now transpose it to the root ④ D chord.

**Example 102: The "D" Boogie Pattern, Variation 5**

## Teacher Suggestions
- Play program 47.
- Variation 5 is based on the guitar riff to the Led Zeppelin song *Rock and Roll*. Rhythmically the riff is similar to Variations 1, 3 and 4. It uses the power 5th, 6th and 7th chords and both the major and minor 3rd of each chord as in Variation 4.
- Write out the E, A and D major scales and demonstrate the minor and major 3rd of each.
- Students learn Example 100 (Variation 5 in E).
- Show that the A and D patterns are exactly the same only transposed to different string sets.
- Students should play examples 100 - 102 with the recordings.

**Teacher Note:** On the recording, the minor 3rd of each chord is played with a quarter tone bend. This is done by pulling the string down slightly, forcing the note sharp.

# Rock Lesson 21: Boogie Variation 5

**Guitar Rock Shop 1**

### Boogie Pattern, Variation 5
### (The "Rock and Roll" Pattern)

Example 103

## Teacher Suggestions
- Example 103 places Variation 5 in the context of a 12-bar blues progression. Play program 48 using the complete listening sequence described on page 19.
- Students should sing the blues progression root movement with program 48 (example 103).
- Students should play example 103 with the recording.

**Listening Suggestions:** Led Zeppelin's *Rock and Roll* from the album *Led Zeppelin*.

# Guitar Method 1

## Lesson 22: The Rest

**New Concepts**
Whole rest
Half rest
Quarter rest
Eighth rest

### The Rest

A rest is a period of silence. Each type of note has a corresponding rest:

Whole Rest: 𝄻 = 𝅝 = 4 beats     Half Rest: 𝄼 = 𝅗𝅥 = 2 beats
Quarter Rest: 𝄽 = ♩ = 1 beat     Eighth Rest: 𝄾 = ♪ = 1/2 beat

When playing a note followed by a rest you should stop that note from ringing. To stop a fretted note from ringing, release the finger pressure on that note. To stop an open string from ringing, you can either gently touch the string with your left hand, or use the palm of your right hand to deaden the note.

Count out loud and tap your foot in the following studies.

**Rest & Roll**

Count the following exercise carefully. Move your pick in a constant down-up motion. When no note is played on the downbeat move your pick down anyway—only miss the string. This will put your hand in position to play the next note with an upstroke.

**Eighth Rest Etude**

This excerpt from *A Little Night Music* utilizes both the quarter and eighth note rests. Count carefully and tap your foot on each beat. (The foot should go down on beats 1, 2, 3 and 4 and up on "and.")

**A Little Night Music**

Medium tempo                                    Wolfgang Amadeus Mozart

**Objective**
- Learn the rest

**Teacher Suggestions**
- Listen to programs 69 and 70.
- Students should first count out loud and clap the rhythm to *Rest & Roll*.
- Listen to program 71.
- Practice *Eighth Rest Etude* with a constant down-up motion of the pick. The pick should "miss" the strings on each rest.
- Use the complete listening procedure described on page 19 for *A Little Night Music* before having the students practice it.

**Listening Suggestions:** Various recorded versions of *A Little Night Music* (*Eine Kleine Nacht Musik*).

# Theory Lesson 22: Rests

## Guitar Theory 1

**Reinforces**
Counting and playing rests

### Rests

The duration of musical silence is indicated by different types of rests.

In 4/4 time a whole rest receives four beats:

A half rest receives two beats:

A quarter rest receives one beat:

An eighth rest receives 1/2 of a beat:

In the next exercise, fill in the missing beats with rests. Use only one rest in each measure, then clap the rhythm.

Add the bar lines, then clap the rhythm:

Fill in the blanks:

One whole rest equals _____ beats.
One quarter rest equals _____ beat.
One half rest equals _____ beats.

Use after page 43 of *Belwin's 21st Century Guitar Method 1*.

This page correlates to Method book page 43.

## Teacher Suggestions
- Explain each fill-in example.
- Do part of each example with students.
- Have students complete the examples on their own or as homework assignments.

# Guitar Rock Shop 1

# Rock Lesson 22: Lead Riffs and Patterns

## New Concepts
Lead Riffs, Target Tones

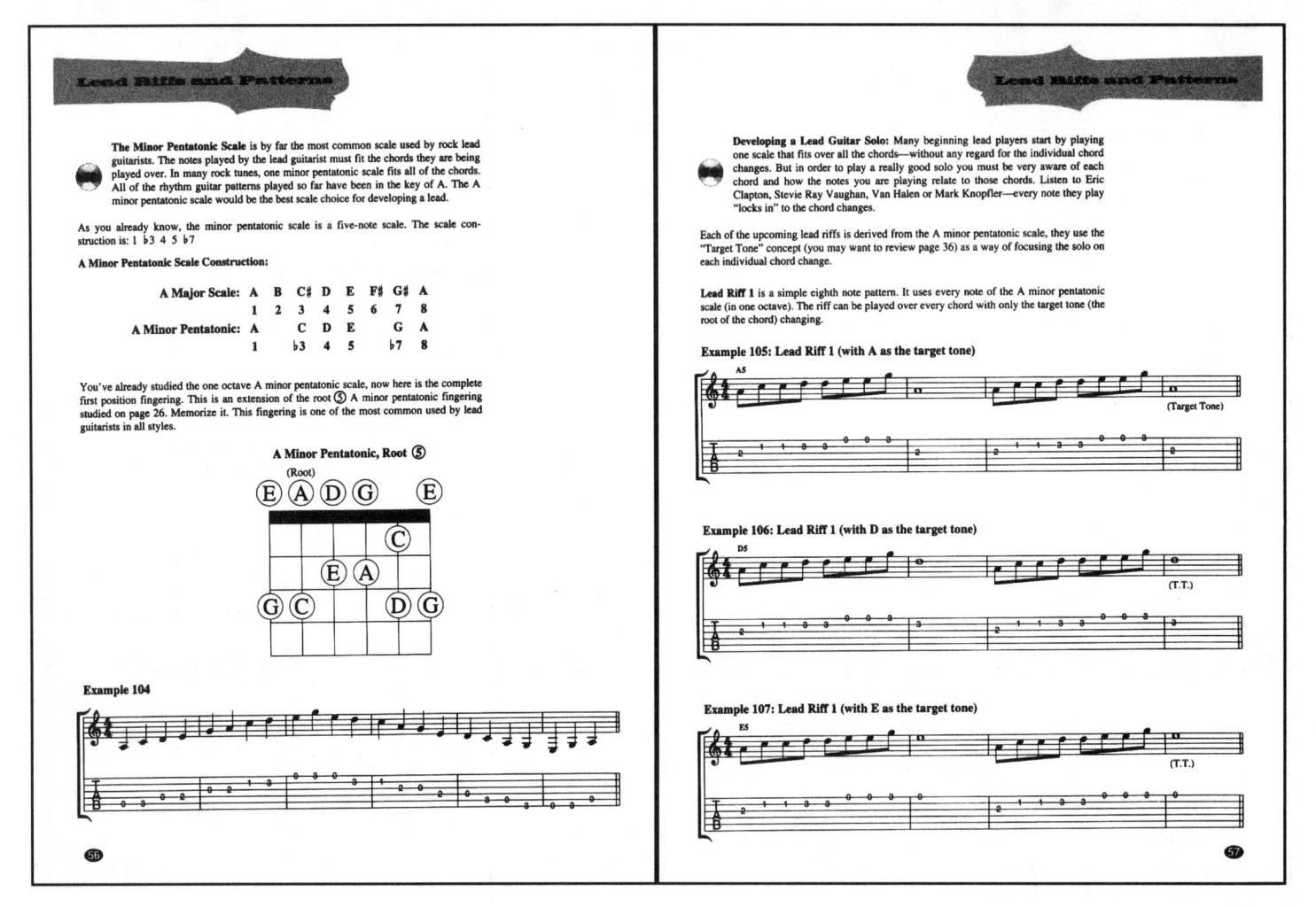

---

### Lead Riffs and Patterns

**The Minor Pentatonic Scale** is by far the most common scale used by rock lead guitarists. The notes played by the lead guitarist must fit the chords they are being played over. In many rock tunes, one minor pentatonic scale fits all of the chords. All of the rhythm guitar patterns played so far have been in the key of A. The A minor pentatonic scale would be the best scale choice for developing a lead.

As you already know, the minor pentatonic scale is a five-note scale. The scale construction is: 1 ♭3 4 5 ♭7

**A Minor Pentatonic Scale Construction:**

| A Major Scale: | A | B | C# | D | E | F# | G# | A |
|---|---|---|---|---|---|---|---|---|
|  | 1 | 2 | 3 | 4 | 5 | 6 | 7 | 8 |
| A Minor Pentatonic: | A |  | C | D | E |  | G | A |
|  | 1 |  | ♭3 | 4 | 5 |  | ♭7 | 8 |

You've already studied the one octave A minor pentatonic scale, now here is the complete first position fingering. This is an extension of the root ⑤ A minor pentatonic fingering studied on page 26. Memorize it. This fingering is one of the most common used by lead guitarists in all styles.

**A Minor Pentatonic, Root ⑤**

**Example 104**

---

### Lead Riffs and Patterns

**Developing a Lead Guitar Solo:** Many beginning lead players start by playing one scale that fits over all the chords—without any regard for the individual chord changes. But in order to play a really good solo you must be very aware of each chord and how the notes you are playing relate to those chords. Listen to Eric Clapton, Stevie Ray Vaughan, Van Halen or Mark Knopfler—every note they play "locks in" to the chord changes.

Each of the upcoming lead riffs is derived from the A minor pentatonic scale, they use the "Target Tone" concept (you may want to review page 36) as a way of focusing the solo on each individual chord change.

**Lead Riff 1** is a simple eighth note pattern. It uses every note of the A minor pentatonic scale (in one octave). The riff can be played over every chord with only the target tone (the root of the chord) changing.

**Example 105: Lead Riff 1 (with A as the target tone)**

**Example 106: Lead Riff 1 (with D as the target tone)**

**Example 107: Lead Riff 1 (with E as the target tone)**

---

## Objective
- Begin improvising using specific minor pentatonic riffs that can be used over each change in the blues progression
- Introduce the "target tone" concept as a means of focusing the solo on each individual chord change

## Teacher Suggestions
- Play program 49. Here we introduce the complete 1st position fingering for the A minor pentatonic scale.
- Review the construction of the minor pentatonic scale and compare the A minor pentatonic to the A major scale.
- **Teacher Note:** I begin teaching improvisation by using specific licks or riffs drawn from the minor pentatonic scale. Often a student is given a minor pentatonic scale fingering and told to "go for it." This is akin to giving a non-English speaking student a large selection of English words and telling them to string them together any old way. Each style of music has its own "sentence structure" and the best way to develop a feel and an ear for it is to learn all the licks, riffs and cliches you can.
- Even though the same riff is played over each chord, ending the riff on a "target tone" (usually the root of the chord) will make the solo "lock in" on the chord changes rather than just rambling through the scale.
- Play program 50.
- Students learn Example 105 (Lead Riff 1 in A). Show that the E and D patterns are exactly the same only transposed to different string sets and with different target tones.
- Students should play examples 105 - 107 with the recordings.

# Rock Lesson 22: Lead Riffs and Patterns

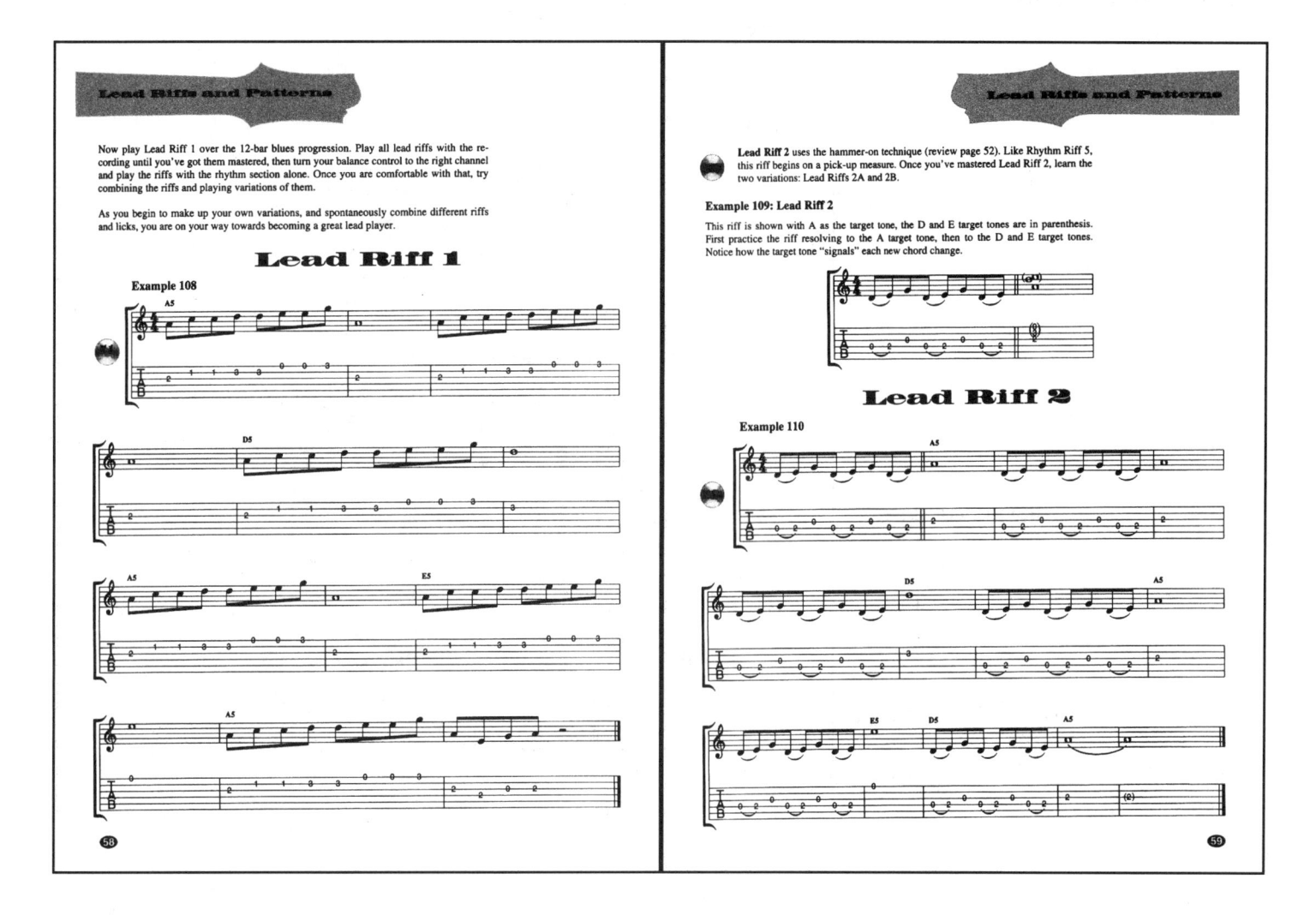

## Guitar Rock Shop 1

## Teacher Suggestions
- Example 108 places Lead Riff 1 in the context of a 12-bar blues progression. Notice how the target tones make the solo fit the changes. Play program 51 using the complete listening sequence.
- Lead Riff 2 is demonstrated on program 52. Have students listen to program 52 and then practice Example 109 ending on each different target tone. Notice that Lead Riff 2 begins on a pick-up measure, resolving to the target tone on the first beat of each chord change.
- Example 110 places Lead Riff 2 in the context of a 12-bar blues progression.

# Guitar Method 1

## Lesson 23: Rock Workshop 104
## The Blues Boogie Pattern

**New Concepts**
Two-note power 6th chord
Boogie pattern

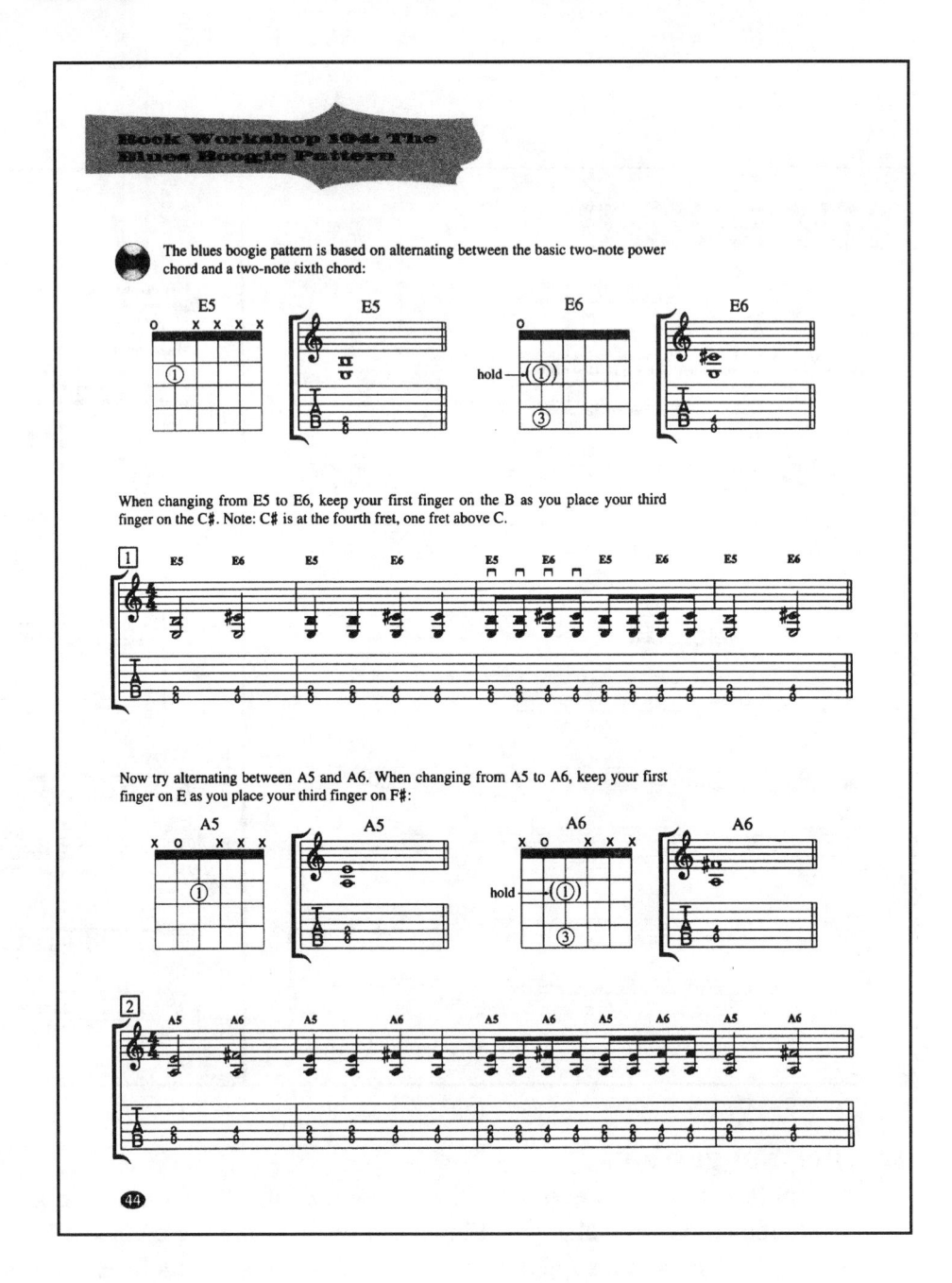

### Rock Workshop 104: The Blues Boogie Pattern

The blues boogie pattern is based on alternating between the basic two-note power chord and a two-note sixth chord:

When changing from E5 to E6, keep your first finger on the B as you place your third finger on the C♯. Note: C♯ is at the fourth fret, one fret above C.

Now try alternating between A5 and A6. When changing from A5 to A6, keep your first finger on E as you place your third finger on F♯:

**Objective**
- Learn the basic E, A and D boogie patterns (alternating power 5th and 6th chords)

**Teacher Suggestions**
- Play program 73.
- Review the derivation of the power fifth chord (root/5th) and explain the power sixth chord (root/6th).
- Demonstrate that the E boogie pattern (ex. 1) is exactly the same as the A and D boogie patterns (exs. 2 and 3) only transposed to a different set of strings.
- Have students play examples 1 - 3 with the recordings.

# Lesson 23: Rock Workshop 104
## The Blues Boogie Pattern

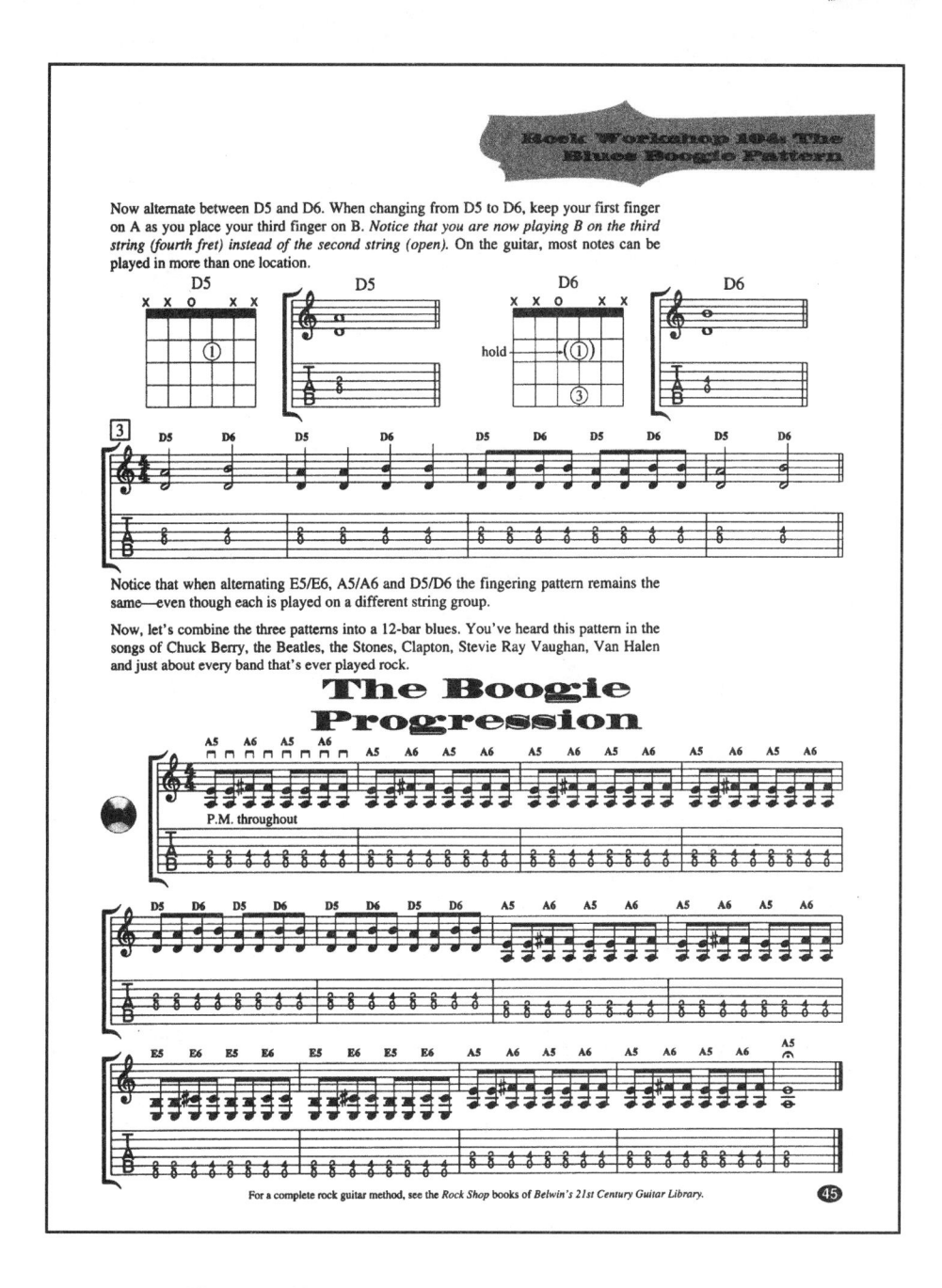

*Guitar Method 1*

[Sheet music page: Rock Workshop 104: The Blues Boogie Pattern, showing D5 and D6 chord diagrams, and "The Boogie Progression" — a 12-bar blues in A]

## Teacher Suggestions
- Play program 74. Use the complete listening procedure described on page 19.
- The *Boogie Progression* is a complete 12-bar blues boogie pattern in A. Students should sing the blues progression root movement with program 74 (*The Boogie Progression*).

**Listening Suggestions:** Any straight-eighth rock boogie songs. Chuck Berry, Bob Seger, the Beach Boys and Stevie Ray Vaughan have all recorded many songs of this type.

**Optional Song Book:** Students are now prepared to play *409* on page 28 *Song Trax 1*.
**Optional Ensemble Book:** Students are now prepared to play *Goin' Home Boogie Blues* on page 29 of *Guitar Ensemble 1*.

# Guitar Theory 1

## Theory Lesson 23: The Boogie Progression

**Reinforces**
E6, A6 and D6, The Boogie Progression

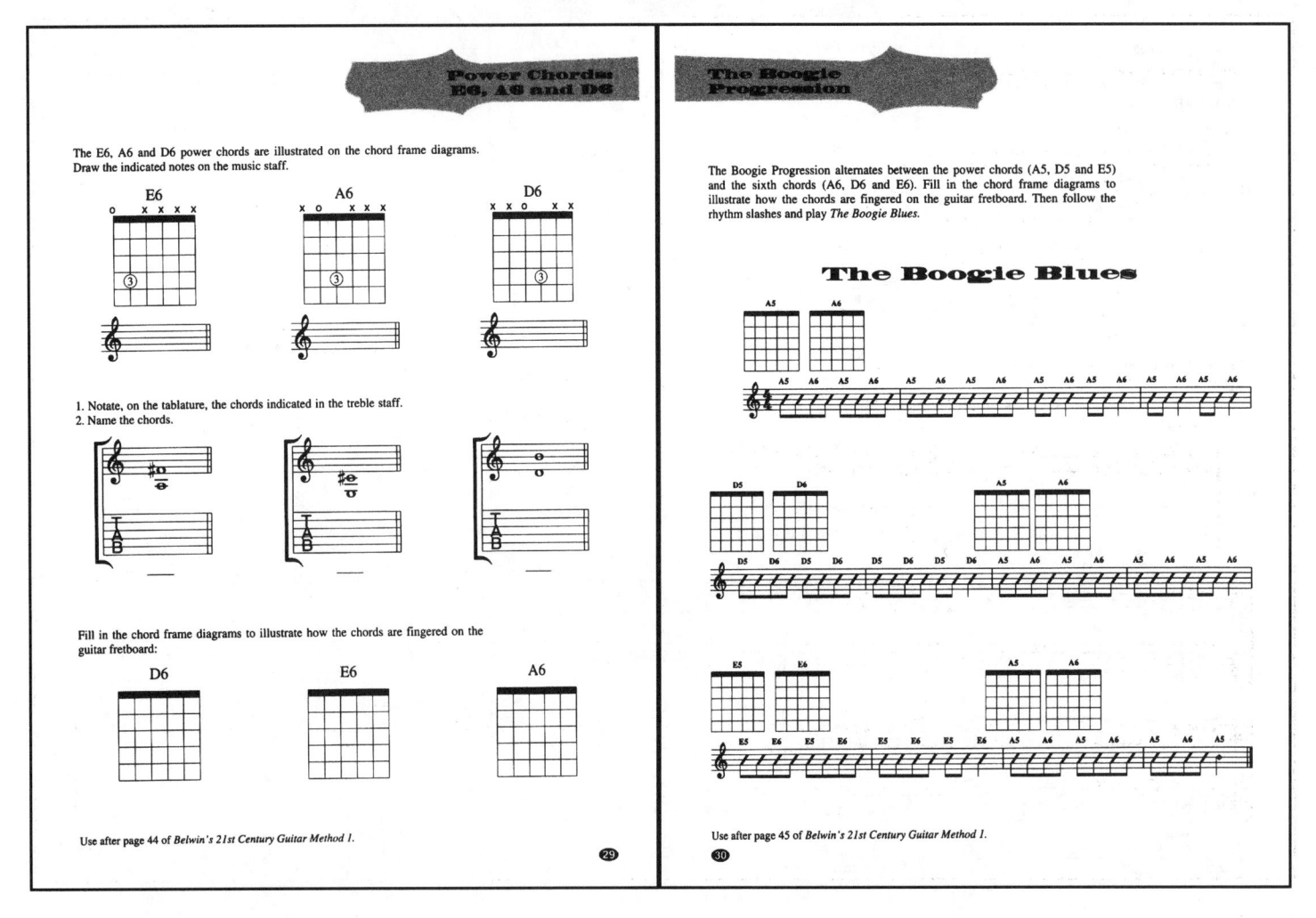

These pages correlate to Method book pages 44 and 45.

## Objective
- Develop the students ability to understand and visualize note locations and chord fingerings on the neck of the guitar
- Reinforce the blues/boogie progression

## Teacher Suggestions
- Explain each fill-in example.
- Do part of each example with students.
- Have students complete the examples on their own or as homework assignments.

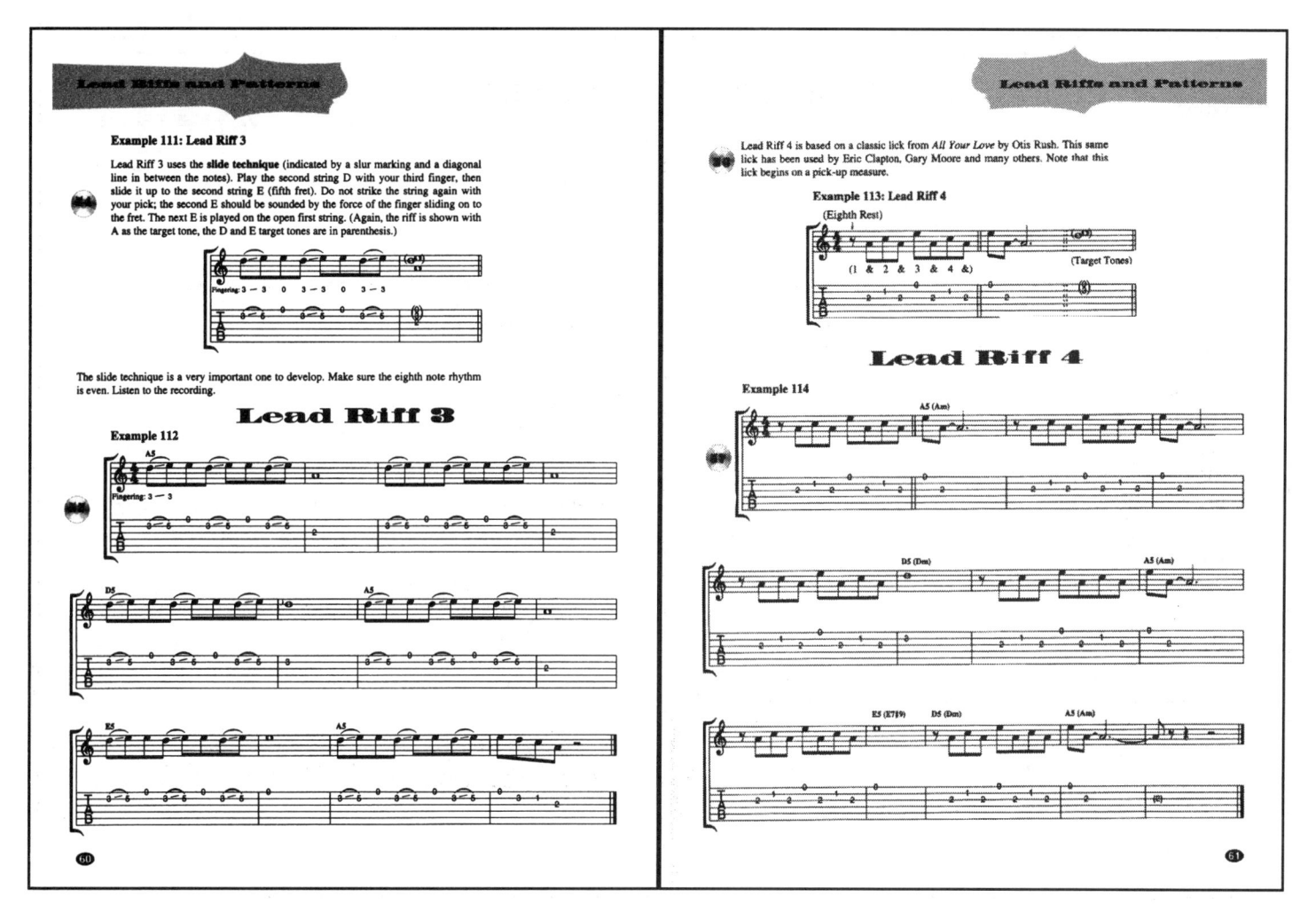

# Rock Lesson 23: Lead Riffs and Patterns

**Guitar Rock Shop 1**

## New Concepts
The slide technique

### Lead Riffs and Patterns

**Example 111: Lead Riff 3**

Lead Riff 3 uses the **slide technique** (indicated by a slur marking and a diagonal line in between the notes). Play the second string D with your third finger, then slide it up to the second string E (fifth fret). Do not strike the string again with your pick; the second E should be sounded by the force of the finger sliding on to the fret. The next E is played on the open first string. (Again, the riff is shown with A as the target tone, the D and E target tones are in parenthesis.)

The slide technique is a very important one to develop. Make sure the eighth note rhythm is even. Listen to the recording.

### Lead Riff 3

**Example 112**

### Lead Riffs and Patterns

Lead Riff 4 is based on a classic lick from *All Your Love* by Otis Rush. This same lick has been used by Eric Clapton, Gary Moore and many others. Note that this lick begins on a pick-up measure.

**Example 113: Lead Riff 4**

### Lead Riff 4

**Example 114**

## Objective
- Learn two new lead riffs that can be used over each change in the blues progression
- Reinforce the "target tone" concept as a means of focusing the solo on each individual chord change

## Teacher Suggestions
- Play program 54. Lead Riff 3 introduces the slide technique: play the 3rd fret D and slide up to the 5th fret E. Do not strike the note a second time. Make sure the eighth note rhythm is even.
- Students should learn Example 111 (Lead Riff 3) and practice ending on each different target tone.
- Example 112 places Lead Riff 3 in the context of a 12-bar blues progression. Play program 55 using the complete listening sequence. Point out how the target tones make the solo fit the changes.
- Students should play example 112 with the recording.
- Play program 56. Lead Riff 4 is based on a minor arpeggio. Major and minor chords have not been explored theoretically yet but you can use this as an opportunity to do so. Write out the E, A and D major scales and explain that the major chord is constructed from the root, 3rd and 5th of the scale and the minor chord from the root, b3rd and 5th.
- Students should learn Example 113 (Lead Riff 4) and practice ending on each different target tone.
- Example 114 places Lead Riff 4 in the context of a 12-bar blues progression. Play program 57 using the complete listening sequence. Point out how the target tones make the solo fit the changes.
- Students should play example 114 with the recording.

# Guitar Method 1

## Lesson 24: Old Time Rock and Roll

**New Concepts**
8-bar blues form

**Reinforces**
I, IV and V chords, A boogie pattern, D boogie pattern, E boogie pattern

## Objective
- Reinforce all material learned so far with a popular rock song

## Teacher Suggestions
- Explain the 8-bar blues form.
- Play program 75, use the complete listening procedure. Notice that the rhythm guitar part, not the melody, is isolated in the right channel.
- Have students play *Old Time Rock and Roll* with the recording.
- **Group Class:** Have part of the class play the melody while the rest play the rhythm guitar part, then reverse.

**Optional Song Book:** Students are now prepared to play *Tube Snake Boogie* on page 30 of *Song Trax 1*.

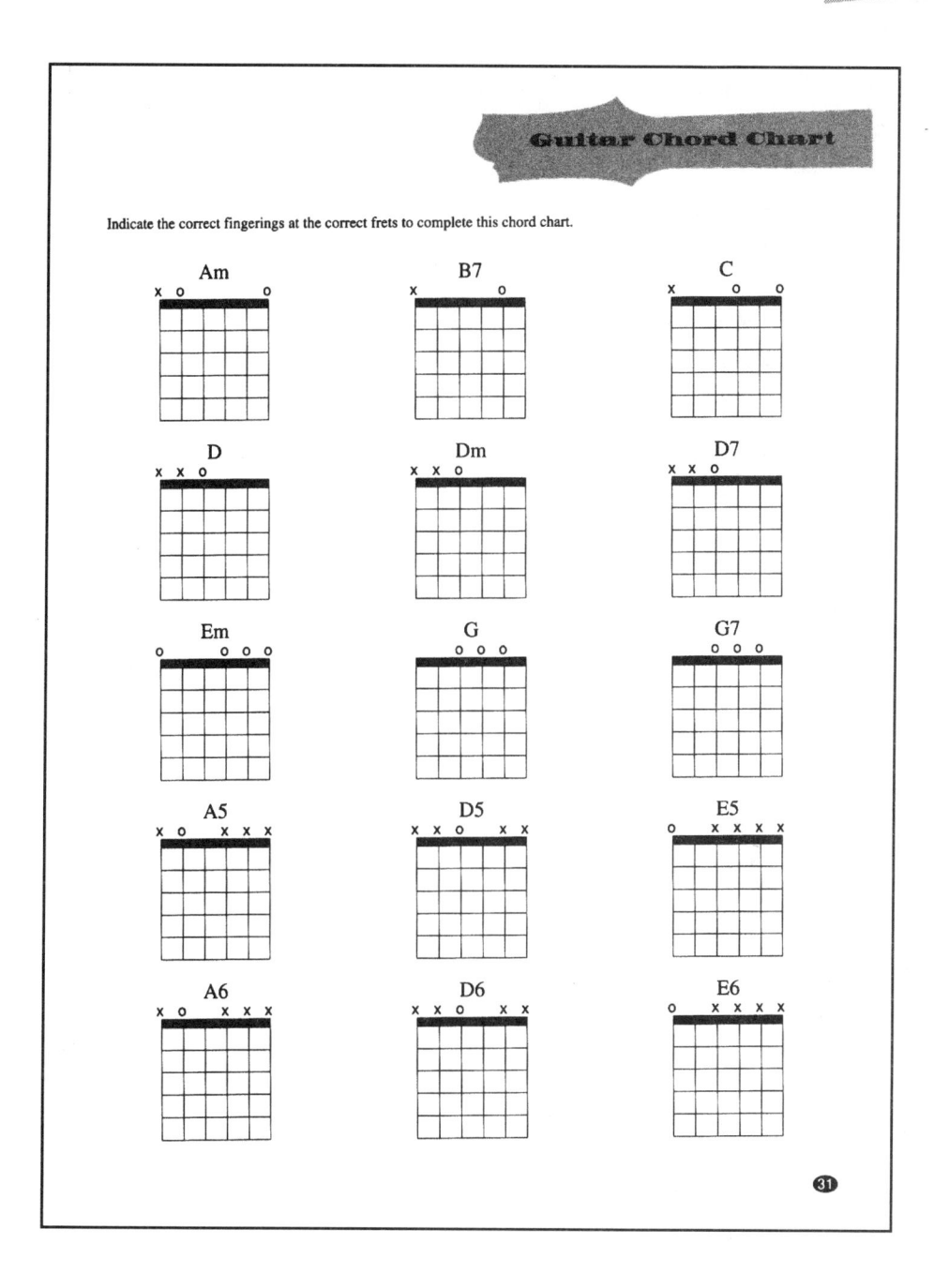

# Theory Lesson 24: Guitar Chord Chart

**Guitar Theory 1**

## Guitar Chord Chart

Indicate the correct fingerings at the correct frets to complete this chord chart.

| Am | B7 | C |
| D | Dm | D7 |
| Em | G | G7 |
| A5 | D5 | E5 |
| A6 | D6 | E6 |

**31**

**Reinforces**
Chord knowledge
Fretboard visualization

## Objective
- Develop the students ability to understand and visualize note locations and chord fingerings on the neck of the guitar.

## Teacher Suggestions
- Have students fill-in each chord frame and then play the chord. Students can refer to page 48 of the *Guitar Method* book for most of these chords.

109

# Guitar Rock Shop 1

## Rock Lesson 24: Lead Riffs and Patterns

**Reinforces**
All lead riffs

### Lead Riffs and Patterns

*Getting It Together* is an example of how each of these riffs can be combined, altered and varied. Keep experimenting—remove the lead guitar from the recording and play along with the rhythm tracks. Each lick, riff, pattern, scale and idea you learn must be practiced until they are second nature and come easily to you.

#### Getting It Together

**Example 115**

(Lead Riff 1 (one octave lower), Lead Riff 2, Lead Riff 4, Lead Riff 3, Descending A minor pentatonic scale)

## Objective
- Show that memorized patterns can be combined and altered to create new ideas
- Reinforce the "target tone" concept as a means of focusing the solo on each individual chord change

## Teacher Suggestions
- Explain that when improvising, the student should constantly be trying to combine, alter and utilize everything they know in new ways.
- Listen to program 58. Students should play example 115 with the recording.
- Students should try removing the lead guitar from this or any of the other programs and practice improvising solos over the rhythm tracks.

# Rock Lesson 24: Riff Review

## Guitar Rock Shop 1

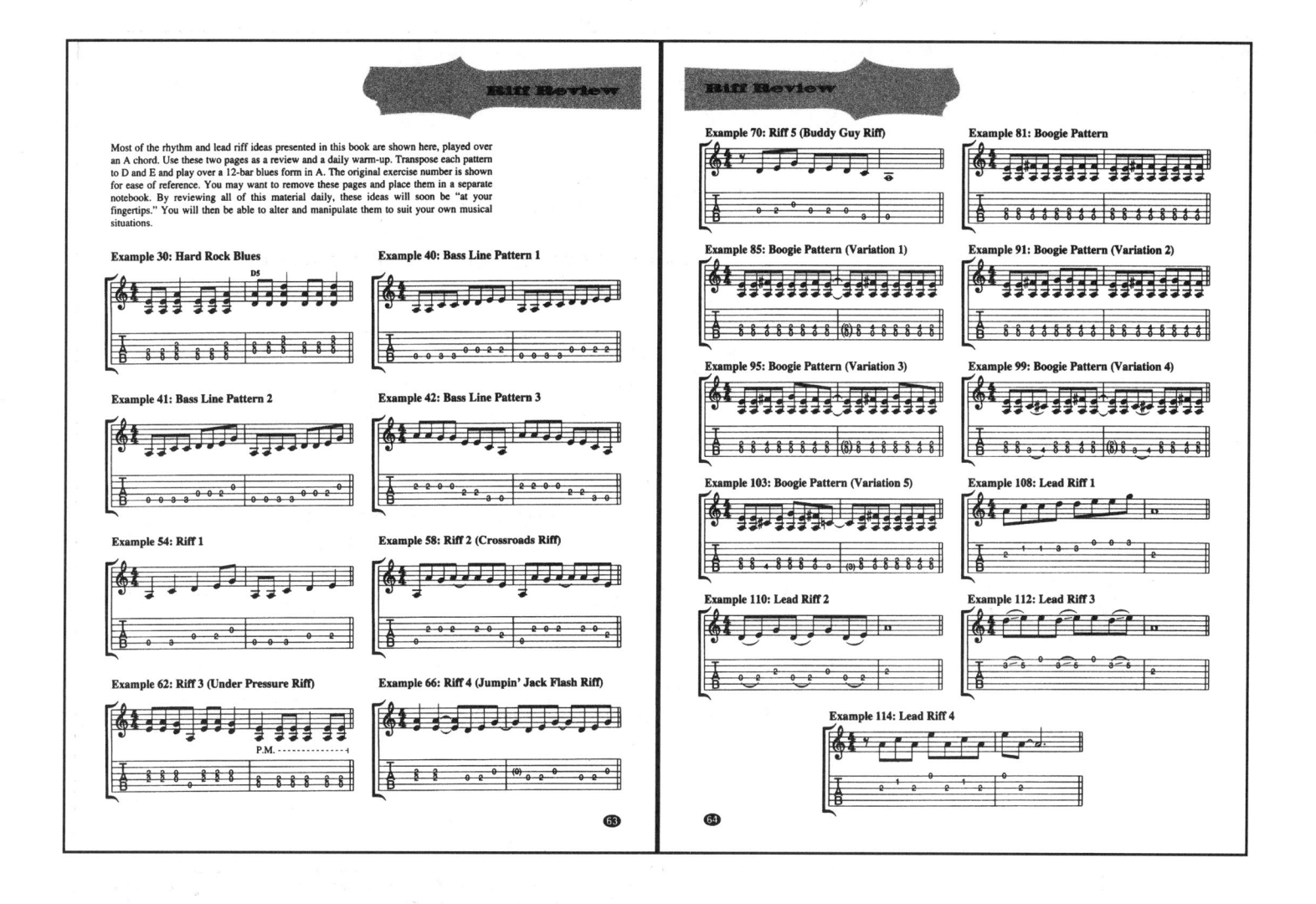

## Objective
- Review all riffs and patterns

## Teacher Suggestions
- These two pages provide a synopsis of every riff and pattern learned in Rock Shop book 1. Each pattern is written in A.
- Students should first play each pattern in A and then transpose to D and E.
- Then play each pattern over a 12-bar blues from in A.
- Students can use these two pages as daily warm-up exercises.

# Attention Teachers!
# Belwin's
# 21st Century Guitar Library: Level 2

Level 2 of *Belwin's 21st Century Guitar Library* begins a more in-depth exploration of the guitar in terms of technique, theory, and musical content. Level 2, like level 1, is supported by a full complement of supplementary books.

*Guitar Method 2* includes:
- Music Theory
- The Keys of C, G and D
- Fretboard Exploration
- 2nd Position
- Syncopation
- Rhythm and Lead Guitar Techniques
- Cut Time
- Solo Guitar Style
- Rock Workshops
- Pop and Classical songs like Margaritaville, Romanza and Classical Gas.

*Guitar Rock Shop 2* includes:
- Moveable Power Chords
- Moveable Minor Pentatonic Scale Patterns
- Triplets
- The Rock Shuffle Rhythm
- String Bending
- Vibrato
- Classic Rock Rhythm and Lead Riffs.

*Guitar Theory 2* is correlated by page to *Guitar Method 2*. This book is designed to increase fretboard understanding through the use of fretboard, chord frame, tablature and notation fill-in type exercises.

*Guitar Song Trax 2* includes not only the melody and chords but authentic rhythm and lead guitar parts to songs by Creedence Clearwater Revival, the Everly Brothers, ZZ Top, Bryan Adams, the Doors and Garth Brooks.

*Guitar Ensemble 2* includes a mix a classical, popular, bluegrass and rock songs arranged for three guitars with optional bass, drums and piano. The level of material is correlated to *Guitar Method 2*.